AF661060

DECOLONISING INDIAN ANTHROPOLOGY

Decolonising Indian Anthropology

A CIVILISATIONAL APPROACH TO THE INTER-RELATIONSHIP AMONG PEOPLE OF THE FORESTS, HILLS AND PLAINS

SACHCHIDANAND JOSHI
RAGHVENDRA SINGH
K. ANIL KUMAR

Foreword by
S. GURUMURTHY

कला वस्मिन् प्रतिष्ठिता:
INDIRA GANDHI NATIONAL CENTRE FOR THE ARTS
इन्दिरा गाँधी राष्ट्रीय कला केन्द्र

Vivekananda International Foundation

MANOHAR
2026

Cover illustration: Warli Painting from the IGNCA
Janapada Sampada Archives collection.

First published 2026
First eBook edition 2026

© Indira Gandhi National Centre for the Arts and
Vivekananda International Foundation, 2026

All rights reserved. No part of this publication may be
reproduced or transmitted, in any form or by any means,
without prior permission of the authors and the publisher.

ISBN 978-93-6080-195-3 (hardbound)
ISBN 978-93-6080-996-6 (eBook)

Published by
Indira Gandhi National Centre for the Arts,
Janpath, New Delhi - 110001
in association with
Ajay Kumar Jain *for*
Manohar Publishers & Distributors
4753/23 Ansari Road, Daryaganj
New Delhi 110 002

Cover design by Manoj Kumar

Typeset by OGAI Technologies Pvt. Ltd.,
Chennai 600032, Tamil Nadu

Printed and bound in India

Contents

Illustrations

Foreword

The theory of Western anthropology that later became modern anthropology was originally founded on the colonial ideology of Rudyard Kipling's *The White Man's Burden*, which regarded the Whites as civilised, all others as 'the other people'. The other people and their civilisations—read 'all colonized societies'—were first characterized as 'savage' and 'barbaric'. Later, as the White West became a bit liberal, that description was moderated to 'primitive'. Still later, as a 'tribal'. And currently as 'indigenous'.

But whether it is savage, barbaric, primitive, tribal or indigenous, in substance, it meant the same thing—even after the West labelled itself as modern, later as liberal—non-white or non-Western. Even now, this is the neo-Western perspective of original anthropology.

After the colonized societies became independent, the colonial education they had instituted continued and that left the post-colonial national societies divided into two: the civilised and developed plains and their inhabitants and the primitive and backward forests and hills and their inhabitants.

The discipline of anthropology in the post-colonial societies consequently transformed into studying the forest and hill dwellers from the perspective of the national people of the plains, who inherited the status of colonizers as civilised people, as 'the other' people, that is, those who were primitive and backward relative to the plains people.

This was obviously on the Western experience of Europe and the Americas, where new people occupied the local people's land and drove them into forests and hills and called them indigenous people. This is in total contrast to how forests and forest-dwellers are perceived in the Indian civilisation. Even the United Nations' (UN's) studies have confirmed that there are no indigenous people as distinct from the plains people in Asia and Africa.

Contrary to the Western view of forests as backward, Indian civilisation considers the forest as a place of higher learning and forest-dwelling as spiritually superior to living on plains. Because of this paradigm difference, there is an irreconcilable contradiction between the Western view of forests and forest-dwellers and the Indian civilisational approach to both.

There are essentially four fundamental, irreconcilable contradictions between the assumptions of Western anthropology and the Indian civilisational position on forests and forest-dwellers. First, unlike in the West, where forest and hill people and people of the plains were isolated from each other, in India there have been common civilisational, cultural and legendary links and intercourse between the forest and hill-dwellers and the people of the plains since prehistoric days. There have been continuous civilisational interfaces and migrations between the plains and the forests. This has been testified to by the epics, *Ramayana* and *Mahabharata* and other ancient literature and also by historical evidence from the Mughal period to the pre-Independence days, when forest and hill people had joined the plain-dwellers to fight against common dangers to both.

The isolation of the forests and hills from the plains was intrinsic to the colonial agenda, which carved out the reserved forest areas that stopped the free social and civilisational intercourse between the two areas and peoples. Over centuries, this turned into a development divide, which became an optical, social and civilisational demarcation that did not exist before the advent of the colonialists. Optically, the dress and lifestyle of the plains, forest and hills people were not very different before colonial rule; under colonial rule, the dress and lifestyle of the plain-dwellers changed, but that of the forest and hill people remained as before. This optical difference, plus the development divide, could easily fit into the cultural and social divide in the prism of Western anthropology.

Second, in Indian civilisation, unlike in the Western worldview, people from the plains never considered forests or forest-dwellers as backward. The forest was revered by the people of the plains as a place of contemplation for acquiring higher knowledge and enlightenment. Prince Siddhartha abdicated his throne, went into the forests for enlightenment and deep contemplation and became the Buddha.

In the Indian spiritual worldview, the forest was also regarded as the destination for the last cycle of one's earthly life known as *Vanaprastha*, which meant giving up the plains or normal life and leaving for the forest by renouncing the world or plains to attain *Mukti*. Indian legends are full of stories of great kings who have given up their thrones and taken to the forest for the final lap of their lives. Not only was the forest not backward, but from the perspective of gaining enlightenment and spiritual virtues, forest-dwelling was considered superior to life on the plains—something the West could never even imagine. This approach, which considers the forest as a place of enlightenment, totally contradicts the Western worldview, which condemns the forest to a place of darkness and backwardness.

Third, Vedic ascetics or *rishis* made forests their abode because they believed that the forests provided them an ecosystem to connect with cosmic forces. That was how they gained for the people of the plains the entire knowledge system of India. The *Vedas* and the *Upanishads*—the greatest literature of ancient India—are the gifts of forests and hills to the plain-dwellers. They are called the *Aranyakas*, books of the forest. The Western theory that forest and hill people are unenlightened and backwards and the plain-dwellers are enlightened and developed, is totally rejected by the Indian civilisation.

Fourth, the people of the plains never regarded the forest books, the Vedas and Upanishads, as ordinary books; this is still the case today. If these texts are no ordinary books, the people who authored them, the forest-dwellers and the hill-dwellers, could not be ordinary people. The people of the plains in India believe that the *Vedas* and the *Upanishads* contain such higher and mystic knowledge that the forests and the people who authored such books could never be regarded as backward. It is because of the serene ecosystem of forests, free of pollution that human greed produces in the plains that the *rishis* sought the forests to connect with the higher reaches of knowledge that lay beyond the Newtonian world.

That was how they could discover and propound in the *Vedas* the one universal consciousness as the one and only reality and the physical universe as merely an appearance of reality. This view, once dismissed by colonialists as a fantasy, is now the view of modern science! Nobel science laureates such as Ervin Schrödinger, Werner Heisenberg, Niels Bohr, Brian David Josephson and Charles H. Townes say that the idea of one universal consciousness, which the *Vedas* and the *Upanishads* propound, alone can reveal the secrets of the origin of the universe (which even quantum science cannot explain). The Vedic *rishis* said that the entire creation, the universe—the matter or energy—emanated from one universal consciousness. This view was upheld by Roger Penrose, the Nobel Prize winner for physics in 2020, who said that matter emerged out of one supreme consciousness.

Does it not mean that the Vedic *rishis* dwelling in the forests discovered what the Nobel scientists now say modern science is yet to discover? With such irrefutable evidence from modern scientists about the *Vedas* and the *Upanishads* that came from the forests, can anyone hold a brief for modern anthropology, which says that forests and those who inhabited forests in India are backward?

Our sacred texts were considered to be the fountains of Indian knowledge. This was until the colonialists, ignorant of the higher reaches of scientific knowledge beyond Newtonian mechanics, began trashing the *Vedas* to claim and establish their own superiority. T.B. Macaulay, who devised the colonial education system for India, wrote in his famous Minute dated 1835 on the need for the English education system in India that a single shelf of a good European library was worth the whole native literature of India.

Unfortunately, the Western view was gulped and vomited by mainline Indian historians like Romila Thapar, who wrote that the *Vedas* were 'primitive animism struggling in ignorance'. Can there be a greater testimony to how

Western anthropology has produced dangerous and mischievous consequences that have been destructive to the Indian civilisation?

One of the reasons Western anthropology took root in India was that chronologically, the discovery of Sanskrit in the second half of the nineteenth century by Monier Williams came after the West thought the source of it, the Greco-Roman civilisation, was superior to all other civilisations. Monier Williams discovered Sanskrit as a wonderful language that is more perfect than Greek, more copious than Latin and more refined than either of them. This at once established that the Indian civilisation was superior even to the originating premises of the Western civilisation.

If the discovery of Sanskrit had occurred a century earlier, the Western worldview that its people were superior and the colonized people were savage and primitive would have been disproved by the Indian civilisation. Significantly, Macaulay's Minute on Education, 1835, which trashed the entire Indian civilisation's output as worthless, also preceded the discovery of Sanskrit in chronology. Had Sanskrit been discovered before the infamous Minute, Monier Williams could not have written so disparagingly about the Indian literature.

Thomas McEvilly, a Greek American writer, produced a magnum opus titled *The Shape of Ancient Thought* on the origin of Indian and Greek civilisations in 2001. He commented that the discovery of Sanskrit by Monier Williams proved that 'the language of the colonized Indian people was the language of the colonial masters themselves'. McEvilly went on to theorize by extensive research that the Greek philosophy—of Plato, Socrates and others—had no foundational research laboratory in Greece and that it was only from ancient India that the Greek civilisation, which was the origin of Enlightenment movement that made the West assert its superiority, imported its founding premises. In other words, Indian civilisation was the mother of the Greeks. Half a century before Monier Williams' discovery of Sanskrit and more than two centuries before Thomas McEvilly, Edward Pockoke, another Greek traced the origin of Greek civilisation to India in his book, *India in Greece*, which was first published in 1830 but never saw the light of day during the colonial rule in India.

The issue needs no further discussion. The discipline of anthropology, divorced from the civilisational roots of India, has caused divisions, disruptions, even insurgencies and separatism in forest and hill areas of India. The civilisational approach to anthropology is long overdue. That is the only corrective to perverted conclusions that have emerged from the application of the Western approach to anthropology in India. This long-overdue and delayed exercise has been undertaken by the Indira Gandhi National Centre for Arts (IGNCA), New Delhi and Vivekananda International Foundation (VIF), New Delhi. Both these institutions deserve volumes of praise for the initiative.

I am delighted that the work of the two institutions over the years has yielded an authentic and authoritative book, *Decolonising Indian Anthropology: A Civilisational Approach to the Inter-relationship among people of the Forests, Hills and Plains,* authored by Dr Sachchidanand Joshi, Member Secretary and Executive and Academic Head of the IGNCA; Raghvendra Singh, Senior Fellow, VIF, who was also a member of the Indian Administrative Service and Prof. K. Anil Kumar, Head of the Department, Janapada Sampada, at IGNCA. I am sure that this work will correct the distortions and perversions in the discipline of anthropology caused by the Western approach and lead to a civilisational approach to the study of anthropology in India.

S. GURUMURTHY
Chairman
Vivekananda International Foundation
New Delhi

Acknowledgements

The Indira Gandhi National Centre for the Arts (IGNCA) and the Vivekananda International Foundation (VIF) have collaborated on a joint project, 'Reviving Indian Narratives: Understanding Traditional Communities in Hills and Forests'. The VIF chairman and prominent thinker and author S. Gurumurthy's thoughts on this subject have drawn our attention back to a long-standing problem with Indian history and culture. This work was undertaken under the guidance of S. Gurumurthy and Dr Sachchidanand Joshi, Member Secretary, IGNCA. Five brainstorming sessions were held to kickstart the initiative. This publication is the result of those five brainstorming sessions, a panel discussion and a national seminar that brought together academicians, intellectuals, research scholars and civil society groups from various regions of India.

We extend our heartfelt gratitude to S. Gurumurthy for inspiring us to commence a research on the necessity of an Indian civilisational perspective in studying the forest and hill communities of India. We would like to express our sincere gratitude to our esteemed President IGNCA, Padma Bhushan Shri Ram Bahadur Rai, for his invaluable guidance and unwavering support in bringing this work to fruition. We are deeply grateful to Dr Sachchidanand Joshi for his insightful ideas and valuable feedback to develop the draft of this book. We extend our sincere thanks to Dr Arvind Gupta for his invaluable suggestions in enhancing the quality of the book. Additionally, we express our gratitude to Prof. Sujit Dutta, Distinguished Fellow, VIF, for reviewing the initial draft of this book and providing us with his invaluable comments. We express our gratitude to Dr Anamika, Assistant Professor at Jawaharlal Nehru University (JNU), for her intial assistance in proofreading the book. I would like to extend my sincere appreciation to Shri. Rajesh Singh, distinguished author, for his exceptional assistance in the content editing of this book. His expertise and keen eye for detail have significantly enhanced the quality of the manuscript, ensuring that the ideas are conveyed with clarity and precision.

The discussion in this book begins by addressing the brainstorming meeting, which started with the tribal narratives that Western anthropologists and sociologists labelled the tribes as 'savage', 'barbarians', 'backward' and 'primitive'. In many parts of the world, indigenous tribes were split apart by colonial and Western ideas. In forcibly separating and isolating the tribal people from the inhabitants of the plains in India, colonial scholars created a gap among the people, pitting 'us' against the 'others'.

The experts who participated in the brainstorming meeting expressed the view that tribals were not a separate category as conceived by anthropologists and sociologists. Hence, the so-called tribals are to be referred to as 'Jana' and the whole concept of Scheduled Tribes must be seriously viewed from an Indian point of view. One needs to relook at the whole process of conceptualization of tribal narratives. New narratives can be built on the basis of facts that were either not known to the colonial writers or were deliberately glossed over.

From the brainstorming sessions, there was a larger consensus to bring forth Indian narratives on the traditional communities residing in forests, plains and the hills of India, on the following aspects pertaining to the understanding of traditional communities of India:

- The term and concept of 'indigenous' does not apply to India, as clearly highlighted in the UN's document titled, 'State of the World's indigenous Peoples'.
- Further, the Western narratives on traditional communities labelling them as 'savage', 'barbaric', 'primitive', 'aboriginal' and 'indigenous' should be denounced and condemned by all.
- There is an immediate need to revive the Indian narratives on the traditional communities of India and also review the existing literature on tribal cultures from an Indian perspective using new research methods sans Western approaches or perspectives.
- Also, extensive and intensive research should be carried out across India to bring out the inherent and embedded 'social capital' of traditional communities of India.

This book attempts to summarize the issue by emphasizing the salient features of previous studies. The book critically evaluates how anthropologists have viewed and studied Indian tribes. It also calls into question the ontological and epistemological foundations of their knowledge production concerning the Indian tribal communities. The book also discusses the various issues with Indian tribal discourse.

A national seminar was organized in collaboration with the Indian Council of Social Science Research (ICSSR) on 15–16 November 2023, at the IGNCA, focussing on the theme, 'Reviving Indian Narratives about Traditional Communities Living in the Hills and Forests', to deepen the understanding of the ongoing discussion. This event saw participation of numerous academicians and research scholars across various disciplines. Following extensive discussions and deliberations, all delegates concluded that a revival of the Indian narratives concerning traditional communities living in the hills and forests is essential for a proper understanding of these communities.

Members who took part in the deliberations held in various parts of the country felt that there was an immediate need to understand the Indian communities residing in the forests, hills and the plains. Through an in-depth study, the Indian narrative has to be established, something that is not an alternative narrative but rather which stands the test of objective interpretation of the gathered empirical data.

We thank the members for their active participation and contributions. We express our gratitude to the following experts who participated in the brainstorming sessions, as their cooperation and contributions were indispensable in completing this book:

- Dr Arvind Gupta, Director, VIF
- Lt. General R.K. Sawhney, Senior Fellow, VIF
- Shri. Raghvendra Singh, Senior Fellow, VIF
- Padma Shri. Nivedita Bhide, Vice President, Vivekananda Kendra, Kanyakumari
- Padma Shri Dr J.K. Bajaj, Chairman, ICSSR
- Prof. Umesh Ashok Kadam, Former Member Secretary, ICHR
- Padma Shri Ashok Bhagat, Secretary, Vikas Bharti
- Shri. Harsh Chouhan, Former Chairperson, NCST
- Prof. P.C. Joshi, Former VC, Delhi University
- Prof. K.K. Misra, Former VC, Utkal University of Culture
- Prof. S.M. Patnaik, Former VC, Utkal University
- Prof. Satya Narayana Munda, Former VC, Dr Shyama Prasad University
- Ranendra Kumar, IAS (Retd.), Director, Dr Ram Dayal Munda TRI
- Prof. P. Venkata Rao, Former Dean, Hyderabd Central University
- Prof. B.V. Sharma, Director, AnSi, Kolkata
- Prof. Amitabh Pandey, Director, IGRMS, Bhopal
- Prof. K. Anil Kumar, HoD, JS Division, IGNCA
- Prof. R.C. Gaur, HoD, Kala Nidi Division, Dean (Admin), IGNCA
- Prof. Pratapanand Jha, Dean Academic, IGNCA
- Prof. Aun Bhardwaj, Head Academic, IGNCA
- Prof. Sudhir Lall, HoD, Kala Kosa Division, IGNCA
- Prof. Achal Pandya, HoD, Conservation Division
- Prof. Vijoy S. Sahay (Retd.) Department of Anthropology, Allahabad University
- Prof. Debal Singh Roy, former Director, ACD, IGNOU
- Prof. Rashmi Sinha, former Director, SOSS, IGNOU
- Prof. R.P Mitra, Department of Anthropology, Delhi University

- Prof. Molly Kaushal, Former Director, NMCM, IGNCA
- Prof. D.C. Choubey, Head (EAP & Area Studies, IGNCA)
- Dr Richa Negi, HoD, Rock Art Division, IGNCA
- Dr Prathibha Kumari, Deputy Registrar General
- Dr Sunita Reddy, Associate Professor, JNU
- Dr Ganesh Murmu, Vinoba Bhave University
- Dr Rukshana Zaman, Assistant Professor, IGNOU
- Dr M. Kishan, Assistant Professor, Delhi University
- Dr Rabindranath Sarma, Associate Professor, Central University, Jharkhand
- Dr Binod, Assistant Professor, IGNOU, New Delhi
- Dr Swadesh Singh, Assistant Professor, Delhi University
- Dr Ramakar Pant, Former HoD, JS Division, IGNCA
- Dr Sapam Ranabir Singh, IGNCA Regional Director, Guwahati
- Dr Rembemo Odyuo, Assistant Professor, JS Division, IGNCA
- Dr Arun Reddy, Assistant Professor, JS Division, IGNCA
- Dr Vandana Kumari, Assistant Professor, JS Division, IGNCA
- Dr Arpita Anant, Research Fellow, VIF
- Dr Steffy Teresa Murmu, Visiting Faculty, Ranchi University
- Dr Pradeep Munda, Assistant Professor, BIT, Mesra
- Shri. Ajit Kumar, Project Director Mausam, IGNCA
- Shri. Abhay Mishra, Assistant Director, NMCM
- Shri. Santosh Kiro, Department of Journalism, St. Xavier's College, Ranchi
- Ms Laxmi Rawat, AFA/AO, JS Division, IGNCA
- Ms Shatabdi Manna, Project Associate, JS Division, IGNCA
- Ms Kanupriya, Project Assistant, JS Division, IGNCA
- Mr Dharamvir, JS Division, IGNCA
- Mr Dilip, JS Division, IGNCA
- Mr Murari, JS Division, IGNCA
- Mr Rajesh, JS Division, IGNCA

To facilitate additional dialogue and to gather broader perspectives, the IGNCA organized a special panel discussion on the theme, 'Decolonising Indian Anthropology: A Civilisational Approach to the Inter-relationship among people of the Forests, Hills and Plains', at the Indian Anthropology Congress 2025 (IAC-2025), 21–23 February, which was held at the Anthropological Survey of India, Kolkata.

More than 450 academicians and scholars from approximately 60 universities and 40 other research organisations and national museums across the country attended the IAC-2025. The panel session was attended by many distinguished anthropologists, scholars and policymakers across the country and the panellists on the dais were Prof. P.C. Joshi. Former Vice Chancellor, University of Delhi,

Prof. K.K. Basa, Chairman, Monument Authority of India, Prof. Sabita Acharya, Vice Chancellor, Utkal University, Bhubaneswar, Prof. P. Venkat Rao, Former Dean, University of Hyderabad, Prof. A. Chella Perumal, Former Director & Head, Pondicherry Central University, Prof. K.R. Rama Mohan, Head, Department of Anthropology, Sikkim Central University, Prof. M. Romesh Singh, Head, Department of Anthropology, University of Hyderabad and Prof. K. Anil Kumar, Head, JS Division, IGNCA.

The panel was convened under the chairmanship of Prof. P.C. Joshi that aimed to provide a platform to critically examine Eurocentric frameworks in Indian anthropology and explore ways to integrate indigenous perspectives into academic discourse. The discussion emphasized the urgent need to reform Indian anthropology by cantering indigenous voices, revising colonial classifications and shifting towards a civilisational approach. Moving forward, curriculum changes, policy reforms and greater representation of indigenous scholars will help create a more inclusive and decolonised discipline.

In order to re-establish the indigenous narrative, confront colonial prejudices and suggest an unbiased, data-driven civilisational approach to comprehending India's tribal groups, the panel envisaged for substantial research. Dr Sachchidanand Joshi graced the valedictory function as the chief guest. In his address, he emphasized that the diversity of Bharat should be comprehended solely within the framework of the Vedic tradition in anthropological discussions.

CHAPTER 1

Introduction

The people of the forests and hills constitute an important segment of the Indian population and account for nearly 8.6 per cent of the total population. Studying them has been a matter of interest since the late sixteenth century. It was around this time that Western anthropologists came to know of communities and cultures that were very different from theirs. The study of tribal communities commenced with anthropologists' interest in the study of 'other cultures'. In fact, anthropology as a discipline in India emerged from the study of tribes.

The British colonial administrators, anthropologists and ethnographers in India were trailblazers in the survey of tribes and expeditions in their habitats. However, their methods were often questionable, and their survey reports and papers served as valuable sources of information about a particular province and a tool for the ongoing development of colonial administration in India. Through the use of official machinery and tours for collecting data, they circumvented the ethical considerations of research. Not surprisingly, therefore, their writings distorted tribes as being characterised as backward, uncivilised and barbaric.

India's hills and forest communities were identified and enumerated as tribes during the British rule. It becomes apparent that the Western perspective about them has been at variance with the Indian view. Western anthropologists and social scientists labelled these communities as 'savage' first, 'barbaric' next, 'primitive' later, 'tribal' thereafter and finally, indigenous. All these terms were used interchangeably to denote groups of people deemed different from the mainstream societies. In other words, if people are indigenous, they were per se barbaric or primitive or savage!

The European colonisers distinguished themselves from the people of the land they occupied by using the terms mentioned. This was not the case in India. The word 'tribe' in India was used in the census record after a long period of colonial contact. Moreover, the term was not used to designate all Indians, i.e. the entire population of the territory they colonised, as they did in other countries. It was the colonial mindset of 'divide and rule' that guided the British motive of segregating the Indian population on various grounds. Colonial administrators divided the Indian population into tribes (people without a caste system) and caste non-tribes (people having a caste system).

Since the inception of Western historical curiosity about India, scholars have rationalized the existence of tribal communities residing in the forests and mountains of the region by asserting that they represented the original inhabitants of the land, displaced to these remote areas by incoming immigrant populations who settled in the plains. With the emergence of the theory of Aryan invasion, the notion of indigenous groups being pushed down by Aryan invaders gained widespread acceptance, almost becoming an established historical fact. In Indian archaeological writings, this theory took on a slightly altered yet interconnected manifestation. Certain prominent Indian archaeologists categorized the nation into distinct divisions: 'areas of attraction', 'areas of relative isolation' and 'areas of isolation'. However, critics argue that this classification overlooks the fact that regions lacking agricultural richness can still possess significant non-agricultural resources like minerals, forests or strategic locations along trade routes.

The Western narrative, it must be reiterated, was founded on the basis that the people of the forests and hills are backward and the people of the plains are advanced. But, the Indian reality, to reassert, is that forests and hills are the places of contemplation and the very origin of the highest knowledge—the Aranyakas of *Vedas* (forest texts), which contained the highest wisdom, according to great men of the world, including many Noble laureates. The Western narrative is almost entirely an outcome of colonial history, which distinguished between the original occupants of colonised territories and those who invaded them. But the Indian reality is different, as no one invaded or occupied the territories of the original occupants.

Western narratives insist that the people of the forests and those of the hills are separated from each other by differences in history, culture and faith. The Indian reality is that the people of the forest and hills have a strong bond and a shared history, culture and faith with the people of the plains. The Western narrative is premised on the total segregation of the forest and the hills' people. But Indian history shows continuous migration between the forests and the plains. In the Indian subcontinent, the problem is more observed due to the pervasive reality of what the post-Indian anthropologists call 'tribes in transition' or the tribe-caste continuum.

According to the scholar and anthropologist, N.K. Bose, in the categorisation of 'Jana and Jati,' i.e. tribe and caste, respectfully, the Jana had been interacting with the Jati in significant ways since time immemorial. Bose explained the process how Hindu society integrated tribal groups by incorporating them into the caste system, ensuring their place within the social structure. Bose emphasised the 'Hindu method of tribal absorption' as a key factor in maintaining Hindu society's ability to accommodate diverse, productive elements and withstand various challenges over centuries.

Forest and hill communities are characterized by their diversity, which encompasses various aspects such as their historical and civilisational backgrounds, languages and linguistic traits, ecological surroundings, physical attributes, population size, predominant means of livelihood, level of development and social hierarchy. But colonial administrators and anthropologists have not utilized a civilisational approach to comprehend this remarkable history and diversity.

S. Gurumurthy's view is that no civilisational approach for the forest and hill people of India is in line with the current anthropological discourse, which is trying to take a post-colonial India-routed stand. In his paper, Gurumurthy states that the Indian establishment is still blind to and ignores the reality of these groups, even after 75 years of the country achieving freedom. It is alarming to observe how the Western colonial anthropological approach and its strategies for interacting with hill and forest communities in colonized nations, continues to shape public opinion and the establishment narrative in India—they are still institutionalised without question. He believes that a study of India's hills and forests people requires an Indian civilisational approach. The plainsmen of Indian civilisation migrated to the forests in search of greater knowledge, and they also supported and protected the foresters' right to stay there and reflect on the depths of human consciousness.

Indian civilisation was jointly developed by the plains people and foresters. In that light, the plains populace seems less like contributors to the beginning and growth of Indian civilisation and more like consumers. Thus, in the Indian civilisation, the hill people and foresters serve as co-partners in developing the civilisation rather than as the 'other' people, in contrast to the plainsmen (Gurumurthy, 2023).

In August 2022, at India's 75th anniversary of independence, Prime Minister Narendra Modi delivered his ninth speech in a row, from the Red Fort ramparts, urging the people of this historic civilisation to eradicate all traces of the colonial mindset. Gurumurthy's recent insights have refocused our attention on the longstanding issue concerning Indian history and civilisation, and to which Prime Minister Modi referred. In this context, the present paper attempts to outline the problem by highlighting key aspects of the existing research.

THE ANTHROPOLOGICAL DISCOURSE

Tribal studies have been relevant in many ways. In the seventeenth century, studies on tribes commenced with an aim to understand them as a representative of the earlier stage of human civilisation. They were seen as social fossils, and experts believed that they could reconstruct the past of human society and culture by studying them in depth. The seventeenth and eighteenth centuries were also the era of expansion of Western colonisation. Many of the tribal areas of Africa, America and Southeast Asia came under the control of colonial powers. With this, there was an urgent need to understand the tribal communities in order to govern them. The colonial powers vigorously promoted tribal studies with the ostensible objective of serving administrative interests.

The word 'tribe/tribal' brings a general picture of people with arrows and spears in their hands, feathers on their heads and speaking an unintelligible language. They were associated with savagery. They were projected as animistic and uncivilised, their life as brutish and short, their art as crude and their religion as a medley of superstitions. All the early explorers and administrators, including professional anthropologists and historians, academicians, religious leaders and missionaries, vied with one another in using uncomplimentary adjectives to describe the 'tribals'.

Interestingly, the term 'tribe' has not been derived from those being called tribals, but rather the classification was imposed on them. In fact, along with colonisation and the spread of Christianity, the word 'tribal' became more popular. India, despite being the largest democratic country in the world, has failed to define in the Indian context what tribe means, and has merely inherited the definition given in the Imperial Gazetteer, i.e. 'A tribe is a collection of families bearing a common name, speaking a common dialect, occupying or professing to occupy a common territory and is not usually endogamous though originally it might have been so'. The term has been used by different persons differently over the decades. Sahay (1969) and S. C. Dube (1977) had, after conducting a detailed examination of various definitions given by different authors, came to the conclusion that the term 'tribe' 'has never been defined precisely and satisfactorily in the Indian context'.

During the early nineteenth century, it was mainly the British administrators and Western anthropologists who started the convention of categorizing certain groups in Indian society as tribes. Intending to give them administrative and political concessions, lists began to be prepared of the Indian tribes. The lists of Scheduled Tribes attached to the Constitution of India had its origin from this colonial exercise. Since independence, anthropologists have more or less accepted this list without critically examining its rationale.

The categorisation of the Indian population into two distinct groups: tribes and caste, came up in the first Census of India, 1891; in a report prepared by Baine, the tribal groups were clubbed under the category of 'forest tribes', which constituted a part of the 'agricultural and pastoral castes'. This population was estimated at 16 million at that time. In the 1901 Census report by Risley, they were renamed as 'animists', based on their religious practices, while in the 1911 Census report by Gait, they were termed as 'tribal animists' or the people following the 'tribal religion'. In the Census report of 1921, Hutton classified tribes under 'hill and forest tribes' with a population of 22 million. In the 1931 Census, they were named 'primitive tribes'.

The renaming continued. In the Government of India Act of 1935, they were termed 'backward tribes', and the 1941 Census report used the term 'tribes' (cited from Misra, 2013; Atal, 2013). It was only in the 1948 Census report that they were called 'Adivasi'. In 1950, to offer them special treatment in the Constitution of India, they were categorised as 'Scheduled Tribe'. Colonial rule institutionalised the term 'tribe' as an administrative category. 'Native law and custom' became a central feature of this administration. The colonial judicial system dealt with only the most serious crimes; most local disputes were to be resolved by tribal courts using 'customary' law.

Risley (1892) utilized anthropometric techniques to gather data on the origins of various castes and tribal groups, including measuring the facial features of different members. Paul Topinard, a French physician and anthropologist, adopted this methodology, which was later used by the Government of British India and the Asiatic Society of Bengal for an ethnographic survey in India. Thurston and Rangachari (1909) also employed a similar method in their survey of southern India, while Russell and Hira Lal (1916) relied on Vedic literature instead of Risley's racial theory. Despite facing criticism for his racist methods, Risley was respected by the British Empire; he would become the president of the Royal Anthropological Institute in 1910, reflecting a colonial mentality within the academic community.

The British colonial expansion into the hills, plains, forests, mountains, rivers and islands of India led to an increase in writings about the different communities, eventually referred to as tribes (Bhukya, 2008, 2017, 2021; Xaxa, 2008). To support the extension of their colonial authority over new territories, colonial administrators recruited amateur ethnographers, missionaries, explorers and colonial ethnographers to provide information (Eliot, 1794; Wade, 1800; M'Cosh, 1837; Lewin, 1869; Butler, 1875; Hunter, 1876; Mackenzie, 1884; Aitchison, 1892; Sandys, 2008). According to Wouters (2012), colonial administrators, travellers, missionaries and early anthropologists made efforts to comprehend, categorize and classify the caste and tribes in a manner that would serve the interests of the government and provide comprehensive information to their Western audiences. The British Empire then used this information to further expand its territory in the hill areas.

The British rule in India created some social categories, with tribes being one of them. This category came in due to the colonial policy of 'divide and rule'. The other one is the 'criminal tribe', which later became the de-notified tribe in free India. The colonial policy of exclusion of people from their traditional livelihoods resulted in those people resorting to petty crimes as an alternative source of livelihood. Instead of understanding the reason for their criminal tendencies, they were brought to task by enacting criminal laws and applying them on these 'criminals'.

Throughout history, both Western and Indian anthropologists have struggled to provide a definitive definition of the terms, 'tribe' or 'tribal', from an Indian perspective. The common contention in all the writings is that the appellative is an imposition of anthropologists and missionaries. Tribe, therefore, in India has no proper explanation and thus has a limited scope of application to the diverse situations of the population. Revitalizing the thrust of liberation from the old perspective is an urgent call so that this education becomes a powerful tool in liberating the so-called tribals from backwardness. For that, one has to go back in history to find the values that existed and were practised among the so-called tribal people of India.

Most Western and Indian anthropologists have not given much serious thought to the problem of creating a definition of tribal society that fits the Indian context. They have swung continually between textbook definitions of tribe and prevailing classifications of Indian society into tribal and non-tribal. It is still not clear as to what 'tribal society' means or how this term should be used in India.

Tribes in India have been living with dignity alongside the non-tribal communities since time immemorial. The British government viewed the tribes from their own perspective and tried to bring them to their administrative fold. Since then, the state's interest has been directed towards the tribes, and as a result the search for policy measures became a priority among scholars and administrators for a long time.

Research on the communities labelled as tribes by the British colonial officials evolved into what is now known as tribal studies. This venture was formalised with the establishment of the Asiatic Society of Bengal in 1784. The *Journal of the Asiatic Society of Bengal*, initiated in 1832, focused on studying the inhabitants of hills, plains and mountainous regions of British India for the benefit of the colonisers. One of the early studies conducted by M'Cosh, titled, 'Account of the Mountain Tribes on the Extreme N.E. Frontier of Bengal', referred to the tribes as 'barbarous and independently savage'. This language, although shocking and derogatory, was common in the publications of colonial administrators and ethnographers, who continued to publish with a free hand on the people of India. Among their notable works were the *1872 Descriptive Ethnology of Bengal* by Dalton, the *1892 Tribes and Caste of Bengal* by Herbert Hope Risley, the *1909 Castes and Tribes of Southern India* by Edward Thurnston, The *Caste and Tribes of the Central Provinces (1916)* by Robert Vane Russell and Rai Bahadur Hira Lal and the 1868–1875 compilation of eight volumes, *The People of India* by Watson and Kaye.

Anthropologists trained under colonial rule began to systematically study the tribes after 1930, contrasting with earlier colonial ethnographers who lacked formal anthropology training and served as administrators, explorers and missionaries. An example of an early-trained colonial ethnographer who arrived in India in 1936 was von Fürer-Haimendorf. In 2012, Wouters identified him as the initial genuine anthropologist to research the tribes of north-eastern India.

Trained in Vienna and London, he was heavily influenced by Malinowski, whom he encountered in London. Like Malinowski, he conducted ethnographic fieldwork in Pangsha Naga village in Nagaland, resulting in *The Naked Naga* (von Fürer-Haimendorf, 1939). In his fieldwork in the Naga village, his main goals were to observe the practice of head-hunting and gather ethnographic material for display in British museums. According to Wouters (2012), von Fürer-Haimendorf's ethnographical accounts are more detailed and grounded in anthropology than earlier colonial administrators. However, his choice of titles like 'The Naked Naga', reveals a racist attitude, perpetuating stereotypes through terms such as 'nakedness' and 'head-hunting' (Wouters, 2012, p. 116). Kamei (2021) argues that such projects objectify the tribal people, while Ziipao (2013) highlights the colonial biases, a feeling of cultural supremacy and Eurocentric views that too are blatantly racist in many aspects.

Tribal studies in India were dominated by colonial ethnographers and explorers, a trend that persisted through post-colonial India, where studies on tribes were controlled by a dominant male caste. During the British era in India, colonial ethnographers and trained anthropologists had a unique approach to writing about the tribals. For over 150 years, until India gained independence in 1947, they continuously produced writings without acknowledging the importance of reflecting on their own perspectives and responsibilities. These works consistently portrayed the tribal people as lazy, wild, savage, naked, primitive, exotic, degraded, warlike, sexist, barbaric, uncivilised and criminal. Not done with heaping such negativity on the tribals, they highlighted their habits of drinking, gambling and wearing dirty clothes, among others.

The studies by these colonial ethnographers and anthropologists stated that the tribals, backward in everything, were in need of assimilation into the mainstream society for the purposes of getting 'civilised'. This attitude reflected the scholars' own privileged social positions and biases. Scholars, influenced by uncritical methodologies of Malinowski and such others, failed to approach tribal studies with sensitivity, further perpetuating the dominant caste perspective. As a result, the tribals of India were consistently marginalized within this framework, lacking recognition as non-caste societies or as equals within caste societies. Colonial anthropologists pursued their work in the interests of the colonisers in terms of the concepts and theories they developed as well as the roles they played.

Following India's independence in 1947, intense debates ensued among anthropologists, administrators and social workers regarding the classification, terms and the position of the tribes in the country. The discourse revolved around integrating them into an independent India, exemplified by the scholarly exchanges between Elwin and G. S. Ghurye. Elwin's perspective on tribal communities, as presented in his work, *The Baiga* (1939), questioned whether tribes should remain isolated or be assimilated into the mainstream. Elwin advocated for maintaining isolation, suggesting they be kept separate from the dominant society, akin to being in 'national park[s]'.

Gurumurthy in his paper discusses the influence of Verrier Elwin on the post-independent Indian establishment, highlighting his background as a Christian evangelist-turned-anthropological adviser to the government. Elvin's work focused on forest-dwellers, shaping government policy and his ideas. His work on forest-dwelling people became the Bible for the government, and for which he received many awards, including the prestigious Padma Bhushan. Elwin appreciated the tribal culture and desired its preservation without interference from their civilisational cousins in the plains—thus displaying a lack of understanding of the millennial commonality between the plainsmen and foresters. He was blind to the fact that forcing the forest people to convert, a process he actively encouraged, would destroy their culture.

Elwin essentially had the same position as the Westerners towards the people of the forest, considering them to be 'other people' compared to those who lived on the plains. Elwin lacked the chance to delve into India's Vedas, *Puranas* and philosophical traditions concerning foresters and hillmen, thereby missing out on the deep civilisational connections between the forest-dwellers and the plainsmen. His judgement was clouded by the vast and contradictory diversity among the Indian people in both the plains and forests. Elvin's perspective did not align with the original Indian civilisational viewpoint, leading to a disconnect in understanding the forest-dwellers' situation in the context of colonial history and development.

Elwin faced significant criticism from anthropologists of his time, including Bose (1941), Ghurye (1963) and Srinivas (1976). Ghurye strongly disagreed with Elwin's theory of isolation and advocated for assimilation instead (Ghurye, 1963). However, Ghurye was often criticized for being a scholar who relied heavily on library research (Venkatesan, 2002). Ghurye's perspective, influenced by his upper-caste position, labelled the tribes as inferior to the dominant *Savarna* (or upper) caste society and argued for their assimilation into Hindu society (Ghurye, 1963). This viewpoint reflects broader debates on the 'tribe-caste-class continuum' (Xaxa, 2008; Akhup, 2013). In contrast, G.S. Ghurye argued that isolation at the root of social backwardness and assimilation as the only way out.

Other anthropologists of the time, such as Majumdar (1937) and Bose (1941), shared similar opinions, with Bose proposing a process of 'the Hindu method of Tribal absorption' (Bose, 1941; Xaxa, 2008; Akhup, 2013). Scholars say that both these scholars abandoned their respective positions later and opted for integration. The lack of a civilisational approach has placed tribals at a significant disadvantage when the outside world has encroached upon their society, whether through colonial rule or the establishment of a national state. The clash of cultures that accompanies the development process often leaves them in a worse condition than they were previously.

CIVILISATIONAL CONSCIOUSNESS WORLDWIDE

The global shift in civilisational consciousness, once dominated by post-World War II political and economic ideologies, is now being driven by Asia's economic and geopolitical advancements over the past decade. Even communist China, previously focused on eradicating its own civilisational consciousness, now proudly embraces its ancient civilisation as a model for the future, transitioning towards a neo-Confucian philosophy. The emergence of new civilisational consciousness is believed to have the potential to reshape international relations and order, even as the weakening of Western universalism leads to a dispersal of global power and a rise in national civilisations' awareness. Questions are being asked about the exclusivity of the West as the sole source of modernity, with the recognition growing that modernity can stem from various cultures such as Indian, Chinese and Japanese modernity.

Although historically rooted in a West-centric perspective, even the United Nations (UN) has begun to acknowledge cultural diversity through platforms such as the Cultural Diversity Convention (2001). The world is gradually realizing the importance of embracing and recognizing the plurality of cultures in shaping the global landscape and fostering mutual understanding among nations. The UN shifted its approach and endorsed a culture-focused development model for all in the 2015 Millennium Development Goals. It recommended this directive for the rest of the world to embrace Western modernity in the Measures for the Development of Underdeveloped Economies in 1951. The world is undoubtedly undergoing a new era of cultural transformation.

India is no exception to this global trend. Ancient India has been a civilisation since time immemorial. It was no surprise that the Indian freedom movement itself was civilisational. In his foundational treatise, *Hind Swaraj*, Mahatma Gandhi defined India's struggle against the British as a civilisational project. His chosen successor, Jawaharlal Nehru, said in an article on the freedom movement in the *Foreign Affairs* magazine in 1938, that India's battle for freedom was cultural. Decades later, Prime Minister Modi stated that India's soil had civilisational consciousness that has protected and saved the nation since ancient times, even as many great civilisations have perished. Addressing a programme on 'Meri Maati Mera Desh' campaign's Amrit Kalash Yatra at Kartavya Path in New Delhi, the Prime Minister emphasized on the significance of soil and its connection to spirituality and explained why soil is used as an element for the culmination of Azadi Ka Amrit Mahotsav. He cited the words of a poet to say that it was the soil of the land throughout history, where civilisation had flourished, humans had progressed and that it held the imprint of eons.

The independence struggle thus brought about a strong sense of civilisational consciousness among the millennials. But this consciousness gradually faded after independence due to the overwhelming economic, secular and ideological politics of the time. This loss of civilisational consciousness profoundly impacted various aspects of India's existence, including national security. However, in recent decades, there has been a revival of pre-independence Indian civilisational consciousness, coinciding with the increasing global awareness of culture. That said, it is also true that there has been a lack of effort to adopt a civilisational approach in an important area of national life—the relationship between the plains dwellers and the forest people. With rising global civilisational consciousness worldwide, there is an immediate need to understand communities residing in hills, forests and plains of India, from an Indian civilisational approach.

RATIONALE OF THE STUDY

Anthropology in India was introduced in the early nineteenth century. During this period, many British anthropologists and sociologists came to India to conduct studies on communities residing in the hills and the forests, and in the plains as well. Apart from anthropologists, British administrators also collected data on them. Missionaries, too, were attracted to ethnographic and linguistic research. Anthropologists have defined tribes in varied ways but if we survey the literature on tribes, some consensus can be reached. The tribes are conceptualized in anthropological literature as isolated. Most of the scholars were especially influenced by such early British anthropologists working elsewhere. That is how Western narratives on the traditional communities began in India. Forcibly separating and isolating the hills and the forest people from the inhabitants of the plains in India, colonial scholars created a gap between 'us' and 'them'.

The colonial perspective of forest and hills people in the Americas and Pacific region as savage, uncivilised and backward, was inappropriately extended to the hills and the forest people of India. For instance, the Portuguese, who ruled Goa, regarded the hills and forest people of the Sahyadri range as uncivilised and backward. The Portuguese divided the Goan population into two categories: (a) the Old Conquests and (b) the New Conquests—the first was converted to Christianity, whereas the latter comprised Hindus. While the converted people were recognised as civilised, the 'others' were regarded as semi-savage and uncivilised.

With the establishment of the Asiatic Society of Bengal and efforts by William Jones and the likes, a new direction and orientation came into existence with Indian and European scholars trying to identify common elements in the Indian and European civilisations. In this narrative, the 'Dravidians' and the hills and forest people were labelled as non-Aryan/tribes, theoretically separated from the mainstream Indians. In myriad racial classifications, this difference was highlighted through morphological, racial and linguistic criteria. Overall, there was an attempt to create a historical narrative that was conducive to colonial hegemonic designs and invidious Indian social, cultural and historical realities. A narrative propounded by the colonial West in the form of the 'Aryan invasion' theory conveniently belittled and brushed aside the great advancements that India had made. The Aryans 'came and conquered and built India' narrative was a wrong theoretical construct, serving ulterior motives of the colonisers by establishing that the first colonisers were the Aryans who had come all the way from the Steppes in Central Asia.

This was to justify the second colonisation by the Europeans. The Indo-European languages were conveniently linked to the European and north-Indian groups of Indo-Aryan with the Asiatic Society of Bengal trying desperately to locate those common threads that connected India and the Great Britain. This approach conveniently divided India into the Aryan and non-Aryan groups. For the Britishers, who claimed that they were the custodians of high civilisation, all Indians (and particularly the ones who were living in forests and hills), represented primitive, savage and barbarian people. In giving identity to the subject Indians, they used the criteria that suited them.

The Britishers needed to identify, classify and even segregate Indian masses in accordance with an agenda of divide and rule. Thus, the more the groups were segregated, the easier it was to deal with them separately. They labelled communities as tribes, criminal tribes, depressed castes and certain areas as scheduled districts, wholly excluded and partially excluded areas, to serve their convenience. The reason given for the exclusion was the fear that if these groups were allowed to be in direct contact with the others, they would be exploited, harmed and annihilated. But the real agenda was different. It was to exclude potentially rebellious groups so that they could be isolated and kept under surveillance. There were also nomadic communities. As it was difficult to contain and control them, the British promptly labelled them as 'criminal tribes', making them one of the most harassed and disadvantaged groups in India.

The U.N. Dhebar Commission Report of 1960–1961says that the isolation of the hills and forest people led to their exploitation by landlords, moneylenders and contractors. This left the forest and hills people at the mercy of government officials. The Dhebar Commission also indicates how the Scheduled Tribes concept evolved, namely, from the policy of isolation by the British, commencing in the eighteenth century, which commended separate administration model for 'wholly excluded areas' and 'areas of modified exclusion'. The Commission did point out the civic, civilisational and historical connection between the hills and forest communities—the Bhils, for instance—and the people of the plains. It showed no isolation of tribes during earlier times, when Bhils were in the administrative and civil service of the Rajputana rulers. The review of conditions of tribals before independence showed that the policy of isolation and drift meant nothing more than maintaining the status quo. It resulted in reducing these communities to a state of penury in most parts of India.

The hills and forest people enjoyed autonomy until the beginning of the medieval period. But by the end of the sixteenth century, they were harassed by the Muslim rulers and gradually lost autonomy. In medieval India, the Nagbansi Raja of Chotanagpur, the head of the Oraons and the Mundas, was reduced to a Malguzar (or a tributary) by 1585 CE. In the reign of Mughal ruler Jehangir, the Muslim governors wanted to extract extra payments from Chotanagpur Raja from the Oraon and the Munda village communities. However, this proved to be difficult. Consequently, in 1616 CE, the king was arrested and released only after 12 years. This was the beginning of the agrarian troubles among the forest and hill people.

The Bhils of western India also felt disturbed. There was a large-scale conversion of the Bhils to Islam. The Bhils were treated mercilessly. Consequently, they retreated deeper into the hills. India's Gonds also met the same fate in the medieval period. In the beginning of the fifteenth century, the Gond dynasty was firmly established in Garha (near today's Jabalpur). In 1564, the Mughal army conquered Garha and the Gonds had to recognize the sovereignty of the new rulers. By 1780, the Gond dynasty had ended when their last ruler was captured. The Banjaras of north India also had to collaborate with the Mughal army when it invaded South India, which resulted in the migration of these people to Andhra Pradesh. When they, with their bullocks, became free from the Mughal army, started trading and thus became a useful medium of transaction between the northern and the southern parts of the country.

The next phase started with the advent of the British rule in the country. When the Britishers first entered Chotanagpur (then known as Jungal Mahal), they faced fierce opposition from the community settled there. Subsequently, these people had to face money lenders and usurers, who exploited them. Encroachment on their forests by alien groups and the government led to the cessation of their right of sole occupation. The forest contractors began to carry away a part of the forest produce. The British land settlement policy also affected the ownership system. Oppression by the usurers and the mahajans, enhancement of the rent by landlords, etc., led to a number of disturbances and uprisings.

Such disturbances and uprisings started in 1772 by the Mal Paharias, and then followed a series of disturbances in 1795, 1800, 1801, 1807, 1808, 1816, 1821 and the Paika rebellion between 1787 and 1830. In 1831–1832 followed the Great Kol Rising. The revolt was, however, suppressed. The Regulation XIII of 1833 was passed and Chotanagpur was declared a non-regulating area. This was the start of the British's isolation policy. The Khond rising in 1846, the Santhal rebellion in 1854, the unrest in Dhanbad in 1869–1870, etc., extended the non-regulating system. In due course, the idea of a distinct and special arrangement for isolated areas was enforced. In 1874, the Scheduled District Act was passed, giving the Executive wide powers, which were generously exercised by the colonial masters. Still, a few uprisings, like the Sardari agitation in 1887, the Birsa movement in 1895, the Tana Bhagat movement in 1914, etc., came up although they were quelled. By then, the agitators had started participating in the freedom movement launched by Mahatma Gandhi.

With the Government of India Act of 1919, two types of exclusions came into force: (a) the 'wholly excluded area' and (b) the 'area of modified exclusion. The acceleration of the freedom movement was a headache for the rulers. In 1935, an Act was passed to incorporate 'excluded areas' and 'partially excluded areas'. Reservations were made for the hills and forest communities and a few other sections of the Indian population. No Act of the then Federal Legislature or the Provincial Legislatures would apply to these secluded areas. This was all at the administrative level. In the British period, the communities faced another encroachment in the form of conversion to Christianity by the missionaries who accompanied the rulers. This resulted in the creation of factions among the local population—tribals and converted tribals. In the north-east, a major population was converted. Together, the religious conversion and the excluded area policy gave rise to a somewhat separate identity in the minds of the people of that region.

However, not much changed after independence. The post-independence Indian establishment studies and public discourses have unfortunately neglected the millennial civilisational relationship in the country. Instead, these studies were influenced by Western scholars and ideas, leading to a division between the foresters and plainsmen, similar to what the colonists did. Regrettably, there has been no systematic effort to study them from an Indian civilisational perspective. However, considering the multitude of historical, epigraphic, and civilisational evidence that has emerged in recent decades across various fields, it is imperative to completely reassess the colonial perspective on the significance of forests and hills. A thorough examination of Indian civilisational evidence will demonstrate the necessity of adopting a methodical and all-encompassing approach to comprehending the communities residing in India's forests and hills; it's an endeavour that has yet to be undertaken. Only through this approach can we truly grasp the intricacies of the Indian reality.

Such a research is not only crucial from a social, cultural and civilisational standpoint but it also holds significant strategic importance for the nation, ensuring its security, peace and harmony. The colonial administration's strategy of dividing rather than integrating different communities from the hills, forests and the plains was a deliberate tactic to fragment and segregate the people of India based on religious, caste, regional and linguistic identities. Unfortunately, even after several decades of independence, Indian academic and administrative institutions have failed to recognize the necessity of re-evaluating this flawed and perilous colonial approach.

The academic, social and political discourse still perpetuates the colonial perspective that the tribal communities living in the forests and hills are fundamentally different from the rest of the Bharatiya population. They continue to be viewed as the 'other people'. This viewpoint implies that the plains people are more civilised and responsible for studying and understanding the tribal communities. The colonialists' original intention to civilise the colonized people—an inherently racist approach—has now evolved into a social science discipline known as the anthropology of modernity. This discipline aims to modernize and civilise the hill and forest communities according to the perceptions and treatment of the plains people.

In the past, research on Indian tribes was primarily conducted by colonial ethnographers and explorers. These studies were taken over by Indian anthropologists in post-colonial India. The studies often portrayed tribes as backward, uncivilised and the scholars believed that the tribes needed to be assimilated into mainstream society to be 'civilised'. The tribal and non-tribal communities in India have co-existed for centuries, influencing each other in different ways in varying degrees. This was also another way of classifying the tribal population of India based on the degree of incorporation into the non-tribal caste-based Hindu society.

Using a variety of written sources, research has been done on the information that is now known about the people who live in the hills and forests. These publications are an excellent place to start learning about the problem. But the most important thing is to assess where these individuals stand in the Indian caste system. In order to do this, a careful reading of ancient texts and literature is required. It is not yet clear if this has been done with the requisite rigour. Without conducting extensive research, academics have observed several aspects of the people living on the periphery of Hindu caste society. Examining the historical veracity and foundation of these observations is crucial. This could be studied from the perspective of either the tribal society or from the civilisational approach.

INDIAN CIVILISATIONAL UNDERPINNINGS

India is unique in that it has a continuity of thousands of years of existence. One may wonder how and why India has lived as a vibrant society for such a long time. Take the case of 'Sindhu Sabhyata', which had well-developed urban centres. This civilisation has, in practice, not vanished. It is still reflected in the customs, traditions and cultural milieu of contemporary India. From the earliest times, the mountains have been considered the abode of Gods and revered and worshipped. There are hundreds of shrines and temples built atop the hills and innumerable caves and monuments dedicated to the divine all over India. *Skanda Purana* has a whole section called *Sahyadri Kanda* that provides descriptions of over a hundred Tirthas in the Sahyadri range.

Hills and forests, which were considered sacred, purer places for study and contemplation, were also regarded as the abodes of Gods and worshipped. Mount Kailash is worshipped as the abode of Shiva. Likewise, the Govardhan Hill in Vrindavan is associated with Krishna. So, the hills in India were not mere natural spots but abodes of higher spirits and centres for those seeking to attain the highest spiritual wisdom. They were not backward places.

An ancient Vedic scripture, the *Purusha Suktam*, speaks of Aranya (forest) and Grama (village) as integral and simultaneous parts of the process of evolution. A forest was neither associated with the uncivilised nor was the village with the civilised. If in Western anthropology, those who lived in plains were regarded as civilised and the inhabitants of forests as primitive and backward, it was the other way around in the Indian civilisation story. Forests were associated with contemplation and knowledge of higher life, and the plains were associated with the mundane. The Vedic texts are divided into Aranyaka, regarded as the book of Forests, and Brahmanas, the book of plains.

The Aranyaka texts are called thus because they were works to be read in the forests, in contradistinction to the regular Brahmanas, which were to be read in the plains. Kol, Bhil and Gond are some of the ancient communities known from the days of *Ramayana*. Gond and Bhil are the top two communities in terms of population size. The anthropological approach in the West, labelling foresters as backward and plainsmen as forward, contradicts the Indian perspective of integrated humans as a whole, as depicted in the ancient philosophical concept of *Isavasyam Idam Sarvam* from the *Isavasya Upanishad*.

Prominent Indian anthropologists and social scientists like N.K. Bose, G.S. Ghurye, S.C. Dube, D.N. Mazumdar, André Béteille and B.K. Roy Burman have established a close historical interaction between tribes and caste societies. According to Ghurye, Indian tribes were never isolated but were part of the Hindu civilisation, and their cultural beliefs reflect a rudimentary form of Hindu society. According to scholars such as Bose, Mandelbaum, Dube and Surajit Sinha, the Juang tribes, Urali tribes, Raj Gonds and Bhumij tribes, respectively, have been observed to undergo a transformation from tribes to castes over a long period of time. This phenomenon has been ongoing since ancient times. The interaction between Hindu civilisation and tribes has been continuing for centuries if not millennia. Tribes like Bhumjis, the Majhis, Bhils, Raj Gonds, Mundas, Oraon, Tharus and Santhals have largely assimilated within the Hindu fold; while in north-east India, tribes like the Naga, Kuki and Mizo have embraced Christianity in large numbers.

What distinguished the people of the plains from those of the hills and forests was not a codified set of beliefs or practices but rather the geographical terrain in which these two cultures coexisted. This ancient civilisation has marked a continuum of elements from the Vana to Kshetra, although with varied changes. This continuum is reflected in the incorporation of hill and forest deities, myths and rituals within the fold of Hinduism, such as the worship of Jagannath or the story of Chenchu Lakshmi of Andhra Pradesh.

The two terrains, Aranya and Janapada, where Aranya is the same as the Vana while Janapada represents the plains, where the recurring and mutual influences of each terrain is found on the other. The biggest factor for such interaction was the gradual expansion of the Kshetra and the selective incorporation of the elements of the Vana by the socio-economic and political structure of the Kshetra. It was not only the traders and merchants who moved through the routes passing through the forests but also saints, ascetics and mystics who ventured along the path. The hills and forest people of eastern India, from Juangs to Munda and Savaras to Oraons, still reflect the influences of Bhakti saints, particularly the Vaishnavite Chaitanya Mahaprabhu, who travelled through their regions. Migration of people, particularly from the Kshetra to the hills and forests, also contributed to this interaction.

There is also a need to understand the dynamics of Indian civilisation as a dialogue between the Great Tradition of the Indian civilisation, that is, the Sanskritic traditions, and the Little Traditions, which were constituted of various regional and local traditions. Through the dialogue, both the Great and Little traditions influenced each other. There is no single explanation to the interaction and assimilation of hill and forest culture with that of plains. The phenomenon can be understood by viewing this interaction as a largely organic and gradual interaction of the constituents of the socio-economic, political and cultural whole, interacting in parts and facilitating mutual transmission of other parts. This interaction was marked by the accommodation, assimilation and co-existence of hill and forest culture within the larger Hindu fold, as opposed to Abrahamic religions, whose interactions are more exclusionary and less accommodative, given the essential nature of their theology constrained by well-defined boundaries. Furthermore, the uniqueness of this interaction stems from the nature of Indian traditions, which enabled the processes of assimilation, incorporation and co-existence to function, rather than from the processes themselves.

REVIVING INDIAN NARRATIVES

In the last decade or so, with rising global civilisational consciousness, there has been an immediate need to understand communities residing in hills, forests and plains of India from an Indian civilisational approach. Through an in-depth study, an Indian narrative has to be established, which is not an alternative narrative but stands the test of objective interpretation of the gathered empirical data.

Scholars such as Bhangya Bhukya (2010) has pointed out that oral traditions, including stories, songs and other forms of cultural expression, offer valuable insights into the lived experiences, social structures and historical narratives of Adivasi communities, which are often absent or misrepresented in the colonial archive. This approach emphasizes the need to challenge imposed Adivasi identities and deconstruct the silencing of marginalized voices by majoritarian perspectives. This new turn underlines the need to move beyond analysing just 'the claustrophobic confines' of Adivasi identity, which was imposed on them by 'the colonial administrator, the colonial anthropologist, the missionary' and to rethink the production of knowledge about Adivasis by unpacking majoritarian voices that silence the marginal ones (Damodaran and Dasgupta, 2022).

Concerns remain regarding the dichotomy pertaining to development and preservation of the tradition of such communities, as modernization has brought about major changes in the lifestyle of these people and diluted the authenticity of many age-old practices related to their socio-cultural aspects. The colonial narrative caused ample harm to these communities. Their philosophy, literature, aestheticism, medicines and agriculture are rich and have existed since time immemorial but suffered greatly during colonisation. Progress is only possible by seeking neither dilute nor destroy the Adivasi language, culture and philosophy. If language dies, then the corresponding identity also dies.

The word 'diversity' was not part of the UN's lexicon for long. It was only in 2001 that it came to be mentioned at the United Nations Cultural Diversity Convention. It was then that it was first accepted as 'cultural diversity'. Until then, terms such as 'human rights' and 'individualism' were the models. The idea of diversity has to be prioritized and highlighted in works that are proposed for future on the Janjati Samuh (Samaj).

Social capital is the capacity of the people to work together. One can be a beneficiary of social capital but not the owner of it. Social capital cannot be established like a bank or company; it evolves. For example, a family is a social capital—one cannot form a family by law. Likewise, a community is a social capital too. A focus on the recognition of community as a social capital will automatically help remove the politics of identity. When social capital plays an important part in the progress and development of a society, such development becomes more sustainable. The social capital of Janjati Samuh (Samaj)—the capacity of people to work together, to relate together—needs to be emphasized. Also, the Janjati community's 'asmita', 'astitva', 'aastha' and 'vikas' should be prioritized while conducting any empirical research. To understand the asmita of the tribes, researchers should focus on original stories, spiritual aspects, worldview, lifestyle and continuity. The identity of this diverse group should be understood holistically.

The history of forests and hills people in India has often been seen through an anthropological and ethnic lens, leading to stereotypes of backwardness, nudity and isolation. These studies have been influenced by the colonial scholars' politics of knowledge-making, which has marginalized the forest people. The fact is that the forests and hills people have a long-standing notion of state and sovereignty, as seen in the rich histories of tribal dynasties like the Cheros, Gonds and Ahoms. Despite this, the post-colonial period has witnessed a reluctance to recognize and respect them. The emergence of tribal history challenges these misconceptions and narratives, which have been supported by caste politics in India. It is crucial for academics to reconstruct and highlight the true narrative of these people and portray them as sovereigns rather than subalterns in their regions.

Any fresh research should prioritize insider narratives from the Janjatiya Samuh members. Scholars/academicians/researchers from the community should be encouraged to conduct an in-depth study on their own culture(s). The renewed research studies should not be reactionary, thus leading to a counter-narrative. The Western research methodology must be completely abandoned in order to bring out embodied experiences and perspectives of the hills, forests and plains communities of India.

The Indian holistic view of looking at the Janjatis of India should be adopted. For example, the art, craft and celebrations of the community is not an exhibitory event but a participatory one. Oral tradition is a major part of the history of the Janjati Samuh. It is important to treat the oral tradition as a pillar to understand their narrative. According to communitarian philosophy, nature and humans are a single entity and the ancestors (spirits) also co-exist. All this has to be taken care of, while working with the Janjati Samaj. In undertaking the study of the *Vedas* and *Itihaas*, the strands reflective of the commonality of history should be highlighted. *Mahabharata*, *Ramayana* and other such pan-Indian texts needs to be studied in depth to highlight the narratives of common history and cultural heritage of this ancient land and its people.

The understanding of the Janjati Samuh should be from the perspective of sensitivity rather than from the Western anthropological modernity. Field views should be given more importance than bookish knowledge. The research should involve collating, collecting, analysing and critiquing the existing literature before starting fresh research; however, fresh research should focus on understanding local wisdom, knowledge and practices and instead of carrying extensive research on each and every tribe of India, a representative study across India can be carried out. The geo-cultural context should be an important basis for understanding the Janjatiya Samuh.

Oral histories/stories of these communities, in their setting, should be particularly documented. Also, their role in the freedom movement, with a special focus on prison reports, first information report (FIR) and court proceedings instituted by the British, should be recorded. These documents and reports of the Raj period would provide deeper insights into the realities of the society of that specific period. The narrative that hills and forests are not backward regions but places of enlightenment, needs to be assertively established. The ethos of the Janjatiya Samuh should always be a priority while undertaking such research.

The names given to some of the Janjatiya Samuh, as recorded in colonial reports and further recognised, should be revisited. There is an immediate need for terminological dignity to be accorded to these communities. A good case in point in this regard is, for example, the Birhor tribe, which translates to 'forest man'. This specific terminology has been given to the Birhor by neighbouring dominant groups.

Our earlier discussion has highlighted a major issue with tribal studies, which is the perception of tribes within a colonial social structure. Tribes have been historically portrayed as primitive, savage and inferior, and this perception persists to this day. Anthropologists have attempted to challenge this notion but tribes are still categorized as societies with the minimal division of labour, lacking complexity, and without literacy skills. Anthropology has viewed the changes occurring within tribes as a transition towards becoming peasants, castes or socially diverse groups, resulting in the erosion of tribal identity. Unfortunately, the fact that tribes constitute their own distinct societies has been overlooked, and anthropologists tend to view tribal societies as eroding and assimilating into castes and peasant communities. In the post-colonial era, anthropologists have started to analyse tribes through the lens of castes, as caste is primarily an occupational category. Tribals have been equated with castes but in order to truly transform the discourse and decolonise the study of tribal communities, it is essential to view tribes as societies similar to any other.

The characteristics defining a Telugu society, for instance, are found in tribal societies like the Gond and the Kolams indicating no fundamental differences. The colonial legacy categorized tribes, leading to a narrow focus on their social and economic backwardness in anthropological writings. This perspective overshadowed the broader political economy context, marked by land appropriation, displacement and exploitation. There is a need to decolonise the understanding of the tribal narratives and social identities in order to revolutionise the colonial narrative in India. The study of forests and hills' people is no longer solely within the realm of anthropology; it has become a subject that spans across various disciplines. A comprehensive approach is needed to comprehend the narratives of forest and hill communities, which calls for an interdisciplinary and trans-disciplinary framework to be implemented across the disciplines.

KEY ISSUES NEEDING ATTENTION

With the desirability of a new framework, it is crucial to highlight the subsequent focal points that necessitate further investigation. This will enable the acquisition of fresh perspectives from scholars and researchers across different disciplines, thereby fostering a dialogue on the multifaceted narratives of forest and hill communities in India. It suggests that academics need to prioritize the showcasing of authentic narratives of these communities as independent entities rather than marginalized groups. A holistic comprehension of forest communities' historical, cultural, social, economic, environmental and political dimensions can be attained through a combination of multidisciplinary, interdisciplinary and cross-disciplinary approaches. To encapsulate:

- It is vital to reassess the imposed colonial narratives that depict a dichotomy between the plains people and the forest people, and that which have affected India's Janjati communities.
- It is essential to comprehend the Janjati Samuh of India within their unique ecological setting, along with gaining knowledge about their creation stories, traditional tales, spiritual beliefs, perspectives on the world, philosophy, way of life and enduring traditions.
- There is a fundamental need to preserve oral histories of and narratives from the Janjati communities, as they provide valuable insights into their rich cultural heritage. Additionally, it is important to safeguard references to the Janjati communities that can be found in classical literature, ancient Indian writings and vernacular works, as they contribute to a deeper understanding and appreciation of their traditions and contributions to society.
- It is necessary to have a comprehensive understanding of the shared rituals, customs and traditional cultural practices that binds the communities together. This will offer valuable insights into the relationship between the Janjati villages and the Indian plains.
- The documentation of present literature is essential to conserve local wisdom, indigenous knowledge, traditional conflict resolution techniques and community-driven practices as a valuable social capital for our future generations.
- A detailed list of reference materials that accurately portray the Indian stories of the Janjati Samuh must be included in the university curriculum.
- The time has come to revive the colonial names or labels that were enforced on the Janjati communities of India.
- The critical analysis of the working and relevance of Schedule-V and Schedule-VI areas mentioned in the Constitution of India is of utmost importance and requires immediate attention.

- The role of the Janjati Samuh in the Indian independence movement can be examined through a critical analysis of jail reports, FIRs and the judicial processes established by the British colonial authorities.
- To investigate the nationalist trends in the writings of Indian anthropologists both in the pre- and post-independence periods, which aimed to serve the Indian nation.
- To understand tribal history, it is important to identify its sources and make an attempt to uncover the historical convergence between the plains and forest tribes.
- There is an urgent need to write an integrated history of India from a civilisational point view that brings out how the forests and hills people lived harmoniously with other people.
- This research aims to enhance the existing anthropology syllabi and curriculum in India by incorporating the insights gained on the nationalist tradition of Indian anthropology.

THE METHODOLOGY

In the beginning, there are generally two approaches used by researchers working in the domain of tribal studies: 'evolutionary' and 'civilisational'. The evolutionary approach has been typically used by the Western social scientists to understand the tribes of Africa, Australia and New Zealand, while the civilisational perspective appears more suitable to study communities of the hills, forests and plains of India. The civilisational approach tends to look into aspects of co-existence and continuity among people residing in a specific geographical setting.

Anthropologists have been following the models, theories and concepts coming from the West, and this has resulted in a shocking lack of originality in the Indian context. These concepts merely imitate the Western models. Anthropologists are uncritically adopting concepts and terms that have come from the West and they have resorted to essentialistic constructions of the tribal communities. The major problem with this method is that it does not contribute to the understanding of diversity. Also, in these narrations, the scholars miss the subaltern voices, i.e. the voices of the people. There is a realisation that over a period of time, we are resorting to what has been termed as 'scientific colonialism' and 'academic dependency'. These terms are used for the way in which they have connected us for decades as a colonial agency. This academic dependency is established through various research institutions, funding agencies and research publications, many of which are controlled by certain publishing houses cumulatively, resulting in a kind of perpetual dependency on the West.

For the colonisers, all non-Western people, non-white people and non-Christian people are pagans or tribals. However, outside Europe, there are only tribals and pagans. Later, in the course of grappling with the complexity of the Indian situation, a distinction was made between tribe and caste, and essentialization was done to create a model in anthropology. Anthropologists follow Robert Redfield, who gave a definition of ideal folk society as essentially 'isolated', 'illiterate', 'homogenous', 'custom bound' and 'tradition bound'. The colonial writers made a distinction between tribes and caste, thereby treating tribes as a distinctive category. They know that they ignored the processes of tribe caste continuum, tribe caste mobility, tribe-like caste and caste-like tribes, thus leading to an essentialized identity.

Scholars such as Guha and Gadgil (1992), Sundar (1997), Skaria (1999), Prasad (2003), Misra & Basa (2005) and Anil Kumar (2011) highlight the role of indigenous communities as sustainable guardians of the environment that challenge colonial forestry policies. Additionally, the works of Venkatesan (2012) and the Xaxa Committee Report (2014) argue that post-colonial anthropology should progress beyond viewing indigenous peoples merely as 'subjects' and instead emphasize their agency and lived experiences. Smith (1999), Shah (2010), Bodhi (2018), Sunder (2007) and Balaram (2021) advocate for a collaborative and participatory approach that respects indigenous epistemologies. They emphasize the importance of ethnographies co-authored with indigenous communities, as well as the incorporation of oral traditions, folklore and community histories, as a framework for decolonising anthropology. Scholars such as Baviskar (2023), Tripura (2023) and Shah (2024) collectively emphasize the necessity of reassessing anthropological methodologies in India, promoting strategies that elevate indigenous perspectives and question colonial paradigms. The aforementioned researchers recognized the need for methodological changes in the decolonisation of anthropology.

Therefore, to move away from the colonial constructs/narratives and their perspectives or framework, the new methodology shall include the following to understanding the Janjati Samuh of India:

1. Indological approach
2. Phenomenological approach
3. Ethno-methodological approach
4. Autoethnography

Indological approach: Indology can contribute to a deeper understanding of the cultural, social and historical dimensions of the Indian subcontinent and its diverse communities. The incorporation of indological perspectives into anthropological research on the Janjati Samuh of the Indian subcontinent allows for a more nuanced and contextually rich analysis. Researchers can draw on historical texts, classical literature and cultural insights to obtain an in-depth understanding of the lived experiences of communities and individuals in the region. This interdisciplinary approach serves the purpose of a holistic comprehension of the complex and dynamic cultural landscape of the Indian subcontinent.

Phenomenological approach: In anthropology, phenomenology is often used to explore and understand the lived experiences of individuals within specific cultural contexts. By incorporating phenomenological approaches into anthropological research, scholars can gain insights into the intricate and often subtle aspects of human experience within diverse cultural settings. It provides a framework for understanding the meanings individuals attribute to their actions, relationships and the world around them.

Ethno-Methdological approach: The ethno-methodological approach focuses on the study of everyday social interactions and the methods people use to make sense of their social world. Also, ethnomethodology seeks to understand how individuals create and maintain social order through their everyday actions. It encourages reflexivity, meaning that researchers should be aware of and reflect on their own assumptions and biases. This self-awareness is considered important for understanding the subjectivity inherent in the study of social interactions.

Autoethnography: Autoethnographic research is needed to explore personal experiences within a cultural context, offering insights into phenomena that traditional research methods might overlook. It allows researchers to bridge the gap between personal narratives and broader social or cultural meanings, fostering a deeper understanding of human behaviour and experiences. This approach is particularly valuable for examining under-researched areas or for providing insider perspectives on cultural practices.

These correct techniques and approaches were not followed by colonial anthropologists when they studied the tribal people. Post-independence, many Indian anthropologists used the civilisational approach to study Indian society and culture. This approach, first developed by Robert Redfield, placed folk and urban societies in an evolutionary 'continuum'. The 'Little and Great traditions' conceptual framework was used in the Indian context to argue about the circulation of cultural elements at two levels. Nirmal Kumar Bose applied this approach to argue about the continuity of Indian culture through cultural assimilation, accommodation or unification. While Bose followed a cultural model of 'tribe-Hindu continuum' to explain 'assimilation', his later anthropological works mainly concentrated on explaining how the tribals were an integral part of the Indian civilisation, which was one of the main political discourses at that time. His analysis of bringing out the beauty of unity in the diversity of Indian civilisation reflected his concerns for a united India. These research interests and the focus of the study bring out the freedom-fighter in Bose and his capability to use anthropology to address some of the important debates of that time.

L.P. Vidyarthi's focus was to provide dimensions of the study of civilisation through a sacred complex of Gaya and Kashi and the nature-man-spirit complex. The earlier studies concentrated mainly on the tribe, and the rural and urban continuum to understand the civilisational aspect of India. Vidyarthi offered different recluse in understanding the Indian civilisation. In furthering the analysis of the sacred complex, he, in collaboration with B.N. Saraswati and M. Jha, studied Kashi. Together, they tried to understand (a) cult of Thirthas, (b) cult of Vishwanath, (c) cult of the Ganges and (d) cult of Smasan, offering their analysis of how they can be understood as dimensions of understanding the civilisation and its characteristics. With his analysis, Vidyarthi proved that it was not necessary that one should not only restrict oneself to tribal, rural and urban dimensions and their interchangeability but also understand the sacred complexes such as Gaya and Kashi to offer dimensionality in the study of Indian civilisation.

Bose and D.N. Majumdar widened the scope of anthropology by venturing into streams such as civilisation, nationalism, cultural change, urbanization, industrialisation and so on. Surajit Sinha's 'tribe-caste-peasant continuum' model introduced structural factors and flexibility to explain 'integration'. Such an understanding led us to conclude that civilisation as a social process transcends religious traditions and does not work similarly for all. But, after these classic research works, not many anthropologists used the above methodology. Researchers using an indological approach can gain a deep grasp of the lived experiences of the local communities and individuals by referencing historical texts, classical literature and cultural ideas.

The research on the understanding of forest and hill people should be carried out on three important aspects: (a) 'asmita' (identity), (b) 'astitva' (existence) and (c) 'vikas' (development). Researchers must focus on history and civilisation, original stories, spiritual aspects, worldview, lifestyle and continuity. The identity of this diverse group should be understood holistically. The proposed fresh research should prioritize insiders' narratives from the forest and hill members.

Scholars/academicians/researchers from the 'Janjatis' should be encouraged to conduct in-depth studies on their own culture(s). The proposed fresh research studies should not be reactionary, leading to a counter-narrative. The Western research methodology should be abandoned entirely to bring out embodied experiences and perspectives of India's hills, forests and plains communities.

CHAPTER 2

The Janjatis of India

India is a melting pot of cultures and the Janjati communities are an intrinsic part of India's diverse cultural treasury. Our country has the largest number of Janjatis compared to any other country. There are 705 notified ethnic groups, as per Article 342 of the Constitution of India, spread across various states and union territories. The population of Janjatis, as per the 2011 Census, is 10.45 crore. The Janjati communities constitute 8.6 per cent of the country's total population and 11.3 per cent of the total rural population. The population of Scheduled Tribes (ST) males is 5.25 crores and that of ST females is 5.20 crores. Janjati communities live in about 15 per cent of the country's areas, in various ecological and geo-climatic conditions, ranging from plains and forests to hills.

A majority of the Janjati population is concentrated in the eastern, central and western belts covering the nine states of Odisha, Madhya Pradesh, Chhattisgarh, Jharkhand, Maharashtra, Gujarat, Rajasthan, Andhra Pradesh and West Bengal. About 12 per cent inhabit the north-eastern region, roughly 5 per cent in the southern region and about 3 per cent in the northern states. The Janjati communities in India are enormously diverse and heterogeneous, in respect of languages spoken, art and culture and mode of livelihood.

THE CONCEPT OF JANJATIS

In ancient Indian literature, there was no equivalent for the English term 'tribe'. Hill and forest people are known by different names, meaning either the 'denizens of hills and forests' or the 'original inhabitants'. The tribals of India generally live in the forests and hills. In the Indian context, the term tribe refers to 'Jana'. The terms Adivasi (first/original settlers), Girijan (hill-dwellers), Vanvasi (forest-dwellers), Vanyajati (forest caste), Adimjati (primitive castes), Janajati (folk people/communities), Vanvasi (inhabitants of forest), Pahari (hill tribe/mountain dwellers), Anusuchit jati (Scheduled Tribes) and so forth, are of recent origin. Among them, Adivasi is known most extensively and Anusuchit Janjati (Scheduled Tribe) is the constitutional official term that covers the gamut of these communities. According to Hardiman David (1987), the tribal people in Gujarat are referred to as Kaliparaja or the 'black people'. Additionally, Persian terms like Qabila and Qabilewale were commonly used to describe tribes. There is empirical evidence suggesting that the term 'jati' was used as a suffix for tribal communities, such as Adivasi jati, Vanyajati and Janaj-jati, which translates to 'kind of forest dweller'. Denis Vidal (1997) further explains that in Sirohi, Rajasthan, the term 'jati' was often used interchangeably to refer to both castes and tribes.

'Jati' in India does not carry the same meaning as its English equivalent 'caste'. Instead, it signifies a 'kind or type' rather than a caste. In various contexts, 'jati' is used to refer to different categories such as *manushya* jati for humankind, *devta* jati and *danav* jati for gods and demons, respectively, *stri* jati for women, *pashu* jati for the 'category' of animals and *vanaspati* jati for plants.

According to the eminent Indologist and historian, Nihar Ranjan Ray (1972), the term 'tribe' in the Indian context suggests that, during ancient times the Sanskrit term 'Jana' referred to these primitive communities of people. He has suggested 'Jana', used earlier to denote tribal communities, such as Savaras, Bhils, Nagas, Kirat, Pulindas and Kols, in place of the term 'tribe'. He argues that the terms Jana and Jati are both derived from the root Jan, which means 'to be born' and 'to give birth to' and, hence, have a biological meaning. This implies that the term Jana in ancient times referred to the autochthonous people, such as the Savaras, the Kullutas, the Kolhas, the Bhils, the Khasas, the Kinnars and a countless number of others whom we now know as 'tribes'.

Over time, each of these communities lent their names to the territories they inhabited and the territories came to be known as Janapadas. In his work, Ghurye refers to the tribes as 'backward Hindus'. This terminology aligns with the objective of 'nation building', which aims to establish a national identity centred around Hinduism by bringing together people from diverse backgrounds under a unified category.

Tribal communities often have different names assigned to them, sometimes by using common terms. These designations are often created by outsiders and the people belonging to those communities are not known to the outside world by their original indigenous names. Tribes refer to themselves by their own community names, such as Munda, Santhal, Gond, Baiga, Sahariya, Gaddi, or by the term 'jati' or 'Adivasi jati.' These outsiders may include neighbouring tribes or clans. For example, the Laju Nocte tribe, known to outsiders and other Nocte clans by this name, refers to its people as Olo. Similarly, the Khamptis identify themselves as Tai, even though the term 'Khampti' has significance in their language system.

The tribals, or Janajatis, have been an integral part of Indian civilisation. Various elements in ancient India were contributed by the tribals. It is believed that they were the earliest among the present inhabitants of the country. The ancient and epic literatures, such as the *Vedas*, the *Puranas*, the *Ramayana* and the *Mahabharata*, present good accounts of the tribal people of India, naming them as Janas, Sabaras, Nishadas, Kiratas, Yaksas, Mundas, Bhils, Nagas, among others.

There is no referable meaning and definition of the term 'tribe' or 'tribal' in Indian history. One reason for that could be that, in the ancient Indian languages, there was no term equivalent to 'tribe'. The common contention in all the writings is that the appellative is an imposition of anthropologists and missionaries. The term 'tribe', therefore, in India has no proper explanation and thus has a limited scope of application to the diverse situations of the population. Revitalising the thrust of liberation from the old perspective is an urgent call so that this education becomes a powerful tool in liberating the so-called tribals from backwardness. For that, one has to go back in history to find the values that existed and were practised among the so-called tribal people of India. This system of de-tribalisation could become a powerful instrument for the liberation, dignity and identity of people groups.

The long debate over the definition of a tribe has proved sterile. Still, it may be best now to view it as an ethnic category defined by real or putative descent, as well as a corporate self-identity and a wide range of commonly shared cultural traits. In other words, tribals believe that they have a common descent, consciously hold a collective self-image and possess a distinctive cultural ethos—many elements of which they collectively share. Shared cognitive orientation and perception of belonging impart cohesion and unity to the ethnic groups. They often develop individual identities and function as the principal unit of larger group loyalty beyond kin, clan and residential local groups. Racial, religious and linguistic groups can also acquire ethnic characteristics and we must consider tribal ethnicity alongside the ethnicity of such groups.

Indian anthropologists have been acutely aware of a certain lack of fit between what their discipline defines as a tribe and what they are obliged to describe as tribes. Yet, they have continued with the existing labels. The anthropologists themselves have not made any significant attempt to arrive at the criteria of tribes located in different contexts. The word 'tribe' has long been used by both anthropologists and laypersons, but recently by few Indian anthropologists it has come under attack as a derogatory term, implying an inferior and backward way of life.

Groups and communities identified and enumerated as tribes during British rule came to be re-classified as Scheduled Tribes after the Constitution of India was adopted in 1950. Article 342 of the Constitution provided for listing these groups in the Schedule so that certain administrative and political concessions could be extended to them. Thus, a distinction was drawn in the form of the tribe as a social and cultural entity and the tribe as a politico-administrative category. The Constitution came to an understanding that tribes in India deserved special protection. Accordingly, the 'scheduling' device was adopted to enable the identification of tribal communities and tribal areas for the extension of such protection.

The 'scheduling' of tribal communities was done on colonial administrative arrangements. The 'partially excluded areas' became 'scheduled' under the 'Fifth Schedule' of the Constitution, while 'wholly excluded areas' were scheduled under the 'Sixth Schedule'. However, there were many tribal groups inhabiting neither of these regions. Over a period of time, continued political and social mobilisation has resulted in the addition of newer areas for inclusion in the Fifth and Sixth Schedules of the Constitution.

Many committees and commissions were set up to suggest criteria to enable the identification of tribal communities/groups for their inclusion in the list of Scheduled Tribes under Article 342(1). The Lokur Committee was set up in 1965 to look into matters relating to scheduling groups as Scheduled Tribes. It was this panel that delineated the criteria for scheduling, which continues to operate to this day. The committee recommended five criteria for identification, namely (1) traits, (2) distinct culture, (3) geographical isolation, (4) shyness of contact with the community at large and (5) backwardness. Then, there are other groups within the Scheduled Tribes known as Particularly Vulnerable Tribal Groups (PVTGs). These have been identified based on the following criteria: (a) Forest-dependent livelihoods, (b) Pre-agricultural level of existence, (c) Stagnant or declining population, (d) Low literacy rates and (e) Subsistence-based economy. Several tribal-populated and tribal-dominant areas across the country that are not Scheduled Areas are not covered by the protections offered under the Fifth Schedule.

Certain parts of north-east states are covered by the Sixth Schedule of the Constitution and a host of other legal and administrative arrangements for the protection of tribal autonomy. Historically, tribes of this region have seen 'isolationist' policies of the colonial British, who labelled many hilly tribal tracts of the north-east as 'wholly excluded' areas. Wholly excluded areas were later included in the Sixth Schedule of the Indian Constitution by the Constituent Assembly. The British policies of 'protectionism' and 'isolationism' were replaced by policies of development and integration of the north-east through the Sixth Schedule of the Constitution. The primary objective of the Sixth Schedule is to protect tribal areas and interests by prioritising self-governance through constitutional institutions at the district or regional level. In addition to these, there are also the statutory Autonomous Councils, Autonomous District Councils in Assam and Hill District Councils in Manipur. These were established by the Acts passed by state legislatures.

Siva Prasad, in his article titled 'Is Tribe a Fiction', discussed that as anthropologists, we always use the term 'tribe' with the confidence that we know about it clearly. Yet, we do not know what it implies. We study the 'tribal' communities as demarcated by the constitutional categories and we presume that with the approval of the government, a community attains 'tribal' status. Isn't it paradoxical that we study communities which are categorised as 'tribal', yet not tribal?

There are plenty of examples that one can cite. 'Tribal' communities are so varied that we find there are situations where even some of the communities follow caste-like hierarchies and claim a status akin to Kshatriya or another caste status (such as the Raj Gond, Bagata, etc.). This is not to suggest that tribes are castes, or vice versa. What needs to be highlighted here is that in certain aspects, there are overlaps between tribes and castes in terms of some social characteristics, as tribes and castes have had regular contact for a long time (Fürer-Haimendorf, 1977).

The Constitution of India makes special provisions for the protection and welfare of its Scheduled Tribes, which are more of legal-administrative categories within the Union. During the debates of the Constituent Assembly, when Jaipal Singh, one of the members, pleaded for the use of the word 'Adivasi' for Indian tribes, it was rejected by B.R. Ambedkar, the chairman of the Drafting Committee of the Constitution, with the argument that it was a general term that had no specific legal de jure connotations—and hence, the term 'Scheduled Tribe' should be used in the Constitution under Article 342. Given this, it is not surprising that the definition was left vague in the Constitution and no attempts were ever made later to define who should be included in the SC, ST and OBC categories and who should be left out.

With independence, the hiatus between tribes and castes was sanctified by the Constitution and over the years, due to political compulsions, internal ethnic divisions and phonetic variations, the number of tribes has increased from 212 in 1950 to more than 427 and they constitute about 7.5 per cent (42 million) of the country's population. In short, a tribe in India is basically a politico-administrative category and has little objective socio-cultural or economic connotation. But anthropologists, who until recently were de facto tribal researchers, have uncritically accepted the administrative category. For all the tribal researchers of today, a tribe is a tribe that is included in the official list of Scheduled Tribes. A few years ago, there were some attempts to define a tribe, but the definitions were not only dissimilar but also contradictory to one another (Pathy et al., 1976).

Though there are all-India tribal organisations and periodic conferences of the emerging category, they still do not evoke powerful loyalty using one or the other of these names. Only a fraction of the 400-odd Scheduled Tribes are drawn into such organisations and gatherings. In specific regional contexts, however, there is evidence of tribal identity contributing to the 'we' and 'they' distinction. 'We' includes, first, an individual tribe and, second, also all other tribes of the region. 'They', on the other hand, includes all non-tribals. Within the cluster of tribes, the 'we' category still refers to one's own tribe; however, for the total population of the region, it is also used as a classification device to distinguish between the tribal and the non-tribal groups. The regional tribal identity gains strength through the articulation of shared interests and collective action; without a foundation of common goals, this identity remains weak and ineffective.

However, the identity problem is more complex than it looks at first sight. There are significant 'we' and 'they' differences among the tribes themselves of a region and they often lead to intense competition and even conflict. A common tribal name, such as Naga or Gond, does not fully subsume the loyalties of individual groups or sub-groups. A Naga is first an Angami, or a Sema, or a Lotha, or a Konyak, or some other named group. How strong and durable, then, is the 'Naga identity'? The same is true of the various groups bearing the generic name Gond. Even some of the smaller tribes—the Kamar, the Saora and the Khond, for example—have divisions, which for all practical purposes constitute individual tribes. A close examination of the situation would suggest that new tribal identities are still evolving. As new identities emerge, old ones are obliterated or subsumed. In the process, old tribal names are discarded and new ones are adopted and mythology and tradition are modified and revised. Alternative bases of solidarity-building are discovered to forge wider links to evolve articulate, aggressive and viable identities.

In the Indian context, the term tribe has never been defined precisely and satisfactorily. Little work has been done so far on tribal self-image (their own ideas, estimations and concepts about themselves) and identity (the way they identify themselves). Most anthropological studies depict tribal life from a researcher's angle and not from a tribe's point of view. A few studies of reference groups and stereotypes of some Indian tribes like the Santhal, the Oraon and the Munda have been attempted, but these are generally psychologically oriented. In these circumstances, we are left with only the choice of reading the relevant literature on Indian tribes and building our profiles of tribal self-image and identity from there (Dube, 1977).

As the tribal groups are presumed to form the oldest ethnological sector of the population, the term 'Adivasi' (Adi = original and Vasi = inhabitant) has become current among certain people. In classifying them, different and sometimes contradictory criteria tend to be used by administrators, anthropologists or social workers, who may take as a basis for their designation skin colour, language, customs, living conditions, or other considerations that they consider necessary. The International Labour Organization has classified such people as 'indigenous' (GoI Dhebar Commission, 1960–1961).

The discrepancies between Indian reality and the Western perspective will be resolved by a few historical accounts from India that date back thousands of years and discuss the link between the plains and forests and the people who inhabit them. And it would be sufficient to demonstrate how incorrect, or perhaps absurd, it is to apply the Western perspective to the Indian forest and hill people.

Diversity or heterogeneity has been termed one of the hallmarks of Indian society. Religion, language, region, caste and tribe are considered the most important distinctions. However, not all of them have been conceptually and theoretically as contentious as the tribe category. It has generally been said that the categories of religion, language, region and caste have been rooted in the consciousness and the social relations of the people at large. They have also had a long history.

The tribals form an indivisible part of Indian civilisation and culture. The tribal population has contributed to different elements of the ancient Indian civilisation. It is believed that they are the most ancient of the present population of India, which is an amalgamation of four main races and cultures—firstly, Austro-Asiatic consisting of Kol or Munda, Khasi and Nicobaris; secondly, Mongols consisting of Naga Bodo, Kuki-chin, etc.; thirdly, Dravid consisting of Orao, Gond and Khonds; and fourthly, Aryans, who probably were last to come to India. Thus, the first three races contributed significantly to the formation of the present Indian population. In India's ancient literature, their names in Sanskrit would appear to have been Nishad, Shabar, Bhil, Kolla, Kirat, Dasa, Dasyu, Sudra, Dramid and Dravid. The ancient and epic literatures, the Vedas, the Puranas, the Ramayana and the Mahabharata, present good accounts about the peopling of India. All these emphasize that India is inhabited by several types of tribes or people (Vidayarthi and Ray, 1985). The Ramayana tells us about the following some tribal people like Rakshas, Vanar, Nishad, Gridhraj, Sabar, Yaksh and the Nagas (Vyas, 1967). The *Mahabharata* also mentions the Kirata and Mundas (Chatterji, 1968).

In the historical period, as early as the period of Ashok, the tribals find mention in his Shahbazgarhi rock edict No. XIII. In the seventh century, Harshacharita mentions the tribes inhabiting the Vindhyan mountains when Harshvardhana went to search for his sister Rajyashri.

Beyond all other distinctions between the people of the plains and the inhabitants of the forests and hills, there has been a shared and ongoing interface and integration of culture, civilisation and religion in India for several millennia. Nowhere else in the world has there been a civilisational convergence like this. The Dhebar Committee on People of Forests in 1962 conducted a study focussed on tribals, aiming to explore the relationship between forests and plains. In the research, the members of the committee utilised ancient texts like the *Ramayana* and the *Mahabharata* to illustrate the absence of a clear demarcation between these two geographical areas. By referencing these literary works, the committee sought to emphasize the interconnectedness and fluidity of forest and plain regions, challenging the notion of a distinct boundary between them.

The Nagas among the Indo-Mongoloid tribes in India are one of the most fascinating and colourful. It is possible that the Nagas are to be included among the Kiratas referred to in Hindu tradition and mythology. The respect in which the Kiratas were traditionally held is shown in the Mahabharata, which describes Shiva as taking the form of a Kirata, with Parvati by his side in the guise of a Kirata woman, to meet the great warrior Arjuna.

The Savaras/Saoras are a large tribe inhabiting the Andhra Pradesh Agency districts of Koraput and Ganjam in Odisha. They are believed to be the descendants of the Sabaras, referred to in the Aittareya Brahmans, *Ramayana* and *Mahabharata*. According to the Korni copper plate, Kamarnava, the founder of the Kalinga-Ganga dynasty, defeated and killed Dantaruva Sabaraditya, the ruler of Srikakulam. Sabaraditya, as the name suggests, must have been a Saora.

The Saoras have ancient associations with Hindu tradition through Sabari, a household word in India. Valmiki's Ramayana describes how Rama and Lakshmana, during their search for Sita, met the aged ascetic Sabari, who offered fruits to them and showed them her hermitage. Many tribals in South India, such as the Gonds, Koya, Pardhans, Kolams, Thoti, Chenhcu Erukala, Andh, Konda Reddi and Konda Kammara, etc., also worship Hindu Gods and Goddesses in addition to their tribal deities (GoI Dhebar Commission, 1961).

The Dhebar Committee said that, because of the continuous migration between the forests and the plains, it had been difficult to distinguish between those from the forests and those from the plains. One of the reasons for this must have been the impact of political and administrative changes and economic factors, resulting in the loss of land. The population growth and pressure on land led to a two-way process: non-tribal people entering the areas inhabited by the tribes and the tribal people migrating to other regions alien to them.

According to the commission, a significant number of Oraons have reportedly been converted to Christianity, but among the Christian Oraons, the dormitory institution is slowly disappearing. Additionally, the Dhebar panel report stated that several Nagas had converted to Christianity.

Niharranjan Ray says tribals are not a separate category as conceived by anthropologists and sociologists. Hence, to him, the so-called tribals are to be referred to as Jana and the whole concept of Scheduled Tribe must be seriously viewed from an Indian point of view (Niharranjan Roy, 1972).

It has been noted that the names given to tribal communities, as documented in colonial reports and subsequently acknowledged by the Indian government, should be re-looked. There is an urgent necessity to grant these tribal communities the respect and dignity in terminology they deserve. The term 'Janjati' or 'Janjatiya' or 'Janjatiya Samooh' could be used in place of 'Tribe'.

The concepts of 'tribe' and 'indigenous' are both constructs of colonialism. However, in India, the term 'indigenous' does not hold the same meaning as it does in America, Canada, Australia and Africa. Anthropologists and scholars have attempted to find a more suitable label for these groups, which are identified differently in academic, administrative and constitutional settings, but have not succeeded.

In India, 'tribe' is a colonial construct. There is no disagreement among the scholars of tribal studies that the concept of tribe is a colonial legacy. The consciousness of the Europeans to situate the self against others got favourable wind in a political situation that involved the dominance of the white people of the colonial power (Channa, 2008). Naturally, the conceptual apparatus of categorising people as 'Tribe' lost the generality and specificity of its application to cross-cultural situations across the globe, which is diverse (Behera, 2010). The term tribe did not exist before the colonial period. However, most of the people with whom the term is associated used to live in forests and hills. Therefore, in India, the notion of tribe has evolved from these people. Over the censuses during the colonial period, the nomenclature referring to tribes underwent successive modifications, involving primarily changes in the descriptive adjectives like hill and forest tribes, primitive tribe or backwards tribe.

The Constitution of India has dropped the qualifying adjectives and has adopted the notion of Scheduled Tribes for this category. There is ambiguity in providing a universally accepted definition. Anthropologists, sociologists, social workers, administrators and other scholars who have been involved with the tribes and their problems are still not in agreement regarding the concept and the definition of their subject.

One of the most common arguments is that, as far as racial history is concerned, the so-called 'tribals' in India cannot be identified with the term anymore (Thomas and Taylor, 1965). Many studies have shown that there is little scientific basis on which the present categorisation of Scheduled Tribes may be defended. This is because the exclusion or inclusion of a particular group reflects political mobilisation rather than a neutral application of the criteria. The problem in India is identifying the people group rather than defining the people group (Birinder, 2011). Thus, in India, 'tribe' is an inadequate explanation to identify a group as a tribe. At the same time, it is time-neutral and not elastic enough to accommodate the upward movement of the smallest unit of the social organisation of the people group over time and again (Behera, 2010).

Many scholars and academics consider the term 'tribe' derogatory. Similar to the Draft of the National Policy for Scheduled Tribes (2006) and Justice Jasraj Chopra's report on the demand of the Gujjars for recognition as a Scheduled Tribe (2007), the current report also highlights the challenges faced when assessing a community's claim to tribal status. Virginius Xaxa (1999) argued that the state's main focus lies in categorising communities into various groups, particularly in terms of scheduling or de-scheduling tribes, rather than in addressing the criteria and parameters for defining a tribe. The community identified itself with a specific name; however, outsiders, often the political state, tried to classify them into categories like 'tribe', 'caste', 'the other backward class', or 'de-notified tribe'. In India, the term commonly used by a community to describe itself as 'jati', signifies 'kind', 'breed', or 'people with a common ancestry', rather than exclusively 'caste'—as commonly interpreted today (Srivastava, 2016). Several have proposed using the term 'community' instead, such as 'Santhal community', 'Bhil community' and 'Gond community'.

The word 'community' is also employed to refer to members of a caste, such as 'carpenter community' and 'weaver community', as well as urban neighbourhoods. The importance of defining a tribe is evident here, as it provides a clear classification. Nevertheless, some anthropologists who once strongly advocated for defining concepts are now hesitant, believing that social phenomena are too complex to be precisely defined. Efforts to define often lead to confusion, with proponents criticised for relying too heavily on outdated positivism (Srivastava, 2018).

Buddhadeb Chaudhuri (1992) proposes the term 'ethnic group' as an alternative, defining it as a self-perpetuating group with shared biological descent and similar fundamental values expressed through cultural forms. Members of an ethnic group typically communicate and interact within the same field, speaking the same or similar language and understanding its cultural nuances, while distinguishing themselves from other categories. On the other hand, Jagannath Pathy (1988) favours the term 'ethnic minority' as tribes are always subordinate to the majority. Additionally, the term 'ethnic group' has been used as a broad category encompassing castes and religious communities.

Alternative terms such as 'autochthones' and 'indigenes' have been proposed for tribes, but they lack the widespread popularity and acceptance that the term 'tribe' holds. Despite the controversies surrounding its usage, 'tribe' remains the most commonly used social category to classify specific segments of societies.

If we look at the forest and hill people from a historical perspective, these groups were referred to as Jana in the *Ramayana* and the *Mahabharata*. When Ram reached the borders of the forests of central India during his exile, the land was introduced to him as Jana-sthan, the land of tribal people. As has been mentioned earlier, tribes in India have never lived in isolation. Hence, a tribal community is never static. Tribes learned from (Jati) caste-based societies and castes also learned some aspects of the life of the tribals (Jana). Due to this interaction process, assimilation, acculturation and adaptation have taken place between the (Jana) tribal community and (Jati) non-tribal community to different degrees.

The term 'tribe' is commonly referred to as 'Jana' or 'communities of people' in ancient Buddhist and Puranic texts. 'Jana' was used to distinguish these communities from the hierarchical caste system, as opposed to the term 'Jati'. In India, while the term 'Jati' is commonly used for caste-based societies, the term Jana could be considered for tribes as suggested by Niharranjan Ray (1972). If not the term 'Jana', it is apparent from the above discussion that there has been a continuous interaction between tribes (Jana) and non-tribes (Jati), so suggesting the term 'Janjati' (tribe or tribes) or 'Janjatiya' (tribal) or 'Janjatiya Samooh' (tribal communities) (the terms 'Samooh', 'Samudaay', 'Samaj' mean living in a group) may be more suitable than tribe. Because the above conversation makes it evident that so-called tribals are not tribals, but they are people groups like any other people groups or communities (Jati).

The term 'Janjatiya' is significant in the context of Indian anthropology as it represents an attempt to move away from the colonial concept of 'tribe', which is laden with negative connotations and implies a sense of otherness and primitivism. 'Janjatis' is a more inclusive and respectful term that acknowledges the historical, cultural and social contributions of these communities to Indian civilisation. It is derived from the Sanskrit term 'Jana', which means 'to be born' or 'to give birth to' and is related to the term 'Jati'. This terminology suggests a biological and communal connection, emphasizing the autochthonous nature of these communities and their integral role in the Indian social fabric. The term 'Janjatis' thus signifies a people group or community, similar to 'Jati', but distinct from the hierarchical caste system.

The adoption of 'Janjatiya' reflects a civilisational approach that recognizes the diversity and demographics of India's forest and hill people and their continuous interactions with the plains people. It also highlights the need for a decolonised narrative that understands these communities within their own geo-cultural contexts, respecting their local wisdom, knowledge and practices.

The term 'Janjatiya' is significant as it challenges the colonial legacy of categorising and essentialising tribal communities, promoting instead a more nuanced and dignified understanding of these groups as integral parts of India's rich cultural and historical landscape.

Prime Minister Modi referred to forest and hill people as Janjatiya and declared 15 November as Janjatiya Gaurav Diwas to commemorate the contributions of tribal communities to the nation's history and culture, besides inspiring the coming generations to preserve our cultural heritage and national pride. This day is also observed to honour all the tribal freedom-fighters and to re-energise the efforts for the socio-economic development of the tribal regions. Commemorating the sacrifice of tribal freedom-fighters and marking their legacy, the union government decided to observe the birth anniversary of one of the great freedom-fighters, Bhagwan Birsa Munda, as Janjatiya Gaurav Divas with effect from 15 November 2021. For the first time in the country after Independence, the art and culture of the tribal society and their contribution to the freedom movement and nation-building are being remembered with pride and honoured on such a grand scale. This declaration acknowledges the glorious history of tribal communities and recognizes their efforts towards the preservation of cultural heritage.

DIVERSITY AND DEMOGRAPHICS

Though India's tribal population is numerically small, it represents an enormous diversity of groups. These groups vary among themselves with respect to language and linguistic traits, ecological settings in which they live, physical features, population size, the extent of acculturation, dominant modes of making a livelihood, levels of development and social stratification. They are also spread over the length and breadth of the country, though their geographical distribution is far from uniform. A majority of the Scheduled Tribes population is concentrated in the eastern, central and Western belts covering the nine States of Odisha, Madhya Pradesh, Chhattisgarh, Jharkhand, Maharashtra, Gujarat, Rajasthan, Andhra Pradesh and West Bengal. About 12 per cent inhabit the north-east region, about 5 per cent in the southern region and about 3 per cent in the northern states. The state with the highest proportion of scheduled tribes is Mizoram (94.5 per cent) and the union territory with the highest proportion of Scheduled Tribes is Lakshadweep (94.8 per cent). Tribals inhabit all parts of the country except for the states of Punjab, Haryana and Delhi and the union territories of Chandigarh and Puducherry.

As can be seen, among the states, Odisha has the largest number of notified STs (62), followed by Karnataka (50), Maharashtra (45), Madhya Pradesh (43) and Chhattisgarh (42). Sikkim has the least, with four tribes, followed by Nagaland, Daman, Diu and Uttarakhand, with five each. Among the south Indian states (without any Scheduled Areas), Karnataka has the largest number of Scheduled Tribes (50), followed by Tamil Nadu (36) and Kerala (36).

The classification of tribes can be categorised into five main regional clusters, considering various factors such as ecological conditions, social structures, economic activities, administrative systems and ethnic backgrounds. It is important to note that while some intersections and shared characteristics among these groups may exist, they can still be differentiated based on these diverse factors.

1. Himalayan region: It has three sub-regions: (a) North-eastern Himalayan region, (b) Central Himalayan region and (c) north-western Himalayan region.
2. Middle region: It is constituted by the States of Bihar, Jharkhand, West Bengal, Odisha and Madhya Pradesh (including Chhattisgarh), where more than 55 per cent of the tribal people of India live.
3. Western region: It includes the States of Rajasthan, Gujarat, Maharashtra, Goa, Dadra and Nagar Haveli.
4. Southern region: It comprises the states of Andhra Pradesh, Tamil Nadu, Karnataka and Kerala.
5. Island region: The Islands of Andaman and Nicobar in the Bay of Bengal and Lakshadweep in the Arabian Sea.

Within this geographical classification, there is much disparity with regard to the distribution of the tribal population of the country. We can come across a very high concentration of the tribals in the 8 states of central or middle India, comprising about 85 per cent of the total tribal population. This is followed by the eight north-eastern states. At the same time, many tribes are distributed over the states and union territories of the eastern states, comprising about 11 per cent.

The Himalayan region comprises 2.03 per cent of STs in Jammu and Kashmir, Himachal Pradesh, Uttarakhand and Uttar Pradesh; the north-eastern region has 12.41 per cent of STs in Sikkim, Arunachal Pradesh, Nagaland, Manipur, Mizoram, Tripura, Meghalaya and Assam; the central-east Indian region has the largest proportion of STs, about 52.51 per cent in Andhra Pradesh, Bihar, Jharkhand, Madhya Pradesh, Chhattisgarh, Odisha and West Bengal; the western region of Rajasthan, Gujarat, Daman and Diu, Dadra and Nagar Haveli, Maharashtra and Goa has 27.64 per cent of STs; the southern region has 5.31 per cent of STs in the states of Karnataka, Kerala and Tamil Nadu; and finally, 0.11 per cent of STs live in the island region of Andaman and Nicobar Islands and Lakshadweep.

Among the states and union territories, Lakshadweep ranks at the top with the highest proportion of ST population (within the state) of 94.8 per cent, followed by Mizoram (94.4 per cent), Nagaland (86.5 per cent), Meghalaya (86.1 per cent) and Arunachal Pradesh (68.8 per cent). Uttar Pradesh stands last with the lowest proportion of ST population, at 0.56 per cent, followed by Tamil Nadu (1.1 per cent), Bihar (1.28 per cent), Kerala (1.45 per cent) and Uttarakhand (2.89 per cent).

Regarding the distribution of ST population by states, Madhya Pradesh stands first with 14.7 per cent, followed by Maharashtra (10.1 per cent), Odisha (9.2 per cent), Rajasthan (8.9 per cent), Gujarat (8.6 per cent), Jharkhand (8.3 per cent), Chhattisgarh (7.5 per cent), Andhra Pradesh (5.7 per cent), West Bengal (5.1 per cent), Karnataka (4.1 per cent), Assam (3.7

per cent), Meghalaya (2.5 per cent) and the remaining states represent 11.6 per cent of the tribal population. The proportion of the ST population in rural areas is 11.3 per cent and in urban areas it is 2.8 per cent. More than half the Scheduled Tribe population is concentrated in Madhya Pradesh, Chhattisgarh, Maharashtra, Odisha, Jharkhand and Gujarat.

However, when we see the ratio of the tribal population to the total population, we find that it is high in the north-eastern states (except for Assam). It ranges from 64 per cent to 95 per cent in Meghalaya, Nagaland, Mizoram, Sikkim and Arunachal Pradesh and between 30 per cent and 35 per cent in Tripura and Manipur. The ratio is over 90 per cent in the union territory of Lakshadweep, whereas it ranges from 22 per cent to 23 per cent in Odisha and Madhya Pradesh. In the rest of the country, the ratio ranges from as low as 1 per cent to 12 per cent.

There are many differences between these regions and from tribe to tribe. For example, while the north-east is often viewed as a singular and homogeneous entity, the region is highly diverse with over 200 tribes and sub-tribes, each with their own language, culture and political structures. Furthermore, the tribes of the north-east differ from tribes in other parts of India, particularly in terms of their historical relationship with the colonial state and the Indian Union. The tribes of the Andaman and Nicobar Islands, comprising 556 islands, of which only a few are populated, are also distinct.

The islands are governed as a union territory under the jurisdiction of the central government, which oversees their administration and development. These islands are notable for being the habitat of some of the world's smallest and most isolated tribes, including the Great Andamanese, Onge, Jarawa and Sentinelese. Each of these tribes possesses a unique cultural heritage and way of life that has remained largely untouched by external influences. The Great Andamanese, once a larger group, have seen their numbers dwindle significantly, while the Onge and Jarawa continue to maintain their traditional practices in harmony with their natural surroundings. The Sentinelese, perhaps the most enigmatic of these tribes, have chosen to remain completely isolated from the outside world, rejecting contact with outsiders and preserving their ancestral customs. This rich tapestry of indigenous cultures highlights the islands' significance not only as a geographical entity but also as a vital repository of human diversity and heritage.

The tribes can also be differentiated based on their population size, since communities like the Gonds, Bhils, Santhals, Oraons, Minas, Mundas and so on, have a population that ranges from one million to a little over seven million people. In contrast, there are communities like the Andamanese Islanders and tribal groups, such as the Birjia and Asur in Bihar, as well as the Birhor of Madhya Pradesh, which have populations of less than 200 people. The groups most under threat have been identified as the Shompens, Sentinelese and Jarawas of the Andaman Islands; the Bondos of Odisha; the Cholanaickans of Kerala; the Abujh Marias of Chhattisgarh; and the Birhors of Jharkhand.

Besides being classified according to the territory, tribes are also grouped according to language or linguistic considerations. Four broad language groups have been identified among the tribes of India and they are: Indo-Aryan, Austro-Asiatic, Dravidian and Tibeto-Burman.

Indian languages are part of four different linguistic families. Indo-Aryan languages, Dravidian languages, Austric (Austro-Asiatic) and the Tibeto-Burman languages. Approximately three-fourths of the country speaks languages belonging to the Indo-Aryan family, but only a little over one per cent of the tribal population speaks the Indo-Aryan languages—the Bhil and the Halbi tribes being the two main groups among them. Languages belonging to the Dravidian family are spoken by tribes such as the Gond, Khond, Koya, Oraon and Toda. The tribes of the Himalayas and of the north-east speak the Tibeto-Burman languages. The Austro-Asiatic family of languages is spoken by the Santhal, Munda and the Ho tribes.

Besides their zonal and geographical distribution, tribes have also been grouped based on their ecological habitat. They are classified into those who live in the hills (Hill Karbis, Hill Tiwas of Assam), the plains (Bodos, Singphos), forests (Kadars of Kerala), rural, urban and industrial areas.

Scheduled Tribes reside in about 15 per cent of the country's area, in various ecological and geo-climatic conditions ranging from plains and forests to hills. Based on the mode of livelihood or subsistence pattern, Indian tribes can be divided into the following categories: food gatherers and hunters, horticulturists, pastoralists, hill cultivators, agriculturists, simple artisans, folk artists, labourers and industrial workers. Traditional occupations of tribal groups may range from honey collection to hunting small animals, to engaging in metalwork and rope-making (High-level Committee, 2014).

Two other important governmental classifications of tribes, which refer to specific histories and vulnerabilities of these communities, are: PVTGs, De-notified, Nomadic and Semi-Nomadic Tribes. Primitive Tribal Groups are a subset of Scheduled Tribes, while certain communities were unjustly labelled as criminal tribes during colonial times and later de-notified by the government of India.

As mentioned earlier, the tribes that were once referred to as criminal are now the de-notified tribes. These de-notified tribes were previously categorised under the Criminal Tribes Act of 1871 by the British government. Some significant groups listed as criminal tribes included Bawaria, Bhatu, Beria, Bhedkut, Dom, Karwal, Mina, Mantam, Yerkula Sugali, Yandi, Koravas, Lambadi and others. It is worth noting that the population of these so-called criminal tribes consists of a subset of the entire tribe or caste. Therefore, within the category of criminal tribes, one can find individuals who belong to tribes,

Hindu castes and Muslims. From an ethnic perspective, criminal tribes were composed of mixed groups.

The British attitude towards petty crimes committed by some individuals or groups was based on a false notion. The colonial rulers believed that crime was a hereditary calling of these people. It is to be noted that Cesare Lombroso's widely accepted theory of 'inborn criminality' continued to influence the colonial administrators for years. His ideas were key inputs to the Italian School of Positivist Criminology, which believed that criminal tendencies were inherent in some individuals, regardless of their social conditions.

In sum, India's population is characterized by its remarkable feature of unity in diversity. The tribal culture of India plays a significant role in shaping various aspects of Indian culture and civilisation, with its traditions and practices permeating throughout centuries and societies. From the Aryan and Dravidian to the Indo-Tibetan languages, the tribal culture of India has experienced a fusion of diverse cultures inter- and intra-community. Few tribal communities share certain similarities, yet they differ significantly in their religious and traditional beliefs. The festivals in these communities are also much of a delight to watch, with their colourful and joyous celebrations. The tribes of our country indeed form the very basis of incredible India.

CHAPTER 3

Colonial Mindset on Tribes

The concept of tribe has traversed a long academic and intellectual history in anthropology. The conceptual development of the word 'tribe' is mired in controversy because of the close association between anthropology and European colonialism. It is evident that the concept emerged in the context of Africa, Australia and North America, but later, towards the second half of the eighteenth century, the concept became popular in the Indian context to identify and classify Indian populations based on social formation by the colonial government.

During the period of British colonial rule, the hill and forest communities of India were recognized and classified as tribes. British colonial administrators, along with anthropologists and ethnographers, played a pioneering role in the exploration and documentation of these tribal groups.

It is evident that the Western viewpoint regarding tribal communities differs significantly from the Indian perspective. Initially, Western anthropologists and social scientists categorised these groups as 'savages', followed by 'barbaric', then 'primitive' and subsequently 'tribal' and finally referring to them as indigenous.

The term and concept of 'indigenous' does not apply to India, as clearly highlighted in the United Nations document titled, *State of the World's indigenous Peoples*, where in it is mentioned:

The concept of indigenous peoples emerged from the colonial experience, whereby the aboriginal peoples of a given land were marginalized after being invaded by colonial powers, whose peoples are now dominant over the earlier occupants. These earlier definitions of indigenousness make sense when looking at the Americas, Russia, the Arctic and many parts of the Pacific. However, this definition makes less sense in most parts of Asia and Africa, where the colonial powers did not displace whole populations of peoples and replace them with settlers of European descent. (p. 17, 2009)

INDIA'S FOREST & HILL PEOPLE: WESTERN VIEW

Colonial administrators and anthropologists were encouraged to engage in the study of the Indian population. From empirical works, it is clear that the term 'tribe' is not of Indian origin. Administrators and anthropologists have stated time and again that the use of the word 'tribe' in India dates back to the colonial period and this classification was done for better administration purposes rather than driven by anthropological imperatives.

In the late nineteenth century, the British colonial administrators arbitrarily classified and categorised the Indian population into 'caste' and 'tribes'. The colonial government also emphasized the categorisation of community divisions based on race and caste. But colonial anthropology failed to acknowledge the unique characteristics of tribal communities, leading to the stigmatisation of Indian tribals as aboriginal, primitive, savage, indigenous, uncivilised, illiterate, Banbasi or Jangli (forest-dwellers), autochthonous and even 'exotic' (Mahana, 2019, p. 10). Consequently, these communities have frequently been depicted by outsiders as autochthonous, wild, or primitive.

Xaxa (1999, 2008) writes that in India, hills and forest communities were identified and enumerated as tribes during British rule. What becomes clearly apparent is that the Western perspective with regard to them is at variance with the Indians. The term 'tribe' is synonymous with being primitive and with savagery and hence is derogatory in many ways. The term 'Tribe' is one of the most contested, particularly in India; to date, no official definition has been established.

The 1950 Constitutional Amendment order with the full list of Scheduled Tribes recognized at the time was largely based on the list of 'backward tribes' prepared by the colonial administration in 1936 (Behura and Panigrahi, 2006).

The primary focus of Western anthropology became evident in the 1860s, when scholars began studying forest and hill communities, referring to them as 'primitive' and 'savage' societies. Prominent British anthropologists, who have studied Indian tribes, include Sir Herbert Risley and William Crooke, both officials in the colonial government, who published the first two handbooks of tribes and castes in British India in the 1890s—each containing a lengthy ethnographic glossary with entries for individual tribes and castes (Fuller, 2027). Risley, along with William Crooke (1848–1923) and Sir Denzil Ibbetson (1847–1908), developed Indian ethnography and anthropology in the late Victorian period (Fuller, 2017, p. 1).

Officially, anthropology aimed to contribute to scientific knowledge and strengthen and improve British rule. Indian society, as seen by the Britishers, was a 'traditional' society, an antithetical 'other' of modern European society. The society comprised separate religious communities; castes were a distinct social group with the tribal population at the periphery. In his classic works, *The People of India* and *The Tribes and Castes of Bengal*, Rilsey summarized his views on the origin and classification of Indian races based on his historical speculations and anthropometric research. His contemporaries and subsequent writers criticised Risley for giving so much emphasis to the racial basis of caste and stressing anthropometric measurements. The work has been criticised as a colonialist misrepresentation. Verrier Elwin (1947) extensively worked with the Gond tribe and Christoph von Fürer-Haimendorf, known for his studies on the tribes of Northeast India, deserve mention. Elwin's notable works include 'The Baiga' and 'The Muria and their Ghotul' (1947). Fürer-Haimendorf, Christoph von, works include 'Tribes of India: The Struggle for Survival' (1982) and 'The Naked Nagas' (1976). Contemporary Indian scholar G. Kanato Chopy (2021) wrote a paper titled 'Critical Reflections on the Konyak Naga Ethnography', which gives a reflexive analysis of Haimendorf's exotic imageries of Nagas against the backdrop of a rapid sociocultural change facing the community.

Some critics point out that Western anthropologists studying Indian tribes approached their research with a pre-existing frame of reference that was rooted in Western cultural norms and values. This has led to a limited understanding of the hill and forest people, as that understanding cannot fully capture the complexities and nuances of the people under study. Critics stress the importance of adopting a more culturally sensitive and context-specific approach to avoid imposing external biases on the interpretation of the hill and forest people's practices and beliefs.

Early British writings on India did not study groups or communities from a caste or tribal perspective. They were studied in their capacity as human groupings or communities. At the onset of British colonisation, there was a need for information about the local population. This led to the systematic gathering of in-depth studies on the culture and society of the colonized people. The British sought to acquire knowledge of the indigenous political, economic and social structures in order to govern effectively. Their description in caste or tribal terms was a later phenomenon. Therefore, it is unclear in what sense the British ethnographers used the term 'tribe' in India, especially in the early phase.

In the colonial period, there was no discernible attempt to adopt a civilisational approach to the relationship between the inhabitants of the plains and the hill and forest people. Revitalising the thrust of liberation from an old perspective is an urgent call so that this education becomes a powerful tool in liberating the so-called tribals from backwardness. For that, one has to go back in history to find the values that existed and were practised among the so-called tribal people of India.

UNDERSTANDING THE CONCEPT OF 'TRIBE'

In twelfth-century Middle English literature, the term 'tribe' was used to describe 1 of the 12 tribes of Israel. However, the Portuguese later adopted the word to refer to the colonized people in Africa. Consequently, it became a colonial term used to categorise groups that colonial powers perceived as 'others' or distinct from the dominant groups within a country.

The term 'tribe' was explored in the previous section, revealing that it was not utilised in India before British rule. Thus, it is a colonial legacy. The study of tribal communities had captivated scholars since the late sixteenth century, when the Western world first encountered cultures and communities that were vastly different from their own. Anthropologists' fascination with understanding 'other cultures' sparked the beginning of tribal studies. Earlier, anthropologists such as Lewis Henry Morgan (1818–1881) and Edward Burnett Tylor (1832–1917) defined tribe as a primitive social formation; primitive because they were supposed to represent the earlier stages through which the contemporary Western civilisation had evolved. During the eighteenth century, the British government felt the need to have an ethnographic account of different tribes of India with a view to ruling over them easily. They were not anthropologists by training or profession, but their accounts provided ample information on the tribal history of India.

The colonial administrators employed the term to classify certain groups of individuals, while scholars utilised it to analyse social changes through a historical lens, resulting in various definitions of the term. Tribes in India may not always be compared with native tribes of Africa or the aborigines of Australia. Further controversy arose among scholars, reformers and administrators to describe the tribes in India. Risely, Lacey, Elwin, Grigson and others are referred to as the tribes as aborigines or aboriginals. Hutton called them primitive. Ghurye described them as aborigines or backwards Hindus. Some scholars called them Adivasi and those like S.T. Das designated them as 'submerged humanity'. While these classifications may indicate the various traits that a tribal community may possess, it is crucial to understand that not all of these traits are necessarily present in every community.

Singh (1998) writes that the tribe is a colonial concept, an Anglo-Saxon word, defined for the first time in the Census of 1901, in contradistinction to caste. The notion of tribe has evolved over the censuses from a hill and forest tribe to a primitive tribe, to a backwards tribe and finally to the Scheduled Tribe. The British initially used the term 'tribe' in Indian society to refer to groups claiming common ancestry or living in primitive conditions. The usage of 'tribe' evolved, with the sense of primitive living becoming more prevalent in anthropological writings. This shift in concept reflects changes in the historical understanding of the term 'tribe' within Indian society.

Defining a tribe is challenging, as it requires considering the empirical characteristics of human groups across different regions and time periods. Conceptually, a tribe can be seen as an independent unit that forms a self-contained society with a common government and territory. However, this definition falls short when empirical evidence shows tribes like the Nuer and

Dinka having segmental political organisations. Hence, ecological and political criteria alone are insufficient to define a tribe as a society.

Indian tribes have consistently been a focal point of intense debate, particularly within the realms of social anthropology and sociology. Initially, colonial anthropologists established a framework for defining tribes based on specific parameters and academic expediency. Subsequently, scholars from various disciplines have explored the diverse and complex nature of Indian tribes from cross-cultural and transnational perspectives, highlighting the challenges associated with defining tribes within the Indian context while emphasizing their methodological significance. Hence, although social anthropologists and other scholars generated much interest in conceptualising and defining tribe and their socio-cultural aspects, the concept itself to date remains most problematic and controversial.

The tribal communities in India have been experiencing changes at various levels since the pre-colonial era. These tribes are known to move to different locations when their resources are exhausted, leading to a phenomenon known as 'tribes in transition' to describe the evolving nature of tribal communities in India.

The Indian situation has led to the creation of terms such as 'tribes in transition' and 'tribe-caste continuum'. After independence, certain groups were recognized as Scheduled Tribes, including the particularly vulnerable tribal groups (PVTGs). The colonial rulers also labelled certain groups as criminal tribes, but they were later de-notified by the government of India. Some of these de-notified tribes are scheduled in the Constitution, while others are not. Additionally, not all groups classified as tribes are scheduled. Scholars in tribal studies refer to these non-scheduled tribes by this name. There is also ongoing debate regarding whether Indian tribes should be designated as indigenous peoples.

In the Indian context, the concept of tribe is primarily administration-driven. It specifically refers to the Scheduled Tribes, which are the tribes and communities listed in the Constitution of India. Apart from the Scheduled Tribes, there are two other administrative terms related to tribes: the Primitive Tribes and the Ex-criminal or De-notified Tribes. The Primitive Tribal Groups (PTGs) are a subset of the Scheduled Tribes. During the colonial rule, several communities, tribes and other groups were categorised as criminal tribes. Subsequently, the government of India passed an Act to de-notify these communities, designating them as Ex-criminal or De-notified Tribes. Additionally, there are communities that possess all the necessary characteristics to be classified as Scheduled Tribes, yet they are not listed as such in the Constitution. These communities are referred to as Non-Scheduled Tribes.

'Forest tribe' was used in place of 'tribe' in the 1881 census reports. So-called animists were included in the caste group in the 1901 and 1911 censuses. More precisely, Ghurye (1963, p. 205) recommended that the scheduled tribes identified as animists in the census should rather be called 'backward Hindus'. More efforts were made during the post-independence era and there were increased attempts to differentiate between tribes and castes. However, scholars have not yet established a set of criteria for this distinction. It is commonly believed that castes are governed by hereditary division of labour, hierarchy, principles of purity and pollution, as well as civic and religious limitations. On the other hand, tribes are typically characterized by the absence of these caste-related attributes.

British scholars believed that tribes lived in isolation, while post-colonial ethnography emphasizes close interaction between tribes and the larger society. The transformation of tribes into castes is conceived to occur through methods which have been diversely conceptualised. Historians and anthropologists have often discussed the transformation of tribal societies into mainstream civilisation, referencing tribes being absorbed into larger societies, such as Hindu society, as noted by Kosambi (1975) and Bose (1941). Post-independence anthropological works continue to highlight the phenomenon of tribes being assimilated into mainstream society or becoming castes.

Sanskritisation is seen as another method through which tribes are absorbed into Hindu society. The other significant method of tribal assimilation is what Sinha (1962, 1987) refers to as state formation. Sinha argues that in order to fully understand the process of acculturation, Hinduisation and social stratification within the village, it is necessary to examine the data in the broader context of the formation of the principality. He further explains that the formation of the state played a crucial role in transforming the tribal system into the regional caste system, providing the socio-political framework for this transformation.

And yet, concepts such as Sanskritisation and Hinduisation are insufficient to advance the argument in support of the transformation of tribes into castes. Anthropologists and sociologists have never given language the credit it merits in understanding how a tribe became a caste. However, anthropologists have concluded that these tribes either assimilate into Hindu society or develop into castes. Anthropologists have been swift to incorporate tribes into the larger society at the slightest sign of change in their life patterns. The study of tribal society in India has not only focussed on caste but also on peasants. In social anthropological literature, peasant society is often examined in comparison to tribal society. A tribe is typically described as a relatively uniform community with shared governance, language and culture.

The tribes in present-day India have undergone notable changes. Although certain tribes may be perceived as primitive based on measures of development and progress, it is crucial to acknowledge that not all fit into this classification. Many tribes have influential segments that can be likened to the middle class in any other society. In India, the study of tribes focusses on their transformation into castes, peasants and stratified communities. As these are characteristics of Indian society as a whole, tribes are seen as assimilating into the broader society, resulting in the loss of their distinct identity.

In anthropology's conceptualization, tribes are usually perceived as being an isolated civilisation. Second, a tribe is thought to be a unique kind of community. Furthermore, tribes are seen to symbolise a socio-political structure that would eventually advance to a new stage, such as a nation, nationality, or nationhood.

Anthropologists and other social scientists have failed to consider the specific context in which the term 'tribe' is used in Indian society. As we have seen, tribes in India are primarily defined and described as being outside of civilisation. This can lead to complications when tribes coexist with non-tribal societies. While using the term 'indigenous people' may resolve some of these issues, it can also introduce fresh problems. Therefore, the use of the term 'tribe' in the Indian context is both awkward and fundamentally incorrect.

EVOLUTION OF TRIBAL ANTHROPOLOGY

Anthropology in India began under colonial rule. European scholars and British administrators contributed to establishing anthropology in India. Along with this, there appeared on the scene a small number of Indian anthropologists who were being trained by the British masters to assist them in their work. By the beginning of the twentieth century, departments of anthropology were set up in various universities, which in time produced a large number of students.

The beginnings of tribal studies, or documenting and writing monographs on tribal subjects, date back to 1774, when the Asiatic Society of Bengal was established by Sir William Jones. Anthropologists have divided anthropological and tribal studies into four chronological phases of development as per Indian anthropology, viz. (i) The Formative Phase (1774–1919), (ii) The Constructive Phase (1920–1949), (iii) The Analytical Phase (1950–1989) and (iv) The Evaluative Phase (1990–present).

The British government deployed numerous British administrators with scholarly backgrounds to investigate the customs, beliefs and cultural practices of tribal areas in order to streamline governance. These initial studies on the territories and inhabitants were later supplemented by more comprehensive reports from scholars who were heavily influenced by British anthropologists, such as Rivers, resulting in the publication of monographs on various Indian tribes.

Data was collected on the tribes during the Census in 1931 and 1941. The contribution in this direction was made by scholarly British administrators, such as Risley, Dalton, O'Malley, Russel, Thurston and Crooks. Cambell, Latham and Risley published general books on Indian ethnology. These were followed by detailed accounts of specific tribes by Briggs, Shakespeare, Gurdon, Mills, Parry and Grigson.

Apart from ethnographic reports, listings of customs and administrative reports, there were also land revenue settlement reports that gave a more realistic functional idea of Indian rural society. These included the works of Dalton, Buchanan and Lord Baden-Powell. Some missionaries also made important ethnographic and linguistic studies. Among these were P.O. Bodding and J. Hoffman, C.G. Seligmann, B.G. Seligmann and A.R. Radcliffe-Brown.

> In 1911, W.H.R. Rivers's important work, *The Todas*, was published by Macmillan and Co., London. Again, in 1911, Cambridge University Press published the work of B.G. Seligmann and C.G. Seligmann, entitled *The Veddas of Ceylon*. In 1922, A.R. Radcliffe-Brown's work, *The Andaman Islanders*, was published by Cambridge University Press.
> The emergence of writings about the diverse forest and hill communities in India, which were eventually labelled as tribes, gained prominence during the British colonial expansion across the landscapes of the Indian subcontinent, including hills, plains, forests, mountains, rivers and islands. To facilitate the expansion of their colonial rule in these regions, administrators began enlisting the assistance of colonial ethnographers, missionaries, explorers and individuals who considered themselves amateur ethnographers.

After the Asiatic Society of Bengal was founded in 1784, research on the groups that British colonial officials had previously referred to as 'tribes' became organized and became known as tribal studies. For the benefit of the colonists, the *Journal of the Asiatic Society of Bengal* was founded in 1832 with the goal of researching the people living in British India's plains, hilly areas and mountainous regions. *An Account of the Mountain Tribes on the Extreme N.E. Frontier of Bengal* was one of McCosh's important studies that was published in the journal's early issues. In his research, McCosh described the tribes as 'barbarous and independent savages'.

Colonial administrators and ethnographers in India continued to publish extensively about the people of the country. Some notable studies include Dalton's Descriptive Ethnology of Bengal (1872), Herbert Hope Risley's Tribes and Caste of Bengal (1892) and People of India (1908). W.H.R. Rivers' published a study of The Todas (1906), Edward Thurnston's Castes and Tribes of Southern India (1909), Robert Vane Russell and Rai Bahadur Hira Lal's The Caste and Tribes of the Central Provinces (1916) and the compilation of eight volumes titled, The People of India, by Watson and Kaye (1868–1875) too came in the public domain. Risley and Thurnston divide the Indian population into different groups, including tribes and castes.

Rivers characterized the Todas as 'primitive,' failing to recognize their profound appreciation for beauty. In reality, the Todas express their cultural richness through various artistic forms, such as composing songs for numerous occasions and creating internationally renowned embroidery. They also demonstrate a strong commitment to ecological principles and possess a wealth of rituals that illuminate their understanding of cosmology. (Misra, 2022).

In 1939, von Fürer-Haimendorf conducted ethnographic research in Pangsha Naga village in Nagaland, similar to Malinowski's work. *The Naked Naga* was the result of his fieldwork, but his choice of title reveals a racist perspective, perpetuating stereotypes with terms like 'nakedness' and 'headhunting'. Kamei (2021) argues that such studies objectify tribal communities, while Ziipao (2013) highlights how these writings uphold colonial biases, cultural superiority and Eurocentric viewpoints that are inherently racist.

During the Constructive Period (1920–1949), a full-fledged Department of Anthropology was established at Calcutta University in 1920. L.K. Anantha Krishan Iyer, who joined the university, published his Monographs on the Tribe and Caste of Ernakulam. He also wrote and presented a paper on Marriage Customs of the Cochin State and Nambuthari Brahmins of Malabar at the Indian Science Congress in 1914. S.C. Roy was the first Indian ethnographer who worked among the tribal population of Chhotanagpur and he produced a monograph, Munda and their Country, in 1912. In 1921, under the editorship of S.C. Roy, the print journal *Man in India* was started. Many Indian anthropologists, such as D.N. Majumdar, M. Chattopadhyay, I. Karve and T.C. Das, wrote on social institutions. Their works gave the necessary impetus to social anthropology in India. The Changing Hoof by D.N. Majumdar, Marriage and Family in Mysore (1942) by M.N. Srinivas and Hindu Methods of Tribal Absorption (1941) by N.K. Bose produced significant works and they continue to be popular among students of anthropology. Many anthropologists, such as Ghurye, who were educated abroad, later contributed substantially to the discipline.

During the British colonial era in India, colonial ethnographers and trained anthropologists had a unique distinction of continuously producing writings about tribal people for over 150 years until India gained independence. Surprisingly, they never felt the need to reflect on their own positions or epistemological locations, or acknowledge their corresponding responsibility to situate themselves. Their writings consistently portrayed the tribals as lazy, wild, savage, naked, primitive, exotic, degraded, warlike, sexist, barbaric, uncivilised and criminal. Their works highlighted the tribal habits of drinking, gambling and wearing dirty clothes, among other negative stereotypes.

Verrier Elwin, a Christian missionary-turned-anthropologist, spent nearly three decades doing anthropological studies of Indian tribesmen and he is known for his works among the Baigas and Gonds of Odisha and Madhya Pradesh in central India. He also worked on the tribes of north-eastern states, especially the north-east Frontier Agency (NEFA). He produced substantial ethnographic data and was one of the most prolific writers. Elwin wrote about tribal art and culture, their music and dance, their dresses and ornaments and their beliefs and values, which he thought would disappear under the influence of dominant society. His central question was whether (in 1939) tribes should continue to remain in isolation or should be drawn into the larger society. He argued that tribes should be kept in isolation by insulating them from the dominant society. Conversely, Ghurye did not intend to categorise the tribals separately during the Census, advocating for their integration into Hindu society. In contrast, J.H. Hutton viewed tribals as backwards Hindus and believed that they had assimilated into Hindu culture for a considerable period.

S. Gurumurthy stated in his article that Verrier Elvin firmly believed in the preservation of their culture without assimilating with the plainsmen, which contradicted the Western approach of contracting them out for modernization. Upon closer examination, it becomes evident that Elvin's proposal of complete isolation posed a greater threat to national integration and security compared to the Western method of modernising them anthropologically. Additionally, it went against the longstanding history of civilisational interaction between forest and plains communities in India.

After independence, during the Analytical phase (1950–1990), many Indian academicians collaborated with foreign scholars, including Oscar Lewis, Morris Opler, F.G. Bailey, McKim Marriott, Gerald D. Berreman and David Mandelbaum and did fieldwork on Indian villages. A shift was seen as the emphasis moved from descriptive tribal studies to analytical studies on village and caste studies. A large number of monographs were published on village studies, both by Indian and foreign scholars. L.P. Vidyarthi, S.C. Dube, D.N. Majumdar, M.N. Srinivas, B.K. Roy Burman, G.S. Ghurye, N.K. Bose, T.N. Madan and Iravati Karve are some Indian scholars who made significant contributions to village and community studies. A large number of village study monographs were published in the 1960s through the Census of India 1961. These studies generated new ideas and concepts that provided a baseline for future studies.

After independence, initially, the work of Indian anthropologists was not very different from that of British administrators. Tribal people have been studied as different from the rest of the Indian population. While colonial anthropology was more preoccupied with the enumeration and preparation of ethnographies of castes and tribes under the influence of the ethnological tradition, the practice of the discipline in India witnessed a change after the entry of Indian anthropologists and later the replacement of the British colonial government by an Indian national government. The beginnings of the departure were seen in scholars carrying out their fieldwork and not depending on government functionaries for data collection.

A nationalistic perspective can be seen in highlighting a picture of unity in diversity. This was followed by research driven by welfare and development concerns. After establishing anthropology departments in universities, trained anthropologists started undertaking studies on tribes and castes that were more systematic and methodologically superior to the studies made by untrained colonial anthropologists.

Contrary to the perspectives of anthropologists and colonists, the nationalists of the 1930s and the 1940s strongly criticised colonial policies and were hostile towards anthropological writings that glorified cultural primitivism. Supporters of tribal culture believed that the relationship between tribes and peasants was exploitative, advocating for their segregation as the most effective means of modernization. However, nationalist anthropologists and Congress leaders challenged these claims, arguing that the basis of exclusion was unfounded. The Congress engaged in debates with pro-exclusion British officials on two fronts. Firstly, they focussed on their anti-imperialist stance and emphasized the development of a strong Indian identity to mobilise people against colonial rule. Secondly, they contested the social and anthropological justifications put forth by those supporting the government's policies of exclusion and partial exclusion.

On 6 and 9 September 1949, the Constituent Assembly had an elaborate discussion on the 'tribal question', with the main issue being 'reconciling the diversity of custom with the national life of the country'. Nationalist leaders and social reformers supported the 'assimilation' of tribals into mainstream society, whereas the views of Western-trained anthropologists favoured the policy of 'isolationism' and 'protection'. The famous debate between Ghurye and Verrier Elwin reveals arguments both for and against the policy of 'assimilation' and 'isolationism'. While both views were heard, an approach of simultaneous protection and uplift was followed.

Indian anthropology witnessed the emergence of a nationalist movement alongside its colonial roots, gaining momentum during both the pre- and post-independence eras. This movement was defined by socially engaged anthropologists who made significant contributions to nation-building through their analytical research and writings.

One of the pioneers, Sarat Chandra Roy, is rightly considered the 'Father of Indian Ethnography', as he breathed life into the discipline of anthropology in India through his iconic ethnographic works among the tribal communities that were situated in West Bengal, Bihar, Jharkhand and Odisha. Roy, who conducted studies on Munda, Oraon, Birhors and Agaria, was critical of colonial ethnographers like Risely for depending on government functionaries and, as a consequence, rendering unreliable accounts. Most of the time, the lower-level functionaries had no idea about the nature and significance of work or the purpose of the information they were collecting.

Roy, who started as an academic anthropologist, gradually came to adopt the stance of an activist anthropologist (Dasgupta, 2007, p. 133). He played the role of a mediator between administrations and the tribals and acted as a spokesperson for the tribals. Roy advocated the study of anthropology from an Indian point of view. Roy's concern for methodology and his shift towards an Indian approach to methodology can be seen in his combination of Eastern and Western methods (Venkata Rao, 2024).

Roy authored an article titled 'An Indian Outlook on Anthropology' in the journal *Man*, published by the Royal Anthropological Institute of Great Britain and Ireland. This article is considered a pioneering work in the nationalist tradition of Indian anthropology. Roy not only critically assessed Western anthropological theories such as evolutionism, diffusionism and functionalism but also attempted to integrate the ideas of ancient Indian philosophers with Western anthropological concepts. He argued that the essence of Indian thought lies in the subjective process of 'sympathetic immersion' in other cultures and societies, which can be combined with the objective approach of Western anthropology (Abhijit Guha, 2023).

The investigation of cultural data requires not only objective methods but also the enhancement of these methods through historical imagination and a solid understanding of historical and geographical contexts. Additionally, a subjective approach involving deep reflection, or meditation, along with intuitive insights gained from empathetic engagement and self-identification with the society being studied, is essential for a comprehensive analysis (Abhijit Guha, 2023).

In his occasional paper, Abhijit Guha presented a list of ten nationalist anthropologists who learned the methodology of the discipline from the West but did not become blind followers of Europe and America and they also did not want to derive their anthropology from the religious scriptures of the ancient Hindus. Instead, they visualised an Indian character of anthropology, which, according to them, could be used in nation-building, a task that finally could not be developed into full maturity by their own successors. They are Sarat Chandra Mitra (1863–1938), Sarat Chandra Roy (1871–1942), Haran Chandra Chakladar (1874–1958), Bhupendranath Datta (1880–1961), B.R. Ambedkar (1891–1956), Panchanan Mitra (1892–1936), Biraja Sankar Guha (1894–1961), K.P. Chattopadhyay (1897–1963) and Tarak Chandra Das (1898–1964) and Nirmal Kumar Bose (1901–1972).

Scholars believe that, except for a few, most Indian anthropologists did not adhere to the principles of their nationalist predecessors and instead depended more on Western scholars (Abhijit Guha, 2018b, 2018a). In 1929, in his book 'Cultural Anthropology', Bose introduced a remarkable synthesis of Western philosophies with Indian texts and contexts. His incorporation of original ideas drawn from Indian Dharmashastras to interpret Indian civilisation reflects his distinctive approach, blending anthropology, Indology and history in a way that showcases his scholarly originality (Bose, 1929).

In 1938, Jogendrachandra Ghosh wrote an article called 'Hindu Anthropology' in a journal of Calcutta University. In the same year, Sarat Chandra Roy authored an article titled 'An Indian Outlook on Anthropology', in the journal of the Royal Anthropological Institute of Great Britain and Ireland. Roy's article can be seen as a significant contribution to the nationalist tradition of Indian anthropology. In this article, Roy not only critically assessed Western anthropological theories such as evolutionism, diffusionism and functionalism, but also attempted to integrate the ideas of ancient Indian philosophers with Western anthropological concepts. According to Roy, the essence of Indian thought lies in the subjective process of 'sympathetic immersion' in other cultures and societies, which can be combined with the objective approach of Western anthropology.

Sarat Chandra Mitra (1863–1938) was another prolific writer and he published numerous research articles on folklore and social-cultural anthropology. His nationalist spirit was best reflected in his writings on Indian mythology as well as his interest in introducing nature study in the school curriculum as early as 1911 (Mitra, 1911). Haran Chandra Chakladar was a great nationalist and left his government job and joined the Dawn Society at Calcutta, which was very critical of the colonial education in India (Ray Chaudhuri, 1958). Chakladar studied the peasants' wretched condition and the peasant revolt's socio-economic background under forced indigo cultivation in colonial India (Chakladar, 1905). Bhupendranath was the younger brother of the famous Hindu revivalist social reformer Swami Vivekananda. He joined the anti-British struggle and was sent to prison by the colonial government in India. His books Dialectics of Hindu Ritualism (1950) and Studies in Indian Social Polity (1963), though published much later, can be regarded as pioneering works on Indian society and culture from a Marxist perspective.

B.R. Ambedkar's paper on 'Castes in India: Their Mechanism, Genesis and Development' deserves mention. Starting from a fundamental anthropological finding of tribal clan exogamy, Ambedkar was able to show how caste endogamy was superimposed on the former. Secondly, his exposition as early as 1916 of caste as an extreme form of class system was also exemplary. Ambedkar's work was never mentioned or referred to by the world-renowned scholars on caste in India (Ambedkar, 1948).

Panchanan Mitra's book, Prehistoric India, as early as 1923, which was also the first of its kind by any Indian scholar, showed the antiquity, richness and diversity of the culture of humankind in the Indian subcontinent long before the advent of scripts. Biraja Sankar Guha undertook a thorough field survey on the social tensions among the refugees of then East Pakistan to advise the government on how to understand their problems and improve their living conditions. K.P. Chattopadhyay's research on jute mill workers and the workers of the then Calcutta Corporation was pioneering in anthropology inasmuch as it broke away from the colonial anthropological tradition (Roy Burman, 2000). Tarak Chandra Das made a marvellous empirical study, still unparalleled in global and Indian anthropology, on the devastations caused by the Bengal famine of 1943 during the colonial period.

Das was such a courageous academic that, in his presidential address to the anthropology section of the Indian Science Congress in 1941, he criticised the colonial government and Christian missionaries for doing a lot of harm to the tribals of north-eastern India. He had a vision for the application of anthropology to human welfare, but that was forgotten by Indian anthropologists. The critics of Indian anthropology also did not care to look at the socially relevant and nationalist studies of T.C. Das (Guha, 2011). Nirmal Kumar Bose (1901–1972) was a versatile personality in Indian anthropology. His multifaceted interests ranged from temple architecture and prehistory to transformations in tribal life under the impact of Hinduism and modernization (Abhijit Guha, 2023).

Ghurye was not the only nationalist sociologist who criticised pro-exclusionist policies. In an essay entitled 'Hindu Method of Tribal Absorption', Nirmal Kumar Bose laid down his interpretation of the relationship of the dominant Hindu communities with tribes. The stances of both Ghurye and Bose resulted in a defence of Hindu culture and society. They saw the tribal identity as a subset of the larger identity of the caste Hindu society and, therefore, did not consider the assimilation into Hindu society a major problem. But this was not true of all nationalists. Social workers like A.V. Thakkar reflected upon the need to develop a strong nationalist identity.

Indian anthropology in the pre-independence and post-independence eras was shaped not only by colonial influences but also by a growing nationalist trend. Socially engaged anthropologists in India made significant contributions to nation-building through their research and analytical writings. While Indian anthropologists learned methods from the West, they did not blindly imitate European or American approaches. Some Indian scholars delved into Hindu sacred texts to explore Indian civilisation, blending Western theory with indigenous knowledge. Indian anthropologists used Western knowledge to advocate for exploited tribes and marginalized communities, as well as to analyse Indian social reality. The colonial interest in studying tribes for administrative purposes led to the division of Indian society into tribes and castes, drawing parallels from Australian and African experiences.

Anthropological study has the potential to contribute to the promotion of unity in diversity through empathy, which is seen as the essence of human evolution from an Indian perspective. This can be particularly beneficial in a world that is grappling with numerous new and intense interactions, especially between Eastern and Western civilisations (Roy, 1938).

Irawati Karve was India's first woman anthropologist and the founder of sociology at Pune University. She was renowned for her studies of the ethnological and Indological traditions of India. Karve's central ideas focussed on Hindu society and its caste system, as well as kinship organisation in India. She wrote extensively on the *Mahabharata*, wherein her studies treat the protagonists of the epic as historical characters and use their attitudes and behaviour to understand the times they lived in. A nationalistic perspective can be seen in Karve's work, tracing unity in diversity by providing an overarching basis for all the diversity. Following the Indological tradition, Karve (1961) used classical texts to explain contemporary practices. Her range of work stretched from mapping kinship and caste to surveys on the contemporary status of women. To interpret the inner integration of Hindu society, she related Hindu mythologies to modern customs.

The same enterprise was again found in the work, 'Yuganta' (1967). Irawati Karve's retelling of the *Mahabharata* is a literary and sociological text that blends the history, culture and philosophy of ancient times. This work is remarkable as both a literary piece and a sociological study and as an anthropological and cultural document. It is a mirror reflecting human needs and responses alike, both in the past and contemporary times. It won the Sahitya Academy Prize as the best book of that year. The book's subject is secular, scientific and anthropological in the broadest sense.

Nirmal Kumar Bose, a first-generation Indian anthropologist, stood out from all other anthropologists since the subject gained attention in India. His proximity to Gandhi and his experience as personal secretary and co-field worker in Gandhi's field visits to eastern parts of India placed him on a unique pedestal. He restlessly worked for anthropology rooted in India, its philosophical traditions and cultural realities, which are reflected very clearly in his books and articles. A great supporter of revealing the 'Essence of India' through material culture in use at the length and breadth of India, while he was heading the Anthropological Survey of India, he was for understanding the idea of India through text and context. Bose was determined to transform anthropology to suit India and its rich traditions. His vision of India was that of an entity exhibiting cultural unity. He, therefore, saw India as historically or prehistorically interactive and zestful rather than isolated and disengaging. What he wrote was inspired by the classical texts, but was also based on the fieldwork knowledge generated from primary investigations.

The methodology of the study shift is evident in Bose's adoption of a combination of Indology, history and ethnology. The most well-known work on the 'Hindu Method of Tribal Absorption' followed the tradition of acculturation. The processes of accommodation of tribals into the Hindu fold without abandoning their cultural practices, as well as the study of cities, along with writing in vernacular languages (Bengali) in magazines and newspapers, are new improvements initiated by Bose. Mentioning these achievements, Bose (2007) pointed out that a pioneering trend in Indian nationalism began with N.K. Bose.

To comprehend the cultural unity of Indian civilisation, both N.K. Bose and L.P. Vidyarthi have examined the role of Indian pilgrim centres and sadhu traditions, which play an important role. The pilgrim places, or what Vidyarthi would like to call 'sacred complexes', are quite special places, allowing the diversities to come together and discover the connecting thread that joins them to each other and the larger unity. Different people visit these sacred centres for varying purposes. They all subscribe to a different variant of Hinduism and yet can realise a common meaning amidst the differences.

Anthropologists have made significant contributions to the bio-cultural study of ethnic minorities, known by various terms, such as tribes, aboriginals, autochthones, indigenous communities and Adivasis. Another focus of anthropologists has been on addressing the marginalized conditions of these communities and finding ways to integrate them into the mainstream of Indian society post-independence. Despite their efforts, the contributions of anthropologists towards nation-building in post-independence India were often overlooked by planners and policymakers due to the nature of the discipline and the failure to connect micro-level studies with the broader macro context of the nation. The planners of the country's mega five-year plans did not find much value in the detailed empirical studies conducted on specific tribes, castes and villages.

While anthropologists were considered experts in tribal policy at the national level, their role in nation-building or national planning was considered less significant compared to economists. Even though the government understood the importance of anthropological methodology in conducting in-depth field studies, it was not practically feasible to engage a sufficient number of trained anthropologists to assess the social impacts of major events, such as famine, partition, industrialisation, or dam building in post-colonial India. Anthropologists were content with their role as experts on tribes and continued their research on specific communities throughout the country even after independence.

Colonial anthropology categorised the inhabitants of hills, forests and plains in a manner that overlooked their historical interactions and the dynamic cultural exchanges among these groups. Therefore, research should prioritize the following: (a) acknowledging the fluid boundaries that exist between these communities, (b) transitioning from a colonial outsider viewpoint to research that is led by the community, (c) validating tribal and indigenous knowledge as both scientific and legitimate, (d) reforming policies that perpetuate colonial governance frameworks, (e) emphasizing the importance of indigenous voices and community involvement and (f) questioning colonial classifications and the dominance of Western theoretical perspectives.

CHAPTER 4

Decolonising the Indian Narrative

Research on tribes in India was, in the past, primarily conducted by colonial ethnographers and explorers. After independence, these studies were taken over by Indian anthropologists, but such academic exercises continued to be heavily influenced by Western biases. The studies often portrayed tribes as backwards or believed that the tribals could only achieve 'civilisation' through assimilation into the mainstream. To decolonise Indian anthropology, it is essential to critically reassess colonial legacies, acknowledge indigenous knowledge and integrate native perspectives into research and policy development. It is no secret that anthropology in India has been shaped by colonial ethnographers who classified indigenous communities in ways that frequently upheld hierarchical and Eurocentric viewpoints.

British officials and ethnographers, including Herbert Risley (1901) and the Census of India (1891, 1901, 1911), frequently overlooked the dynamic cultural interactions among these communities. Nicholas Dirks (2001) highlighted that colonial anthropology significantly contributed to the establishment of caste and tribal identities in India. Additionally, Verrier Elwin (1943, 1957) and Christoph von Fürer-Haimendorf (1982) contextualised these identities through a colonial developmental perspective.

A well-established critique of Indian anthropology has been articulated by several prominent anthropologists, who argue that the discipline is deeply rooted in a colonial legacy. They contend that Indian anthropologists, for various reasons, have often mirrored the approaches of their colonial predecessors. In 1971, the distinguished Indian anthropologist Surajit Sinha highlighted this issue in an article published in the Journal of the Indian Anthropological Society (JIAS). He noted that, despite significant advancements in research output and the growth of professional expertise in social and cultural anthropology over the past century, Indian anthropologists have largely remained reliant on Western and colonial frameworks (Abhijit Guha: 2025).

The desire for Indigenisation has come with the realisation that the theories and concepts of colonial academic disciplines in Third World countries have been inappropriate. Though attempts towards decolonisation of disciplines existed for a long time, the movement of post-colonialism cutting across disciplines attained significance after independence. Post-colonialism is a stand and a movement against essentialism, that is, the identification of core characteristics of societies and cultures. It questions the essentialist constructions of cultures as distinctive entities. For post-colonial scholars, Western anthropologists looked at Third World societies through the lenses of their own cultures and with an attitude of supremacy. Post-colonialists advocate decolonisation of the disciplines to reverse the effects of colonial understanding and the consequences of colonial domination.

Attempts towards decolonising the discipline in India can be seen in the works following the Indological approach and by using Indian texts, concepts, categories and terms. Anthropologists are well aware of the advantages of using local terms and epic categories as they convey a more accurate understanding of local cultures. Approaching society from the perspective of Indian classical texts has been one way of moving away from colonial tradition.

Indian anthropologists have significantly contributed to the evolution of the discipline and the ongoing decolonization of anthropology. Pioneers such as S.C. Roy, N.K. Bose, B.S. Guha, P. Mitra, J.C. Gosh, L.K. Ananthakrishna Iyer, H.C. Chakladar, S.C. Sinha, T.C. Das and Andre Beteille actively contested the colonial emphasis on racial determinism and the depiction of Indian society as unchanging. Their efforts to establish a distinct Indian tradition in anthropology were particularly noteworthy, as they sought to redefine the field even during the colonial era.

In 1938, Jogendra Chandra Ghosh, in his compelling article "Hindu Anthropology," argued that the Hindus developed various measurements of the human body and its parts prior to the 6th Century B.C. This practice, which can be likened to what is known in Europe as Anthropometry, represents a significant aspect of Physical Anthropology. Ghosh also highlighted that the earliest documentation of these anthropometric measurements is found in the Susruta-Samhita, a medical treatise written by the ancient Hindus (Ghosh: 1938).

In 1933, Panchanan Mitra authored an article that was published in the journal Man in India, under the editorial guidance of S.C. Roy, titled "Research Leads in Anthropology in India." In this significant piece, Mitra not only emphasized the critical role of cultural studies within the Indian context but also highlighted the importance of Indian philosophical thought in shaping contemporary anthropological theories. Furthermore, a group of anthropologists, including H.C. Chakladar, S.C. Roy, B.S. Guha and T.C. Das, despite being from different eras, collectively voiced their opposition to colonial rule with clarity and conviction. They sought to initiate a dialogue on the decolonization of anthropology in India, advocating for a re-examination of the discipline that would reflect the complexities and realities of Indian society rather than the perspectives imposed by colonial narratives. Their efforts marked a pivotal moment in the evolution of anthropology in India, as they aimed to reclaim the discipline for Indian voices and perspectives (Abhijit Guha: 2025).

The use of Indian concepts, categories and terms can be seen in the works of Saraswati Baidyanatha (1970, 1978). He used textual material extensively to bring an Indian flavour to anthropology in his writings. Saraswati used concepts like 'maryada and parampara' to denote descriptions related to social conduct and tradition. He coined a concept called 'Nilakantha syndrome' to explain the accommodation of harmful elements that could be assimilated into society. While many scholars used the terms 'Great tradition' and 'Little tradition', borrowed from Robert Redfield, Saraswati adopted a threefold classification in terms of Sastric (Written), Loukik (Oral) and Naivirtic (Transcendental). A parallel can be seen in the usage of concepts to that of Nirmal Kumar Bose, who mentioned the respectability of Lokachara, Kulachara and Desachara in Indian civilisation.

> Anthropologists consider civilisation as an advancement of cultures characterized by written modes of communication, urbanisation and control by centralised political authority, more complexity and specialisations. The statement by B.S. Cohn, while introducing his book, *India: Social Anthropology of a Civilisation*, reveals the magnitude of the exercise of comprehending Indian civilisation: 'It will be audacity/intellectual arrogance to talk about a 5000 years old civilisation, one of the world's few Ancient civilisations along with Egypt, Mesopotamia, China, Peru, Mess-America, exhibiting immense diversity, which represents a fusion of the past, present and future'. Cohn attempted to capture the enduring aspects or traits as the essence of civilisation—cultural geography and cultural history, social structure, early urbanisation and later urbanisation—in terms of ancient cities and colonial cities. Civilisation represents a continuity of religious symbols, philosophies, social institutions starting from the Indus Valley and discontinuities due to invasions from the west of the sub-continent, Islam, Christianity and the colonial impact (Cohn, 1971). The complexity of Indian civilisation, consisting of different levels, a multitude of variations in historical depth and deficit of conceptual tools to grasp the totality, may be the reasons for not many attempting a holistic understanding of the civilisation. This may be one of the reasons why Indian anthropologists continue with micro-level studies on tribes and villages.

In his examination of the methodology for studying Indian civilisation, Cohn posits that there exists a uniquely Indian essence that can be perceived, documented, enhanced, articulated, or quantified, which underlies the manifestation of a particular trait. This quality is fundamentally Indian or embodies Indian-ness, highlighting that every facet of Indian society is interlinked. He asserts that while it is important to analyse these aspects individually, one must not overlook the interconnectedness of the components involved.

ATTEMPTS AT A FRESH LOOK

Following independence, anthropology expanded its scope to encompass village and caste communities for research. Indian anthropologists, educated in Western universities, conducted studies on tribes, castes, villages, urban areas and sacred cities. They introduced concepts such as Sanskritisation, parochialisation, universalisation and globalization in the examination of Indian civilisation. In order to study civilisation, Redfield established the terms 'Great and Little traditions', 'cultural specialists', 'style of life', 'cultural performances' and 'cultural media'. He defined civilisation as a complex system of customs, role-occupiers and distinctive world views. The terms 'cultural performances' and 'cultural media' were employed by Milton Singer in his methodological research conducted in India. Sanskritisation is the process by which a lower caste or tribe takes on the traditions, rituals and way of life of a higher caste, according to M.N. Srinivas. According to Marriott, universalisation entails preserving elements of the little heritage, whereas parochialisation is a process of localisation and limiting.

N.K. Bose, in his book, *The Structure of Hindu Society*, gives a more civilisational view of Indian society. He has divided it into three parts. The first part mainly belongs to the domain of ethnography, where he presents material based on his own fieldwork. Fieldwork is mainly done among tribal communities. The second part is predominantly Indological, where he presents an account of the theory and practice of Hindu social life. The third part deals with social history.

Archaeologists, on the other hand, have been exploring subjects like the Indus Valley civilisation. Nirmal Kumar Bose highlighted the unity and diversity in Indian civilisation by combining Indology, ethnology and history and functionalism. His interest was beyond civilisation, extending to welfare and nationalism. He was searching for roots of the 'perennial strength of Indian civilisation' and the factors that constrained its creativity in modern times (Sinha, 1986, foreword). The civilisational approach of Nirmal Kumar Bose has inherent directions to the issues of national integration.

Bose is an amalgamation of various personas and interests. He was an anthropologist with a deep interest in geology and architecture, a Gandhian who thrived to understand Indian civilisation in its totality. In order to understand the then-existing discourses about India and its communities, which were generally looked down upon by the colonial administrators, he chose to study the Indian communities and their institutions through a historical approach, thus giving rise to the stream of discipline called 'social history'.

Bose conducted his first independent field research among the Juang tribesmen of Odisha, who practised shifting cultivation. He was struck by the fact that, although Juangs were outside the fold of Hinduism, there were clear indications that Hindu religious ideas had penetrated their culture. They bathe in the morning, they make offerings of sun-dried rice and they use terms such as satya, devata and dharma—all of these prove how strongly Juang religious ceremonies have been influenced by those of the neighbouring Brahminical people. Yet, the Juangs have their own language, they perform their marriage and funeral customs all by themselves, they eat beef and they are not considered by the Hindus to be one of their castes. This brief spell of field research gave Bose important and fundamental insights.

Bose shows that the influence of Aryan or Brahminical civilisation has been more significant in both extent and depth among the Mundas and Oraons than the Juangs or Savaras. It is through influences of this kind that tribal communities become increasingly articulated with the broader society. The process was described as the 'Hindu Method of Tribal Absorption' and according to Bose, it enabled the marginal communities to become a part of Hindu society without requiring them to abandon all their particular customs.

It is interesting to note that Hindu castes like Ahir, Lohar and Midha also join the tribal people in their celebrations and it is difficult to draw a distinction between them. On the nature of the cultural change process, Bose observed occasional fissions within one caste. Also, the absorption of tribal groups from outside into the Hindu social organisation fold, has been noticed. Recruits like Juang or Mundas may not exactly be called Hindu castes now. The reason is that they still need to retain their independent social rites which are not governed by Brahmins. But here we see a method by which the Hindus absorbed tribal groups within their own system.

Bose investigated the co-existence and inter-penetration of two modes of social organisation—'Brahmanical' and 'tribal'—in the field, which clearly indicates his capacity as a field scientist. According to Bose, these modes of social organisation have coexisted in India for a very long time. The first had a superior technological base and was larger in scale and complex than the second. The higher technical efficiency and the right given to all communities to practise their distinctive customs, even when in a hierarchical arrangement, attracted the tribal communities to it. As an anthropologist, Bose was interested not merely in revealing a specific pattern of culture but also in discovering the theory behind the pattern. The theory was an indispensable aid in understanding how the society actually worked.

The civilisational approach of Bose has two dimensions: unity among diverse elements and distinctiveness vis-a-vis other civilisations. He emphasized the importance of studying social history to understand the dynamics of society. In the civilisational approach of Bose, civilisation refers to Hindu civilisation and the institution of caste, which ensured a non-competitive system tolerant of diversity (Gayatri Bhattacharya, 2013). The aspects of the processes that later became popular as culture contact, Hinduisation and Sanskritisation, formed the basic components in Bose's popular article titled, 'The Hindu Method of Tribal Absorption'. Thus, he showed that marginal communities (such as the tribes) were able to become a part of the wider society (i.e., the multi-caste Hindu society) by adopting an occupation and supplying regular services to other castes, that is, getting drawn into the larger economic organisation. The approach of Bose sensitises us to the roots of civilisation and its transformation; this may help give directions to the ways of dealing with internal contradictions and conflicts. His approach highlights the importance of tolerance and cooperation.

Ghuyre advocated the policy of assimilation of the tribals with Hindu society. According to him, tribals have always been in contact with Hindu civilisation. He argued that 'almost all the so-called aboriginal tribes of the region have a Hinduised section, small or large, that they have been in fairly intimate contact with the Hindus for a long time and that they have a common interest with the Hindu in a matter of religion and gainful occupation' (Ghurye, 1963, p. 18). In his view, tribals were nothing more than backward Hindus and he opined that they should be assimilated into the larger Hindu society.

Others have disputed this contention by pointing out significant differences between the Hindus and the tribal religions. It is difficult to determine this issue conclusively because of the following reasons: (1) The Hindu religion does not have any set of criteria to determine an individual's membership into the religion. There is no common ritual, prayer or belief system that all Hindus adhere to, (2) it does not have any church or an ummah whose membership can identify the individual as a member of a particular religious groups, (3) the diversity in tribal religions makes the process of identifying individual tribes that are significantly Hinduised and that which are not, extremely difficult.

Mutually influencing the interaction between the tribes and Hindu civilisation existed from early times. Historians say that Indian civilisation is itself a product of a series of accretions of tribes at different times. Beteille (2004, pp. 71–72) quotes D.D. Kosambi, who says, 'The entire course of Indian history shows tribal elements being fused into the general society. This phenomenon, which lies at the foundation of the most striking Indian feature, namely caste, is also a great basic fact of ancient Indian history'. A known example of the transformation of a tribe into a caste is the Ahoms of Assam, who were originally from outside India and, after a length of time, became a fully integrated caste group within the Hindu caste system. Similarly, the Khasi, regarded as a tribe, has certain Hindu features.

The use of 'civilisation' is scarce in the writings of British colonial writers. Following the training from the American school of thought, many scholars have tried to understand cultures from a civilisational perspective. This perspective attempts to locate each and every component of society and culture in correlation with each other, making it a giant web of networks that provides us with a larger picture rather than studying the individual components independently. Robert Redfield believed that 'civilisation is a complex structure of the great and little traditions'. The civilisational perspective believes that every aspect of society and culture are interlinked and interdependent; one has to study them in their totality to understand the societies and cultures better.

McKim Marriott, in his essay, 'Little Communities in an Indigenous Civilisation', based on his fieldwork in the Kishan Garhi village in Uttar Pradesh, tried to provide us with a civilisational perspective. He elaborated by saying that the village Kishan Garhi reflected the Indian universe (i) through certain aspects of its social structure and (ii) through parts of its religious culture. Marriott, in furthering his arguments, analyses the village social structure, that is, the village as an isolable whole; and yet, at the same time, he explains how it is connected to the other villages and the state through its economy, marriage, kinship, social relationships and politics.

In analysing the religious culture, Marriott also argued how the village has unique religious pantheons and customs (parochialisation) of its own. Yet, it also sought connection and tried to universalise its religious practices. Trying to imitate the social structure of the state and the king by the dominant caste by establishing the jajmani system, the village provides enough evidence that it stands alone. Even so, it is a component connected with the more extensive network to its outside society, revealing the larger picture of how it is a civilisation that one needs to understand.

Milton Singer, through his work, 'The Great Tradition in a Metropolitan Centre: Madras' (1958), tries to argue how the culture of Madras (that can be categorised as 'Great tradition') still resembles or seeks connection with the 'Little tradition'. The continual flow of cultural connection between these two makes it a whole and into a civilisation. He analyses the cultural performances of the Little traditions, such as Bhajans and says that ritual customs were adopted in a manner with which the people could still participate albeit with certain modifications and variations to the versions of the Little traditions. He also analyses how cultural performances such as music and dance are elevated to a more fantastic tradition and yet are firmly grounded in the roots of the Little tradition.

American anthropologists such as Robert Redfield and Milton Singer showed more interest in Indian civilisation. Considering India as an orthogenetic or indigenous civilisation, attention was paid to the cultural role of orthogenetic cities and the role of a multiplicity of networks and centres in integrating the different levels of civilisations. This approach is markedly different from the tribal focus of British anthropologists. The influences of American anthropology led to the study of peasant societies, village studies, civilisational processes, the study of networks and centres. Their concepts of cultural interactions, like Great tradition and Little tradition and the concepts of universalisation and parochialisation go beyond the essentialist, static pictures of society provided by British anthropologists.

Many anthropologists argued that traditional institutions were sometimes obstacles for development. Empirical and contextual studies by scholars like Milton Singer and Scarlett Epstein questioned these notions by arguing that caste did not impede economic growth. Epstein's (1967) studies proved the rationality of the villagers in continuing with inter-caste relations, or breaking away from them. Singer (1972) showed that religious beliefs did not align with the entrepreneurial activities of industrialists in Madras. He demonstrated the behaviour of Brahmins through the processes of 'selective adaptation, compartmentalisation, ritual neutralisation, vicarious ritualisation, abbreviation and consolidation of ritual practices'. Third World scholars like Escobar (1991) were critical of the econometric and techno-centric models borrowed from the West, calling for the liberation of the social sciences from colonial hegemonies. According to Dube (1988) there are several dilemmas that we need to reconcile in the context of modernization and development.

LP Vidayarthi's research on the Gaya pilgrimage centre highlighted its significance as a defining element of Indian civilisation, focussing on sacred geography, sacred performances and sacred specialists. His analysis revealed that pilgrims visiting Gaya contributed to both Little and Great traditions, bringing elements of the former and taking back aspects of the latter, thus enriching the cultural dimension of the civilisation.

In the writings on Indian civilisation, we confront Eurocentric concepts and understanding on one side and an Indological approach on the other. Some scholars highlighted the civilisational achievements, contributions, decline, inequalities and oppression. The contribution of Indian civilisation can be understood from the fact that, when Europe was in the Dark Ages, India exported culture to other Asian countries and prestigious products and goods to several more. The contributions of Indian civilisation can be seen in the fields of astronomy, science, metallurgy, cotton weaving, dyeing, navigation, mathematics (decimal system, zero), geometry, Yoga Sutra of Patanjali, linguistics of Panini, philosophy, logic (quantum physics), Buddhism and medicine (Ayurveda).

Yet the Westerners depicted this country as one of snake charmers and naked sadhus: a country that is backward and needs to be civilised and developed. Nationalist scholars have highlighted the reasons for the decline due to foreign rulers extracting resources and exporting, plundering of wealth, imposition of burdensome taxes, discouraging trade commerce and industries, undermining crafts, and, above all, cultural subordination. Deliberate efforts started during the freedom struggle for unification and mobilisation of the people by highlighting the achievements of the civilisation. Jawaharlal Nehru's book, *Discovery of India*, can be cited here as an example.

Several streams of ideas in the study of Indian civilisation have been hotly debated and countered. There were depictions of India as a frozen civilisation and static society. The oft-quoted statement of Charles Metcalfe, 'Dynasty after dynasty tumbles', is a typical example of a static picture of an unchanging society for centuries. There were projections of Indian villages as little republics, with conservative institutions like the Indian joint family, caste system and Hindu religion—a system of exchange of goods and services was constructed as a *jajmani* system, adding to the descriptions of stagnation at the grassroots level and changes occurred only at the apex.

This sort of picture completely ignored the contestations, mobility and changes that existed in society and were far removed from ground realities. Social historians rightly questioned the static and frozen picture. Even in the colonial government, people petitioned the government with claims and counterclaims over statuses and identities. Stereotypes and essentialisations coming from the colonial period were debunked by scholars like Ronald Inden (Imagining India, 1990) and Nicholas Dirks (Castes of Mind, 2001).

The relationship between culture and development in the Indian context was analysed by Madan (1983). He made a plea for endogenous development models and pointed to the eco-friendly and sustainable nature of prescriptions in Indian philosophies. Madan pointed out that many Western scholars tended to blame the Indian society and culture for the underdevelopment of India. They prescribed the need for social, economic and administrative reforms to promote economic development. Madan underlined how India could achieve a modern, diversified economy with impressive achievements like an increase in agricultural and industrial production, life expectancy and production of skilled manpower through planned development.

He also identified the adoption of inappropriate development strategies borrowed from the West, emphasis on growth while postponing the issue of social justice and the growth of education unrelated to national needs as responsible for the lopsided development in the country. Madan rightly pointed out that economic development, if it were not linked to cultural goals, led to mindless consumerism. He argued for an endogenous development model, an economic development encompassing Indian culture, ethics and philosophy. This actually calls for a redefinition of the goals of development.

More recently, post-modernists raised significant questions on anthropological practices and knowledge and questioned the objectivity of the theories and methods of anthropologists. The works of the post-modernists (Contributors to the volume edited by Clifford, James and George Marcus, 1985 and several others) are critically focussed on the issues related to fieldwork methods, the transformation of data into ethnographies and the interpretations based on the ethnographies. Moving to another dimension, the communities and cultures, which were studied initially by anthropologists during the colonial rule and later under the impact of national government policies, are now experiencing incursions of global forces. Globalization, along with industrialisation and urbanisation, accelerates the disappearance of rich cultural diversity. There is a concern among social anthropologists about the disappearance of cultural variation and identities resulting in homogenisation.

The threat and the fear of globalization have led to efforts towards the protection and revival of traditional practices. In the wake of onslaughts from global forces, various groups are now striving for the revival of traditional cultural practices and education. For anthropologists, the concepts of culture and community have formed the core material. They have understood that, in the wake of globalization, cultures can no longer be studied as internally coherent wholes. They are subject to the influences of multiple sources and traditions and several alternative ways of living have evolved. Traditionally, communities and cultures have been the units of analysis in anthropology. In the post-globalization period, the notion of community can be seriously questioned due to the inherent variety of responses and interests.

The discussion on post-modernism and globalization reveals the predicament of those who carry out anthropological studies in the tradition of fieldwork by selecting traditional topics of colonial times. The practice of anthropology in the post-colonial period requires a different orientation, encompassing global influences and local responses, to capture the dynamics of society and culture. Also, it is time to come out of the entire colonial theoretical and conceptual baggage that labelled the Third World populations as traditional societies, backward and underdeveloped. The ideological underpinnings of imported theories, concepts and categories need to be recognized. To embark on such an exercise, the teaching and learning of anthropology in educational institutions must be closely scrutinised in the wake of post-colonial understanding. This takes us to the question of curricula taught in the departments of anthropology.

Indian anthropologists developed a distinct research methodology to conduct their studies. It included Das (using genealogies to study Purum society), N.K. Bose (spatial distribution technique used to date Indian temples, use of human geography in study of culture-historical issues as well as the use of family histories in studying social change in urban centres), Chattopadhyay and Mukherjee (use of statistics in studying social change), Iravati Karve (text analyses incorporated with kinship studies) and L.P. Vidyarthi (using the concepts of sacred centre, cluster and segment to study sacred complexes). Since Western anthropology, under the influence of British and American, failed to explain the complexity of Indian society, a critical appraisal and reorientation of the discipline was needed for the Indian situation. As a result, many anthropologists have proposed their own theories.

The alternative methodological framework did not merely help establish a refined concept; it also aimed at 'Indianness' for maintaining the quality of national life. In fact, Indian anthropology demands an active, humanistic and critical outlook towards the subject matter in order to overcome the barrier of intellectual colonialism and neo-colonialism. Indian anthropology from the 1990s has been greatly concerned with problems of its own society, both empirical and normative. New types of data are encountered; concepts, methods and theories are continually shaped and reshaped. New ways of looking at new types of data have made Indian anthropology much more distinctive than ever before.

Indian anthropology developed in a unique context compared to British, American and French anthropologies, as it emerged under colonial rule. This posed a challenge for Indian anthropologists in establishing a nationalist and indigenous framework for their discipline. Interestingly, Indian anthropology has not extensively explored its own history and foreign/Western anthropologists who made significant contributions to the understanding of Indian society and culture have shown limited interest in documenting the history of Indian anthropology.

Conversely, Indian anthropologists have made occasional efforts to document the history of the discipline in relation to nation-building in post-independent India. Interestingly, a common critique emerged among prominent Indian anthropologists, suggesting that the field was influenced by colonial ideologies and continued to follow colonial and neo-colonial practices.

In his paper titled, 'Anthropology in India: Need for an Alternate Paradigm', presented at the 14th International Congress of Anthropological and Ethnological Sciences (ICAES) in Williamsburg in 1998, Professor Ajit K. Danda highlighted the detrimental effects of Western models in the curriculum and the complete disregard for indigenous knowledge, that have significantly hindered the advancement of anthropology as a scientific discipline. Similarly, Professor Makhan Jha, in his work, 'Man and His Nature in Indian Textual Traditions', addressed the limitations of Western methodologies in understanding and interpreting Indian realities, particularly focussing on the relationship between man and nature as described in classical Indian texts. Dr A. Capila, in her presentation, 'Understanding Culture Experientially', emphasized that, to truly grasp a culture, researchers must look beyond mere words and attune themselves to the underlying sentiments. Furthermore, Professor S.C. Malik, in his paper, 'Dynamics of Cultural Communication: Anthropology of Experience', challenged the foundational assumptions of post-Newtonian discourse regarding rationality, linear time and the dichotomies of subjectivity versus objectivity and nature versus man, that are often employed to distinguish scientific thought from pre-scientific knowledge systems.

IGNCA INITIATIVES

The Indira Gandhi National Centre for the Arts (IGNCA) has been actively involved in civilisational studies and alternative anthropology, emphasizing a comprehensive understanding of Indian cultural phenomena and noumena in their entirety and interrelation. This initiative encompasses the documentation and examination of folk arts, tribal societies and prehistoric art, aiming to create innovative frameworks for anthropological research. In its efforts to decolonise Indian anthropology, IGNCA has initiated a project named Alternative Paradigms in Anthropology, to investigate alternative methodologies that extend beyond the indigenisation of anthropology. Since its inception, the Janapada Sampada division of IGNCA has concentrated on multidisciplinary lifestyle studies of tribal and rural communities to formulate alternative models for analysing Indian cultural phenomena, taking into account environmental, ecological, agricultural and socio-economic aspects.

The initiatives undertaken by the IGNCA encompass the examination of the community's physical environment, which includes mapping aspects such as water, earth, rocks, soils, minerals, vegetation and energy sources, as well as the interactions among these elements within the ecosystem throughout an annual cycle. The Janapada Sampada Division of IGNCA focuses on the diverse and rich heritage of tribal, rural and small-scale societies through its various programs and research initiatives. These include Loka Parampara, Kshetra Sampada, Northeast India and Ethnographic Collection. Research activities focus on the lifestyle study programmes comprising the Loka Parampara, which revolves around a community and the Kshetra Sampada, which revolves round a region. The division's research emphasizes lifestyle studies, particularly through the Loka Parampara program, which aims to comprehensively explore the cultural knowledge of communities. Traditionally, societies have been analysed in a linear and unidimensional manner by disciplines such as anthropology, sociology and history. In contrast, the IGNCA Centre is developing a holistic model of lifestyle studies that recognizes the interconnectedness of various life dimensions and the complexity of cultural lifestyles among diverse groups. This model seeks to illustrate a multi-layered social space, acknowledging that time encompasses physical, biological, mythical and metaphysical aspects, thus challenging the sufficiency of both evolutionary cultural models and linear historical timelines.

The primary focus of the lifestyle study programs is to explore the intricate connections between nature, ecology, daily life, social structures, worldviews, cosmology, life cycles, routines, annual calendars, knowledge, skills, traditional technologies and artistic expressions. Through targeted community studies, these programs examine the interdependence of the arts, the mutual influences across regions and the relationships among tribal, rural and urban contexts, as well as literary and oral traditions. The findings from these studies often result in comprehensive outputs such as monographs, books, audio-visual documentation and cartographic representations of specific artistic and craft-related aspects. Additionally, the field studies contribute valuable data for developing computerizable modules aimed at facilitating further research. Research has been conducted in the early years on various indigenous groups across India, including the Santhals of West Bengal and Orissa, the Bhuiyans and Paiks of Orissa, the Meiteis of Manipur, the Angamis of Nagaland, the Gujars of the Central Himalayas, the Changpas of Ladakh, the Gaddis of Himachal Pradesh, the Bajara-growing communities of Rajasthan, the Visvakarmas, the forest-dwellers of Karnataka and the Mukkuvars of Tamil Nadu.

Additionally, Lokparampara studies have been conducted on topics such as village India, paddy cultivation practices, living traditions of the *Ramayana* and the *Mahabharata*, the intangible cultural heritage of Indian communities, the Jewish cultural heritage in India, the worldview of Viswakarmas, the confluence of traditions and composite cultures, riverine cultures and Jal Sanskriti etc.

Throughout history, certain regions/ areas have developed into cultural centres attracting people from all parts of India. These centres are places of convergence and radiation, where centrifugal and centripetal forces are evident. Often a temple or a mosque, is the physical or notional centre. So far they have been studied either from the point of view of chronology, history, religion or economics as a linear phenomenon and not a totality from which emanates a multiplicity of creative artistic activity. The IGNCA's research under Kshetra Sampada is broadens this perspective, advocating for a comprehensive examination of regional cultures that are unique yet interconnected. This approach emphasizes not just the significance of a specific location or temple, but also its influence on the community and the intricate interplay of devotional, artistic, geographic, social and economic dimensions that define the sacred center, along with the factors that contribute to its renewal and continuity. Studies have been taken up in the early years on the Brhadisvara Temple, Tanjavur and Vraja Prakalpa. Kshetra Sampada which involves research on temple history, religion and economics. The effort has been to enhance the understanding of the region's cultural diversity. IGNCA's work in this area reflects a broader effort to move beyond traditional anthropological approaches and embrace a more holistic, multidisciplinary and interdisciplinary approach to understanding Indian culture and its diverse expressions.

IGNCA former Professor B.N. Saraswati conducted research on 'Alternative Paradigms in Anthropology'. This exploration for alternatives differs from the pursuits aimed at the 'indigenization of anthropology'. A significant portion of anthropological studies remains influenced by the Cartesian-Newtonian-Darwinian frameworks that emerged during the colonial expansions of the seventeenth, eighteenth and the nineteenth centuries. The works of IGNCA have highlighted the inadequacy of existing anthropological concepts and categories. By acknowledging the connections between mind, man and matter, as well as knowledge, experience, culture and the relationship between man, nature and culture, we seek to establish new paradigms. In his work titled, 'Seeking Alternate Paradigms in Anthropology: An Indian Eye View of the Cosmic Anthropological Principle', Professor Saraswati critically examined the validity of a scientific perspective that categorises humanity into primitive and civilised realms based on physical and technological criteria. He explored what he refers to as 'The Sacred Science of Man', which introduces a series of paired conceptual categories: the many versus the one, man as a microcosm, science as society, theodicy as cosmodicy, mind as matter, word as world, knowledge as experience, knowledge as culture, nature as culture, ritual as language and tradition as hierohistory. Additionally, he provided specific illustrations of the cosmic anthropological principle, including cosmic hierophany, ecological principle, ordering principle and transcending principle.

The IGNCA hosted a special panel discussion on the theme of 'Decolonising Indian Anthropology' at the Indian Anthropology Congress-2025 (IAC-2-25); on the theme, 'Envisioning Anthropology for a Developed India' from 21 to 23 February 2025 at Anthropological Survey of India (AnSI), Head Office in Kolkata. The meet was organized by the Indian National Confederation and Academy of Anthropologists (INCAA), in collaboration with Anthropological Survey of India (AnSI), Indira Gandhi Rashtriya Manav Sangrahalaya (IGRMS), Bhopal and the Indira Gandhi National Centre for The Arts (IGNCA). More than 450 renowned anthropologists, academicians and scholars from approximately 60 universities and 40 other research organisations and national museums across the country attended the congress.

The panel discussion was attended by many distinguished anthropologists, scholars and policymakers across the country. The panelists on the dais were Prof. P.C. Joshi. Former Vice-Chancellor, University of Delhi, Prof. K.K. Basa, Chairman, Monument Authority of India, Prof. Sabita Acharya, Vice Chancellor, Utkal University, Bhubaneshwar, Prof. P. Venkat Rao, Former Dean, University of Hyderabad, Prof. A. Chella Perumal, Former Director & Head, Pondicherry Central University, Prof. K.R. Rama Mohan, Head, Dept of Anthropology, Sikkim Central University, Prof. M. Romesh Singh, Head, Dept of Anthropology University of Hyderabad and Prof. K. Anil Kumar,

Head, JS Division IGNCA. The panel was convened under the chairmanship of Prof. P.C. Joshi which aimed to provide a platform to critically examine Eurocentric frameworks in Indian anthropology and explore ways to integrate indigenous perspectives into academic discourse.

During one of these discussions, Prof. K. Anil Kumar highlighted how the British government had labelled India's indigenous populations as 'primitive' and 'backward' to justify their dominance. By imposing Western theoretical frameworks, early anthropological studies distorted these communities' historical and cultural identities. The interconnectedness of forest, hill and plain societies was overlooked due to their classification as distinct groups. To foster a better understanding of the cultural complexities and socioeconomic realities within India, he argued for a more equitable and inclusive approach to anthropology that acknowledges and values indigenous perspectives.

In his speech, Prof. P.C. Joshi stated that Western perspectives have significantly shaped Indian anthropology, often overlooking local knowledge. Numerous communities were assigned derogatory labels through colonial classifications, which exacerbated existing power imbalances. He cited the 'Jarawa' of the Andaman and Nicobar Islands (whose true name is 'Ang') and the 'Daflas' of Arunachal Pradesh (now referred to as 'Nishi') as examples. Joshi highlighted the importance of anthropologists rectifying historical inaccuracies and adopting the names that communities have selected for themselves. Furthermore, he argued that research methodologies should not be constrained by Western paradigms, advocating for the promotion of community-based participatory research. Proposed solutions included enhancing indigenous representation in academia, revising anthropological curricula and improving policies.

In her address, Prof. Sabita Acharya stated that Western anthropologists have cited indigenous and tribal groups as primitive, thereby reinforcing the belief in Western superiority. British scholars such as William Crook and Herbert Risley utilised the notion of tribal societies as being less advanced to justify colonial dominance. The complex interconnections among populations residing in forests, hills and plains were overlooked in these imperial narratives. A comprehensive approach is necessary to acknowledge the historical, cultural and social bonds among India's diverse populations. Tribal communities are integral to Indian civilisation and should not be regarded as isolated entities. The Indian educational system prioritizes Western theories over indigenous knowledge, continuing to follow colonial frameworks. To decolonise Indian anthropology, it is essential to replace Western-centric methodologies with a civilisational perspective that honours the rich indigenous traditions and relationships among the people of India.

In his presentation, Prof. P. Venkat Rao highlighted the urgent necessity for Indian anthropology to move away from colonial narratives and adopt a civilisational perspective that integrates historical context, indigenous knowledge and linguistic diversity. The historical contributions of indigenous communities have often been neglected in favour of depicting them as separate from civilisation. In opposition to colonial views, anthropologists like N.K. Bose and S.C. Malik advocated an Indian civilisational framework.

To demonstrate the frequent undervaluation of indigenous wisdom in contrast to Western perspectives, Professor Romesh Singh commenced his discussion with the phrase, *ghar ki murgi, dal barabar*' (roughly translated, it means that home-cooked chicken is regarded as equivalent to lentils, or that domestic wisdom is often neglected). There exist systemic issues within Indian anthropology that demand attention. The concept of decolonisation is currently being explored across various academic disciplines, such as political science, sociology and history. The speaker cites academics who have examined this problem including Nandini Sundar, Madhav Gadgil, Ramachandra Guha and Archana Prasad. In India, numerous ethnographies and anthropological studies continue to operate within colonial frameworks. It is imperative that indigenous perspectives and the lived experiences of individuals are prioritized over top-down approaches. The speaker underscores the importance of genuine decolonisation in the field of Indian anthropology.

In 1889, British cartographers and colonial administrators inaccurately categorised the ethnic groups in Sikkim into three primary classifications: the Bhutias, Lepchas and Nepalis. Prof. K.R. Ramamohan discussed how this categorisation had led to ongoing ethnic tensions and political engagement, neglecting the diversity of approximately 20 ethnic communities. These divisions were further solidified in 1975, following the addition of Sikkim to the Indian Union, resulting in political and identity conflicts. To ensure equity, a new commission led by Professor B.V. Sharma has been tasked with reevaluating these classifications. While shamanism has been explored by scholars such as Philippi Sargons, Larry Peters and Pierces Wittabaski, their frameworks do not align with the indigenous practices of Sikkim. The ethnic minorities in Sikkim continue to face challenges in gaining recognition within the current political framework due to the misclassifications from the colonial period.

According to Prof. Chellaperumal, anthropology has its origins in colonialism, with significant contributions from Western scholars such as Malinowski and Radcliffe-Brown shaping its methodologies. The National Education Policy (NEP) 2020 highlighted the importance of incorporating indigenous knowledge into university programs, including anthropology. Despite the attempts of Indian anthropologists like N.K. Bose, D.S. Saraswati and L.P. Vidyarthi to decolonise the discipline, Western methodologies remain prevalent. Indian civilisation was characterized by a complementary structure rather than strict segregation, as illustrated by ancient texts like Sangam literature and Vedic scriptures. American anthropologist Margaret Mead identified 25 unique expressions of love through her in-depth analysis of Tamil literature (Thiruvasagam) and family dynamics, underscoring the critical role of language in understanding culture.

Professor K.K. Basa's examination of tribal culture was somewhat idealised by colonialism, which also generated misleading narratives asserting that colonial ethnography justified colonial governance and reinforced prevailing power structures. To achieve decolonisation, it is essential to confront these biases and inaccuracies in knowledge production. This involves understanding the formation of colonial narratives and contextualising the development of colonial knowledge, as well as objectively analysing and assessing colonial information to eradicate its prejudices. Museums, which were previously marginalized in anthropological discussions, are now playing a crucial role in decolonisation efforts. The Indira Gandhi Manav Sangrahalaya (Museum of Mankind) serves as an example of a post-colonial museum that more accurately represents indigenous cultures. We also have scholars such as S.C. Malik, who have made original contributions to the discourse on archaeology by suggesting that the Harappan civilisation had a caste system.

The panel discussion highlighted the critical necessity for reforming Indian anthropology by prioritising indigenous perspectives, reevaluating colonial classifications and adopting a civilisational framework. To advance this initiative, modifications to the curriculum, policy reforms and increased representation of indigenous scholars are essential for fostering a more inclusive and decolonised field. The panel proposed significant research efforts to restore the indigenous narrative, challenge colonial biases and advocate for an impartial, evidence-based civilisational approach to understanding India's tribal communities.

Dr Sachchidanand Joshi, member secretary of IGNCA, who was the chief guest at the valedictory function, emphasized that India's diversity should be comprehended solely within the framework of the Vedic tradition in anthropological discussions. Dr Joshi recited a poem by Pablo Neruda. He emphasized the significance of this poem for all young scholars and thinkers in anthropology, urging them to recognize that without a shift in our thinking, philosophy and vision, we risk becoming intellectually stagnant. Dr Joshi encouraged young scholars to adopt diverse perspectives, transform the narrative of anthropological studies in India, seek a more India-centric approach and demonstrate to the world that we possess the courage, determination, facts, and, indeed, the truth.

INTER-PEOPLE INTERACTIONS

The interaction between forest and hill people has been a feature of Indian society from the early stages. It can be traced back to the days of *Ramayana* and *Mahabharata*. The tribal groups were referred to as Jana in *Ramayana*.

When Ram reached the borders of the forests of central India during his exile, the land was introduced to him as Jana-sthan, the land of tribal people. The encounter between Guha and the Bhil woman Sabari, mentioned earlier, is a well-known episode in the epic. In the *Mahabharata*, there are mentions of kiratas, Bhim's union with a tribal woman, Hidimba and Krishna's battle against Banasura. These interactions highlight the relationships between tribes and non-tribes in that era.

The indigenous tribes are an integral part of Indian civilisation and culture, having made significant contributions to ancient Indian society. It is believed that they are the oldest among the current population of India, which is a blend of four main races and cultures: Austro-Asiatic, Mongols, Dravidians and Aryans. The first three races played a crucial role in shaping the diverse population of present-day India.

The present-day Mundas and Santhals are believed to be the descendants of the non-Aryan Kolarian group, while the Gonds and Khonds are the prominent Dravidian tribes. The Rig Veda contains the names of several Dasyu warriors and their Aryan adversaries and the Brahmanas, Puranas and Sanhitas provide myths about the origins of non-Aryan tribes such as Nishad, Kol and Asur. The Ramayana and Mahabharata also mention various tribal communities like Rakshas, Vanar, Nishad, Gridhraj, Sabar, Yaksh, Nag, Kirat, Andhra, Madra, Yavan and Paundra.

During the historical era, dating back to the time of Ashoka, the indigenous tribes are referenced in his Shahbazgarhi rock edict No. XIII. In the seventh century, the Harshacharita documents the presence of tribes residing in the Vindhyan Mountains as Harshavardhana embarked on a quest to find his sister Rajyashri.

Tribes such as the Gonds and the Bhumijas established a dynastic presence at certain points in Indian history. The Khamptis, a Buddhist tribe from Arunachal Pradesh, governed the Sadiya outpost of the Ahom kingdom during the early nineteenth century. Furthermore, there exists another aspect to consider regarding the interaction between tribal and non-tribal communities (caste-based societies). Tribes gained knowledge from caste-based societies, while castes also adopted certain elements of tribal life. This process of interaction has led to varying degrees of assimilation, acculturation and adaptation between tribal and non-tribal communities.

During the medieval period, the tribal communities in India enjoyed autonomy. However, with the arrival of Muslim rulers, this autonomous status was lost. For example, the Nagbansi Raja of Chota-Nagpur, who led the Oraons and the Mundas, became a tributary in 1585. The rulers of the Garha kingdom in Central India also faced a similar fate after the defeat of Queen Durgavati in 1564. Despite being nominally under Muslim rule, most tribal states were geographically distant and faced minimal interference in their social and economic systems. They were able to maintain their traditional way of life and their relationship with the land and forests. As a result, tribal resistance during this period was limited and short-lived, leading to fewer tribal revolts under Muslim rule in India.

Since their advent, the British had to face opposition from the tribals. The British rule had created such conditions that were detrimental to the lifestyle and culture of the tribals. The tribal communities revolted in the entire country against the policies and rules of the British government. Tribal leaders held significant positions in several regions prior to the British arrival. There was constant contact between tribes and plains and they possessed some degree of economic power as well as the authority to govern and rule their domains.

It is quite a challenge to categorise tribal communities at one extreme and non-tribal-peasant communities at the other. If we were to position tribal and peasant communities at opposite ends of a spectrum, we would observe numerous tribal communities exhibiting traits of peasant and caste-based societies, as well as many caste-based communities demonstrating characteristics of tribal communities to varying degrees. There exists no void between tribal and caste-based societies positioned at these extremes. A continuum exists between tribal and caste-based societies.

Some examples of the continuum: Anthony Walker (1998), after spending several years with the Toda community in the Nilgiri Hills, concluded that the term 'caste' holds significant value compared to 'tribes', as it situates them within the south Indian cultural framework to which they belong. He finds it perplexing when the Toda are labelled as a 'tribe' in the context used in anthropological and sociological discussions. Similarly, Hockings (1993), having studied the Badaga community in the Nilgiri Hills, notes that they have been classified as a 'tribe', 'caste' and 'Hindu race' in literature since 1922. He, like Walker, emphasizes the need to examine the broader system rather than merely categorising a single unit. The Badaga community migrated from the northern plains to the Nilgiri Hills, exemplifying a caste group that has adopted a tribal model through consistent interactions with the Toda, Kurumba and Kota, who are Scheduled Tribes in the Nilgiri Hills. Hockings views the Nilgiri populace as a 'case of a caste society' that showcases 'multiple distinct indigenous cultures', each with origins rooted in pre-caste social structures.

The interactive approach to tribal studies is undoubtedly appropriate, as tribes do not exist in isolation. Over time, studies are fundamentally historical inquiries, while studies across different cultures at a specific moment can serve as cross-cultural comparisons. However, investigations of tribal studies across space can also explore relational dynamics over time within both tribal and non-tribal contexts. This leads to the essential concept of temporal and spatial convergence among tribes, shaped by the duration and extent of their interactions. Such differences may represent critical distinctions among tribes.

In this regard, spatial studies inherently involve historical inquiries. This perspective is clearly illustrated in Nandini Sinha Kapur's examination of the Bhils in her paper titled, 'The Bhils in the Historic Setting of Western India'.

The research outlines the Bhils' interactions with regional state authorities and the rural communities of Mewar and Dungarpur in southern Rajasthan, as well as the Ahmadabad area and the Panchmahals in Gujarat during the medieval period, specifically from the seventh to the fifteenth centuries. Although it appears to be a historical study, the paper is fundamentally interdisciplinary, as it elucidates the process of acculturation through Kshyatriyaisation or Rajputaisation and peasantisation from a historical viewpoint. Furthermore, the paper utilises a variety of sources, including literary texts and bardic traditions, alongside historical evidence (Nandini Sinha Kapur, 2020).

Indian society exhibits a unique blend of dichotomy and continuity. This distinctive feature allows individuals from all castes and tribes to engage in their customs and traditions, even as it fosters opportunities for social interaction. The coexistence of traditional practices and social engagement defines the essence of Indian society, emphasizing both continuity and evolution. Castes and tribes have long been integral cultural components of Indian society.

During their interaction, the tribals have assimilated certain elements of non-tribal lifestyles. Conversely, non-tribal communities have also embraced tribal customs and traditions. For instance, in Odisha, a tribal deity was incorporated into the Hindu tradition, giving rise to the 'Jagannath Cult'. Nearby tribes influenced the Badaga people of the Nilgiri Hills, while the Karma festival of the Oraons has been adopted by various neighbouring communities in Jharkhand and Odisha.

Placing tribal communities at one end of the pole and the plain communities at the other, is problematic. Many tribal communities exhibit traits of plain and caste-based communities, while several caste-based communities display characteristics of tribal communities to some degree. There is no empty space between tribal and caste-based societies positioned at the opposite poles. Therefore, there exists a continuum between tribal and caste-based societies, referred to as the tribe-caste continuum.

Throughout its history, India has been known for its harmonious coexistence among its people. The acceptance of others has been deeply ingrained in the culture, as evidenced by the peaceful relationships between kings, tribals and rural communities. The tribal population residing in rural areas maintained their distinct identity and way of life, even when interacting with non-tribals. They relied heavily on forest resources for their livelihood, while kings respected their territories and maintained a respectful distance. Interactions between tribal and village communities were primarily centred around trade.

Colonial administrators, census commissioners and anthropologists such as Risley (1915), O'Malley, (1909, 1910), Elwin (1943) and Haimendorf (1977) hold the tribals and non-tribals to be separate. In their view, the tribals did not have more than casual contact with the caste Hindus. Elwin has authored several monographs on the tribes of Madhya Pradesh in different years (Elwin, 1939, 1942, 1947, 1955, 1969), but his writings lack substantial information on inter-tribal relations. On the other hand, Furer-Haimendorf conducted extensive fieldwork among Nagas during his travels in Nagaland in three different years (1936, 1937 and 1969) and published a monograph on Konyak Naga. However, his account of them provides minimal details on the relationships between the tribes and neighbouring communities.

Tribes in India have always been interconnected and have never existed in seclusion. Consequently, a tribal community is constantly evolving and never remains stagnant. To put it differently, the tribal community is undergoing a transition. There is an additional aspect to comprehending the interaction between tribes and non-tribals, particularly those based on caste. Tribes have gained knowledge from caste-based societies and in turn, castes have also acquired insights into the tribal way of life. As a result of this process of interaction, assimilation, acculturation and adaptation have occurred to varying extents between the tribal and non-tribal communities. The interaction between Janjatis and the people of the plains has been a feature of Indian society since its inception and can be traced back to ancient times.

Based on empirical evidence, social anthropologists and ethnographers like Hutton (1955), Bailey (1961), Ghurye (1963), Kosambi (1970), Bose (1971) and Vidyarthi and Rai (1985), have concluded that there is a significant interaction between Caste and Tribe. They believe that various cultural traditions of Hinduism are connected to tribal cultures and vice versa. Social anthropologists and ethnographers such as Hutton (1955), Ghurye (1963), Bose (1971), Vidyarthi and Rai (1985), Bailey (1961) and Kosambi (1970), believe that many cultural traditions of Hinduism have links with the tribal cultures and vice versa. According to them, the tribals have had continuous contact with their neighbouring castes, which has helped them practice settled agriculture and live by a number of specialised manual industries. This contact goes back, at least to the days of the epics of *Ramayana* and *Mahabharata*, when the tribal communities were referred to as Jana.

Extensive studies by scholars present varied nature of the social realities in India between tribes and castes. Though one cannot rule out the existence of isolated tribes in India and also of those tribals and caste Hindus who have been living side by side for centuries, it would be unwise to think that there has been no acculturation process between them. In a given empirical situation, there is every possibility of co-existence of the tribal as well as the caste characteristics. There have been instances of individuals and small tribal groups being absorbed within the Hindu caste system in India. From 1872 onwards, the successive British census commissioners in India noted that throughout the country tribal people were being transformed into castes (Risley, 1915, p. 72; Sinha, 1980, p. 6).

Although Indian tribes have resided in their own physically-demarcated locations, they have never been in isolation. There has been a constant interdependence between them and they have had long-term contacts for exchange, as a result of which their social and cultural features have often been subject to external influences. Mukhopadhyay (2002), from his work among the tribes of Andaman and Nicobar Islands, found that even those communities that are now isolated, were not so in the past. He was of the opinion that the isolation of tribes increased when outsiders (especially the colonial rulers) started entering into their territories in search of precious and non-renewable resources. As surveys of forest and hill territories began, tribal people moved to non-surveyed areas to escape the tyranny of exploitation and suppression. The neighbours of tribes belonged to different cultural and religious categories, varying from one location to another: Hindu, Buddhist and Muslim and in some pockets of Rajasthan and Gujarat.

The UN Dhebar Commission report holds the British policy of exclusion as the reason for the backwardness of the Scheduled Tribes. Its findings testify that they had integrated relations with the people of the plains and the only difference between them was the development gap, which owes itself to the colonial mindset that the tribal people were backward.

Interaction between tribals and non-tribals groups dates back to the early period of Indian history. Many Indian and foreign authors have noted that interaction between the two had existed since the pre-British, pre-industrial and pre-market periods. From the available literature on the tribes of the country, one gets the impression that anthropologists have tended to treat tribes as isolates. In a large number of studies, one finds a detailed description of the life and culture of a people but very little of their relationships with other groups (Roy, 1915, 1925; Elwin, 1942; Majumdar, 1950; Dave, 1960; Das and Raha, 1967). In this section, an attempt has been made to present the material published on inter-tribal relations.

Srivastava (2010) highlighted the fact that tribes, despite having a level of economic self-sufficiency, relied on neighbouring caste communities for certain needs and engaged in interactions with them. They often travelled to multi-caste villages in search of agricultural work, while tribal men and women visited caste villages in Rajasthan to sell various goods like toys, medicines, honey and charms. This long-standing interaction between tribes and castes has been a consistent aspect of their relationship over time. Srivastava emphasized that tribal people maintained connections with different religious beliefs, local cults and sects, particularly within caste society. The initial form of interaction between tribes and caste Hindus involved a process of religious syncretism or 'borrowing'.

Srinivas (1952) stated that most of the interactions of the tribals have been with the majority Hindu community, the structural principle of which is the caste system. It is also a matter of fact that Hinduism has, in some cases, been influenced by tribal religion and vice versa. For example, some prominent Hindu deities had their genesis in tribal gods and goddesses. One of the well-known examples is the Jagannath deity of Odisha, in Puri, which has its origin in the Saora pantheon (Eschmann et al., 1978).

The productive system of caste society influenced the interplay between tribes. Many scholars have been drawn to N.K. Bose's analysis of productive technology and its impact on the spread of Hindu values and the caste system. This perspective on tribal communities is commonly referred to as the 'civilisational approach' (Chaudhury, 2007). Bose believed that tribes in India have always been integrated into the larger civilisation. During difficult economic times, these tribes would join the caste society and adopt occupations to sustain themselves. For instance, the Juangs of Odisha, who were shifting cultivators, had one group become basket makers in a caste village, resulting in a lower status. Another group took up agricultural occupations in Pal Lahara, a small town in Angul district of Odisha and achieved a higher status in the caste hierarchy. This demonstrates how different groups from the same tribe, who were initially equal, became part of two castes with varying ranks.

Chitrasen (1997) examined the dynamics between tribal and caste communities in Sambalpur district, Odisha, focussing on the transformation of a tribal deity into a Hindu one. In a separate study, Arima Mishra (2005) explored the Kandha tribe of Kalahandi district, Odisha, highlighting how their identity as Kutia Kondh extended beyond their village and excluded certain caste groups. Mishra also found evidence of religious and socio-economic interactions between the tribe and the caste group.

The tribal communities coexist with the caste Hindu communities and engage in social and economic interactions. Over time, many tribal groups have adopted Hindu customs and lifestyles due to various economic, social and cultural reasons. These tribal communities have been influenced by Hindu practices since ancient times and some have even attempted to elevate their social status within the Hindu caste system by identifying themselves as warrior or merchant castes. The process of upward mobility in the caste hierarchy, known as Sanskritisation, goes hand in hand with the Hinduisation of tribal people.

Anthropologists have formulated the concept of a tribe-caste continuum based on the interactions between tribal and non-tribal communities. The concept of 'tribe-caste continuum' refers to the transition of a tribal community into a caste-based society. This term was introduced by Robert Redfield to explore the dynamics between tribal, folk, semi-urban and urban populations. Despite the distinctions between tribes and castes, a gradual merging of the two societies has been observed. Anthropological research indicates that tribes often integrate into Hindu society by adopting the lineage and name of a specific caste. For instance, the Toda tribe in the Nilgiri hills demonstrates functional specialisation similar to the caste system. Some tribes settle on the outskirts of villages, take up low-status jobs from caste Hindus and eventually assimilate into the Hindu community. Members of tribal groups may adopt the surname or lineage of a caste and may also intermarry with members of that caste. Wealthy tribal individuals sometimes manage to elevate their social status by aligning themselves with higher castes through the assistance of caste priests.

Bailey (1961) conceptualised the 'Tribe-Caste continuum', suggesting that certain societies exhibit traits of both tribes and castes. Similarly, Surajit Sinha (1965) proposed a continuum between tribe and peasant societies in India. However, categorising janajati communities and plain people communities at opposite ends of a spectrum is challenging because both often display characteristics associated with each other. Therefore, there is no clear division between janajatis and plain societies, but rather a continuous spectrum known as the janajati-caste continuum, where the traits of these communities overlap to different degrees.

Sinha (1959) conducted a study on tribal-caste interactions and introduced several concepts such as tribal-peasant continuum, Bhumij-Kshtriya continuum and Tribal-Rajput continuum. These concepts serve as a framework for understanding the transformation process in middle India. Sinha's research focussed on how the Bhumij tribes in West Bengal and Bihar integrated into the Hindu caste system. Roy Burman also classified Indian tribes based on their orientation towards the Hindu social order, highlighting that some tribes, like Bhumij, Bhil and Gond, have essentially become castes and are indistinguishable from the neighbouring Hindu peasantry. Ethnographic records confirm that the level of interaction between tribes and castes varied from partial isolation to complete assimilation. It is evident from recent studies on tribes in the Himalayan western and middle India that certain tribes have become so Hinduised that they have assimilated into different castes within the caste system.

Majumdar's (1937) research on the 'Khasa' and Srivastava's (1958) research on the 'Tharus' suggest that despite their tribal background and the continuation of certain tribal customs, they have been recognized as Kshatriyas. The 'Kharwars' tribes, through prolonged and consistent interaction with regional Hindu castes, have assimilated into Rajput castes. Many other tribes have also undergone selective acculturation, incorporating certain traits or features of the regional Hindus into their traditional cultures. However, most of them have not achieved any social status within the caste hierarchy, while a few have been integrated into the lower strata of the Hindu social system.

Tribe-caste interaction has been examined through the lens of Great and

Little traditions, specifically in relation to tribes like 'Khasa' and 'Bhil' as depicted in the epics and texts of the Great tradition such as the *Ramayana* and the *Mahabharata*. It is important to note that caste people have embraced certain beliefs, cultures and traditions of the tribals, without hindering assimilation or integration. There is significant overlap between the two groups, as seen in their endogamous nature, presence of exogamous clans and shared marriage ceremonies and joking relationship patterns. Additionally, practices such as seclusion and purificatory baths after childbirth, death, naming of a child and women's seclusion during menstruation are common to both castes and tribes. Furthermore, both tribes and castes practice the disposal of the dead through cremation and burial. This demonstrates the wide spectrum within which change occurs, encompassing shifts in social status, professions and customs.

According to Mandelbaum (1962), Hookings expressed the view that the Badagas of the Nilgiri Hills were initially a jati people but later became a tribe after migrating to their current habitat sometime after the twelfth century. It is possible that they developed some tribal characteristics during their time in the isolated Nilgiri Hills. This would suggest that in recent years, the distinction between caste and tribe has been diminishing for various reasons. Tribes in India are adopting customs, traditions and professions from castes and it appears that they are gradually assimilating into the caste system and vice versa. Therefore, caste and tribes can be seen as two ends of the same continuum.

In his research on the Purum, Das (1945) presents an analysis of the this tribal community's ethnic surroundings and its economic interdependence with the Meithei. Over the past few years, there has been a surge in publications focussing on the tribes of the North-East. Dasgupta (1961) explores the economic, political and socio-religious interactions of the War Khasi with other ethnic communities in the area. Burling (1963) investigates caste-like characteristics in the Garobadha region, where various groups such as the Garo, Baptist Garo, Hindu Garo, Koch, Warang Koch and others reside.

On the other hand, Das (1967) shows how the Assamese culture has adopted ideas, beliefs and institutions of the surrounding Mongoloid population. He argues that there has been a mutual borrowing between the hill people and those of the valley in Assam. This was possible because of mutual exchange of goods through barter, linguistic interaction and interpenetration of religious ideas. Majumdar (1967) describes the social organisation of the Koch of the Garo hills and their gradual merging into Hindu society. He further argues that the position of the Koch in Hindu society is not clearly defined, but they have formed a caste-like hierarchic organisation among themselves and accordingly maintain distance in commensality from each other.

In Oraon villages, Roy (1915) states that in addition to Hindu castes, there are several other tribes such as the Munda, Kharia, Korwa and Asur residing there. The Munda and Kharia tribes held the same status as the Oraon tribe and there was a mutual exchange of services and goods within the village community. Roy (1915) further explains that certain castes and tribes, including the Ahir, Lohar, Gorait, Ghasi, Mahali, Kamar and Jolha, played vital roles in the Oraon country's typical village community.

In his work, Sachchidanand (1964) examines six distinct tribes: the Munda, the Santhal, the Khana, the Ho, the Oraon and the Sauria Paharia. He compares a tribal village with a non-tribal village, highlighting the functional dynamics between various communities, including castes, in the former. On the other hand, Mukherjee et al. (1973) provide a description of the Chero community in Palaman. The Chero people reside in multi-ethnic settlements and engage in interactions with other tribes and castes within their village and neighbouring areas. However, the authors primarily focus on reporting the economic interactions.

Shamrao Hivale (1946) provides a comprehensive account of the relationship between the Pardhan and the Gond communities. The Pardhan serve as the official genealogists for the Gond, with their women playing the role of midwives and tattooing Gond girls. While the Pardhan rely on the Gond for support, their visits to their patrons' homes are celebrated occasions where they reminisce about past events, record births and engage in joyful activities. The Pardhan have a deep appreciation of music, poetry and romance and they entertain their patrons with their quick wit and musical talents.

Fuchs (1960) highlights the bilateral connection between the Gond and the Bhumia. The Bhumia, who are a sub-tribe of the Baiga, reside near the Gond but in distinct settlements. Interestingly, the Gond settlements seem to exhibit greater prosperity. Nonetheless, there is significant interaction and communication between these two communities.

In his paper, Pandey (1962) describes the interaction of tribes and castes in a Bastar village. He has examined the interaction of different groups in informal and formal situations, such as sitting and gossiping, playing games, dancing and singing, friendly meetings, story-telling, participation in rites connected with life crises and quarrels and conflicts. For instance, he describes the seating arrangements of people while they gossip! He goes on to say how members of one group greet others and who can enter whose house.

Furer-Haimendorf's significant monographs from 1943, 1945 and 1948 focus on the Chenchu, the Reddi and the Raj Gond tribes, offering valuable insights into inter-tribal dynamics in united Andhra Pradesh. The Hill Reddi tribe maintains harmonious and mutually beneficial relationships with neighboring tribes like the Koya and the Kammar. The Reddi tribe specialises in basket weaving, which they exchange with the Koya tribe, while some Koya individuals are skilled blacksmiths. Brij Raj Chauhan's (1970) examination of urban areas within tribal communities is worth mentioning. The study stands out in tribal literature on India for its unique and intriguing perspective. It is valuable for our research as it highlights the dynamics of tribal interactions in an urban environment.

The notion that tribals can be separated from the surrounding population is outdated. This has been proven to be untrue even in the case of the tribals residing in the Andaman Islands. Whenever attempts have been made to study inter-ethnic relationships, it has been observed that there are distinct regional patterns of interconnectedness. These patterns can be found in remote areas such as the north-eastern hill regions, inaccessible hills and forests of central India and the remote Nilgiri hills. These regional patterns demonstrate multiple connections with Indian civilisation, especially the caste system.

In India, the sole comprehensive research on interaction was conducted by Prasad in 1974, focussing on three tribes in Bihar: the Maler, the Malpaharia and the Santal. Prasad's study delved into the social, economic and political dimensions of the interaction process among these tribes, attributing cultural disparities in economic activities to ecological factors. Despite the ecological determinism implied by his theoretical framework, Prasad's work sheds light on the interdependence among the tribes, highlighting how interactions with non-tribal groups result in compromise, conflict and competition. Additionally, Prasad notes that cultural exchange, evident in the form of borrowing practices, has emerged as a consequence of the interaction process between the tribes and non-tribes.

Aurora (1972) conducted a study that examines the interaction between the tribe and non-tribe, focussing on the Bhilala community. The study highlights the significant involvement of the Bhilala people in economic activities, religious beliefs and practices, and, to a certain extent, the political sphere. This interaction has resulted in the spreading and acceptance of a more expansive Hindu culture among the Bhilala community.

The Gaddi of Chhamba district in Himachal Pradesh have a unique interaction pattern with non-tribes. They are primarily a semi-agricultural and pastoral tribe but also engage in weaving and minor trade. During winters, they migrate from the high-altitude mountains to the plains of Mandi district, where they spend the season with their sheep. They reside in the plains throughout winter and when summer arrives, they return to the mountains. This allows the Gaddi to interact with non-tribes in two different regions: the hills during summer and the plains during winter. This longstanding interaction pattern has been observed for centuries.

Analysing the interaction process between tribes and non-tribes separately for each tribe would be challenging. Instead, the analysis focusses on geographical regions. These regions are classified based on the territorial groupings proposed by Roy Burman (1972a), which considers historical, ethnic and socio-cultural relations. These geographical regions are:

(1) North-east India comprises Assam, Arunachal Pradesh, Nagaland, Manipur, Mizoram and Meghalaya.
(2) The sub-Himalayan region of north and northwest comprising north and northwest Uttar Pradesh, Bengal and Bihar.
(3) Western India comprising Rajasthan, Gujarat and Maharashtra.
(4) Central and East India covering West Bengal, Odisha, Madhya Pradesh and Andhra Pradesh.
(5) South India comprising Tamil Nadu, Kerala, Karnataka and the different Union Territories, including all the region's islands (Roy Burman, 1972a). The interaction pattern in each geographical region has been discussed separately.

These descriptions illustrate that over time, the interaction dynamics between tribes have ranged from conflict to cooperation and competition, influenced by historical and ecological factors. In practice, conflicts between tribes and non-tribes have been minimal, with tribes increasingly integrating into the broader political framework.

The Khampti community in Arunachal Pradesh exhibits a unique blend of Buddhism and indigenous beliefs. While they primarily follow the Theravada school of Buddhism, they also venerate deities associated with mountains, forests and various animistic traditions. Ancestor worship plays a significant role in their healing practices. This syncretic tradition is highlighted in Subhadra Mitra Channa's research on the Jad of Harsil. The community does not conform to rigid social or religious classifications; instead, its people embody a tradition that exists between Hinduism and Buddhism. The concept of a tribe as a 'closed cultural group' is not applicable to the Khampti or Jad communities (Subhadra Mitra Channa: 2013).

Anthropological analyses have been conducted to comprehend the historical transformation from tribe to caste and vice versa in India and South Asia. Dev Nathan (1997) highlights the tribe-caste continuum resulting from increased cultural contact. Nathan (1997) criticises the ethnocentrism in India, where all communities strive to become Hindu and caste distinctions are blurred. From an anthropological perspective, tribes and castes are observed to merge gradually. Baidyanath Saraswati (1997) further emphasizes the cultural unity of tribes and castes, suggesting that tribes should be treated as castes and castes should be viewed as cultural units. However, this perspective disregards the essence of Indian civilisation, which celebrates unity in diversity and encourages the flourishing of diverse cultures.

Indian literature from antiquity, including the *Vedas*, Puranic texts, the *Mahabharata* and the *Ramayana*, sheds light on the composition and traits of their social system. These writings demonstrate how closely the inhabitants of the plains and the hills and forests are related in terms of history, culture and religion. Interestingly, there is no mention of any forceful subjugation, segregation, or invasion of the hill and forest settlements by nearby monarchs or emperors from the lowlands. Rather, since ancient times, these communities and the inhabitants of the plains have maintained an ongoing flow of people, concepts, information and wisdom.

Irawati Karve, in her seminal work *Yuganta*, articulates that the *Ramayana* serves as a tribute to the archetype of an ideal man, embodied by Rama. Valmiki composed the *Ramayana* to showcase this ideal to humanity, with Sita representing the ideal woman. The narrative is replete with characters that exemplify various ideals, including the perfect brother, the exemplary servant and even the quintessential villain (Karve, 1969). K.S. Singh, in his article, 'Tribal Versions of Rama-Katha: An Anthropological Perspective', posits that these epics function not merely as religious texts but also as historical and anthropological documents (Singh, 1993). T.B. Naik, in his paper, 'Rama-Katha among the Tribes of India', vividly recounts the *Ramayana's* narratives as they are told among diverse tribes across India, from the Western to the eastern regions (Naik, 1993). Furthermore, N.N. Vyas, in his article titled, 'Tribal Versions of Rama-Katha: An Anthropological Perspective', highlights the unique interpretations of the *Ramayana* by India's tribal communities, which are shaped by their experiences in hilly and forested environments (Vyas, 1993). In 2021, Molly Kaushal provided an in-depth exploration of the Gond Ramayani (Kaushal, 2021).

Research across historical, anthropological and literary domains concerning the *Ramayana* has uncovered significant variations in its interpretations, particularly among the janjatis of India. These groups offer unique perspectives that are deeply rooted in their distinct cultural backgrounds and world views. The *Ramayana*, a foundational text in Indian literature, is not merely a story but a canvas upon which diverse narratives are painted, reflecting the values, beliefs and experiences of different communities. For the janjatis, who often inhabit marginalized spaces within the broader societal framework, the epic may resonate with themes of resistance and identity, while women may interpret the text through the lens of gender dynamics and empowerment. This multiplicity of interpretations underscores the richness of the epic also as a cultural artefact, illustrating how it is not only a reflection of ancient traditions but also a living document that continues to evolve and inspire various segments of Indian society.

The millennial civilisational relationship that existed in India has been ignored by the post-independence Indian establishment studies and public discourses, which have instead followed Western scholars and ideas in dividing the foresters and plainsmen, similar to how the colonists did. Unfortunately, there has been no effort to study them from an Indian civilisational perspective. However, recent discoveries in various disciplines have shown the need for a complete reassessment of the colonial assessment of the role of forests and hills. A survey of Indian civilisational testimonies will demonstrate the necessity of adopting a systematic and comprehensive approach to understanding the forest and hills people of India from an Indian perspective, which has not been done so far, in order to grasp the Indian reality truly.

Earlier colonial ethnographers and others treated the tribes as isolates. They described the tribes as if they existed more or less in isolation. To some extent, the observable realities might have seemed to warrant this forty or fifty years ago, when these anthropologists studied the tribes of northeast India. However, it is difficult to believe that the levels of interaction between the tribes and non-tribes could have been so low. A careful study of these ethnographies show that even at that time, the level of interaction between tribes and non-tribes was significant.

EPICS IN INDIAN TRIBAL TRADITIONS

Bharat, the land of supreme culture, light and knowledge, stands as the embodiment of eternal values since unknown times. The *Vedas*, the *Upanishads*, the *Puranas*, the *Kavyas* etc., are the treasures of this land.

The *Ramayana* and the *Mahabharata* are especially noteworthy since they have significantly influenced the development of classical Sanskrit poetry, drama, music, contemporary literature and cinema. These epics continue to inspire artists and writers worldwide, serving as a wellspring of creativity. Furthermore, they have played a crucial role in fostering a sense of national identity and unity in India. As symbols of cultural heritage and national pride, they have contributed to nurturing a shared history and destiny among the diverse people of India.

Various communities, with their unique regional customs, have been drawn towards the core of Indian culture through these epics. These epics serve as a focal point for the amalgamation of Indian civilisation, impacting a wide array of regional cultures. The focus here is to illustrate the influence of the *Ramayana* and the *Mahabharata* on Indian tribal and folk traditions, encompassing heritage, ethnic groups, caste development, oral traditions, folk beliefs, rituals and performing arts.

The *Ramayana* is integral to the Indian Great tradition, alongside the *Mahabharata*, *Puranas*, *Smritis* and the *Brahmanas*. In addition to Sanskrit and Hindu versions, folk and tribal versions of the *Ramayana* and the *Mahabharata* are prevalent in different parts of the country. Tribal communities have been an integral segment of Indian society since the days of these texts.

The Western anthropological approach, labelling foresters as backward and plainsmen as forward, contradicts the Indian perspective that views them as integrated humans within a higher philosophy. Tribes or janajatis in India have never existed in complete isolation. They have been part and parcel of

Indian civilisation even during the days of the epics. Various elements in the ancient civilisation of India were contributed by the tribals.

The *Ramayana* holds a special place in the hearts of the people of Bharat, from the plains to the forests, as it is not just a mere piece of literature but a revered national symbol. Lord Rama is worshipped and respected throughout the country, with over 300 versions of the epic ingrained in the Indian culture, reaching even the remote regions like the north-east and among the forest-dwellers such as the Mizos.

The teachings of Rama in the epic are still recited by millions of individuals from various social backgrounds, residing in different environments such as riversides, forests and hills. Lord Rama did not view those living in the forests and hills as savages, barbarians, or soulless worshippers lacking spiritual understanding.

Numerous versions of the *Ramayana* have spread beyond India into South Asia and Southeast Asia. The 1987 'Ramayana' TV serial was immensely popular; it was watched by an estimated 650 million people, according to the BBC. On Doordarshan, it had the highest viewership in the world—40 million on a single day. There had been requests to change Parliament timings so that members did not miss any episode! Roads and streets would go dry of commuters when the serial was serial was cast. In 2020, after the serial was re-telecast during the COVID-19 lockdown period, on 16 April, the single-day viewership was 77 million, several times more than the total population of many European countries. How do we explain this?

Of course, Indian civilisation is not based solely on the Hindu perspective, but also encompasses folk traditions and ways of those without a written history. The tribal communities, who coexist with caste Hindus, have adopted many aspects of Hindu religious and folk traditions. The interaction between the tribal society's Little tradition and the caste Hindu society's Great tradition has contributed to the unity of Indian civilisation. This unity is maintained through cultural performances and their products, which are institutionalised in festivals, fairs and rituals. Describing Indian civilisation solely through the dichotomy of Sanskritic and Western traditions or the Little and Great traditions would be inadequate.

The *Ramayana* is integral to the Indian 'great' and 'little' tradition, along with the other ancient texts. Scholars like Robert Redfield, Milton Singer and McKim Marriott have utilised the concepts of Little and Great traditions to study social changes in different communities, including in Mexico and India. This approach focusses on civilisation and the social organisation of tradition, which operates on two levels: the folk or unlettered peasants, including tribals and the elite or the 'reflective few'. The Little tradition encompasses the cultural processes of the former, while the Great tradition has those of the latter. However, there is a constant interaction between these two levels of tradition.

A tribal society functions as a cohesive unit, with each social structure being segmentary and distinct. Despite the diverse ethnic tribal groups existing in various cultural and ecological settings, they have interacted similarly with the dominant caste Hindu tradition. During the post-independence era, numerous anthropological works (Bose 1949; Srinivas 1952; Vidyarthi 1963; Sahay 1975; Eschmann 1986; Das, 1988, 2003; Mann and Mann, 1989; Singh and Datta, 1993; Vashishtha, 1997; Behera, 2000; Singh, 2003; Sekhara, 2008; Guillaume-Pey, 2012), have consistently highlighted the occurrence of tribes being assimilated or absorbed into Hindu society, resulting in their transformation into castes. These tribes, including Bhils, Bhumijs, Majhis, Khasas, Koyas, Pardhans and Raj-Gonds, are believed to have embraced the caste system's principles and merged with the neighbouring Hindu peasantry. Consequently, they are often perceived as indistinguishable from the surrounding Hindu population. The discourse surrounding tribes in social anthropology has predominantly revolved around their transition into castes.

This interaction is rooted in the anthropology of knowledge, where the tribal groups, despite varying levels of development, share a common existential basis of living in harmony with nature—in the hills and the forests. Their existence in the midst of nature has provided them with an ethno-methodology that interacts with the Hindu Great traditions in similar ways. It is this tribal existential basis that interprets the Hindu traditions in a specific way. This is the anthropology of knowledge. In other words, tribal knowledge about the Hindi Great tradition, namely, in the present context, the *Ramayana*, is derived from the existential basis of the elements of tribal social structure. The classical story of the epic, as told by the Sanskrit poet Valmiki or the Hindi poet Tulsidas, is given a different and altogether distinctive interpretation by the tribals of the country.

The Ramayana story is widely known among various tribal groups in India, such as the Bhils of Rajasthan, Santhals of Chotanagpur, Korkus, Baiga and Gonds of Madhya Pradesh, all of whom share a similar understanding of the epic. Despite differences in social structures, these tribes have common experiences that shape their interpretation of the Ramayana. The universal tribal reality across the country leads to a consistent anthropological perspective on the *Ramayana* among these diverse groups.

K.S. Singh, in his article 'Tribal Versions of Rama-Katha: An Anthropological Perspective', posits that these epics function not merely as religious texts but also as historical and anthropological documents (Singh, 1993). T.B. Naik, in his paper 'Rama-Katha among the Tribes of India', vividly recounts the Ramayana's narratives as they are told among diverse tribes across India, from the western to the eastern regions (Naik, 1993). Furthermore, N.N. Vyas, in his article 'Tribal Versions of Rama-Katha: An Anthropological Perspective', highlights the unique interpretations of the Ramayana by India's tribal communities, which are shaped by their experiences in hilly and forested environments (Vyas, 1993). In 2021, Molly Kaushal provided an in-depth exploration of the Gond Ramayani (Kaushal, 2021).

Father Camille Bulke emerged as a pioneering scholar who consolidated various versions of the Rama story in his highly acclaimed Ph.D. thesis, which was subsequently published as a book in 1950. Bulke's comprehensive examination of the Rama story across different textual and oral traditions continues to stand unrivalled even today. Bulke collected various extant versions of Ramakatha within the country in Indo-Aryan, Dravidian and tribal languages; he also collected the Brahmanical, Buddhist and Jain versions. He cast his net even wider to collect the central Asian versions, which, again, were influenced by the accounts of traders and missionaries from various parts of India (Bulke, 1950). The release of 'Many Ramayanas' in 1992, edited by Paula Richman, revitalised the exploration of tribal and folk Ramayana traditions. The focus shifted towards 'alternative Ramayanas', viewing Valmiki and Tulsi's texts as dominant and the versions in vernacular languages and among folk and tribal groups as alternative and opposing narratives (Richman, 1992).

The anthropological interpretation of the tribal and folk versions of the two epics, the *Mahabharata* and the *Ramayana*, has garnered significant attention from scholars. In February 1988, the Anthropological Survey of India (ASI) hosted a successful seminar on the folk and tribal versions of the *Ramayana* held at Guwahati University in collaboration with the Department of Folklore Research. This seminar marked a significant multi-disciplinary effort of its kind by scholars from fields such as literature, anthropology, folklore, history, linguistics, etc., to explore our continuing links with the epic traditions. There were some gaps in the material presented but the overall picture that emerged from the discussions was most satisfying. The seminar was made memorable not only by presenting the textual material from all parts of India but also by demonstrating the performing arts connected with Ramlila traditions by cultural troupes from all parts of Assam, testifying to the vibrant traditions of the Ramakatha.

The symposium aimed to continue the research started by the two masters and other scholars in the field of Indian folklore, with a focus on understanding the mindset of tribal people. We gathered scholars who have uncovered and analysed folk and tribal versions of the Ramakatha and are actively sharing their interpretations. Our goal was also to understand the crucial aspects of interaction and integration within the country (Singh and Datta, 1993). Guwahati University's Department of Folklore Research is known for its groundbreaking work in the field. Scholars at the university have uncovered various versions of Rama-Katha, Mahabharata and Puranic traditions of tribes in the north-east, shedding light on the historical and cultural interactions in this frontier region of India.

As a researcher, K.S. Singh gathered a collection of songs about Ramakatha written by both tribal and non-tribal poets. These songs seemed to be direct translations of the story, filled with passion and conviction. They also showed the impact of the Odiya and Bengali versions of Ramakatha, which are widely known in the Hindi belt. However, there were also songs that appeared to be older and more connected to the tribal worldview and customs, indicating that certain elements of Ramakatha had become deeply ingrained within their culture.

During his subsequent study, K.S. Singh encountered various versions of Ramakatha among different tribes like the Mundas, Gonds, Korkus, Kols, Savaras, Bondo, etc. These versions did not indicate the presence of mini-Ramayana or mini-Ramakatha but rather seemed to be echoes from the past, reflecting tribal memories transmitted through generations or teachings from travelling mendicants known as Gossains. The narratives also showed admiration for the heroes and sometimes amusement at their presence in the tribal homeland.

Interestingly, some versions displayed a hint of irreverence, with certain tribes identifying themselves with anti-heroes like Meghanada or Ravana openly and without hesitation. K.S. Singh primarily focusses on Mund, a material exploring the spread, adaptation and revival of Ramakatha traditions within various communities, including those speaking Austro-Asiatic languages. The Munda and related groups offer a compelling interpretation of 'Sita', depicting her as a tribal girl discovered beneath a plough, taken by Ravana while tending to goats.

In his work, Vyas provides an overview of the Ramakatha version that is commonly known among the tribes of Rajasthan and the Nimad region of Madhya Pradesh. Sita, like any other child from the tribe, was born during a period of drought and faced the hardships that came with it. At Sita's request, the golden deer was hunted for its meat, which was a customary practice among the tribes.

Mishra's research focusses on the Ramayana traditions found in Chhattisgarh and western Odisha, specifically among the Bondo, Baiga and Gaur communities. The Ramakatha traditions in this region have been adapted to the local context. One of the rituals performed to bring rain in a drought year is the Rishyashringa Yajna.

On the other hand, T.B. Naik provides a comprehensive description of the Bhilodi Ramayana of the Bhils and the Birhor version, which belongs to the Birhor community of Bihar. Among the tribes in Bihar, the Birhors are the sole people that possess such a detailed account. Interestingly, Rama's fourteen-year exile in the forest, during which he lived a life similar to theirs, seems to have resonated with the Birhor people. As a result, Rama granted the Birhors the skill of trapping and sanctioned their consumption of monkeys and baboons.

Several papers were presented on the influence of the Ramakatha on the tribes in north-east India. Goswami focussed on the Ramakatha traditions among the Bodo Kachari of Nalbari district and discussed its impact on their myths, tales, beliefs and more. Birendranath Datta provided an overview of the Ramakatha traditions among the Karbis, Tiwas, Mizo, Mising, Khamti and those prevalent in Manipur. Numerous scholars presented detailed versions of the Ramakatha in Karbi folk traditions, highlighting their unique ethnic characteristics. The Mizo tribes in the north-east region also possess stories that are influenced by the legend of Rama. In Manipur, the Ramayana is presented through various traditional forms such as Wari-leeba (story-telling), Pena-sakpa (ballad singing), Khongjom parva (narrative singing with dholak accompaniment) and Jatra (folk-theatre).

The impact of the *Ramayana* among the Tiwas or the Lalungs is not as widespread as it is in other communities and is mainly found in scattered stories and tales. However, the Mizo version of the epic shows clear influences from South Asian versions, which in turn have been impacted by versions brought by immigrants from different parts of India. This version seems to have originated in the eastern and southern regions, featuring Ravana with seven or twelve heads. Interestingly, here the hero is Lakshmana and both Lakshmana and Hanumana are given significant importance. In Tripura, the Ramakatha is deeply rooted in tribal and folk traditions, as described by Jagadis Ganchoudhuri. Additionally, there is a Buddhist version of the Ramakatha in the Taiphake cultural tradition, where Rama is depicted as a Bodhisattva. In this unique version, Rama seeks forgiveness from Sita, who then returns to live happily with Rama and their children until the end of their lives, providing a rare happy ending, unlike in other versions.

Indian tribes across the country have been categorised based on their ecological regions, subsistence methods, race, ethnicity and language. These tribes, residing in various parts of India such as the Indo-Gangetic plain, central and western regions, southern areas, Himalayan mountain ranges and valleys and the north-eastern areas with numerous tribal groups, possess a unique Rama lore. The lore can be in the form of a simple anecdote or a detailed narrative, often performed through singing, recitation and dance accompanied by musical instruments to convey the story. While maintaining the coherence of the narrative's structure and themes, these communities incorporate their own texts and underlying messages within the broader storyline.

The Rama theme in art and literature has a vast presence across tribes and non-tribals in India, both spatially and temporally. It is expressed through a multitude of art forms, with katha recitation being the most prevalent among the kathakaras throughout the country. Each region has its unique way of singing and reciting the story, resulting in a diverse range of Rama stories among both tribal and non-tribal communities. Tribal communities in India have developed their own interpretations of the *Ramayana*, incorporating diverse subplots into the central storyline. Various Indian tribes like Bhils, Mundas, Santhals, Gonds, Pardhan, Laura's, Korkus, Rabhas, Bodo-kacharis, Khasis, Missings, Dimasas, Jaintias, Taraon Mishmis Mizos, Tiwes, Karbis and Meiteis have distinct versions of this epic, enriched with narratives reflecting their unique occupations and cultural heritage.

Communities typically integrate their plots and subplots into stories and texts, maintaining a fundamental structural and thematic coherence. The physical and socio-cultural landscape shapes a distinctive local identity and establishes the sacred geography of the area. By connecting the text with indigenous geography and traditions, including songs and narratives from the local repertoire and ensuring that characters adhere to the community's moral and ethical standards, each group presents its own locally and contextually-bound interpretation, often transforming it into an ancestral narrative of its beginnings.

In certain renditions, Ravana is depicted as a heroic figure. The stories of Ram, Sita and Lakshamana are not confined to specific categories of art or regions, as they transcend boundaries between rural and urban, mundane and religious and sacred and secular realms. Various forms of expression, such as literary, oral, kinetic and pictorial elements, blend together to create diverse interpretations of the text in different cultural settings, each with its own unique characteristics. The performative nature of the text allows for flexibility, accessibility and adaptability, contributing to its continued preservation, transmission and mobility across different time periods and geographical locations.

For example, the Pardhan tribes sang the stories of the *Mahabharata* and the *Ramayana*. As a story of the latter epic has been modified in 'Pandubani', similarly the themes of *Ramayana*, called Ramayani, have been modified by the Pardhans. In their Ramayani, the hero of Ramayani is not Rama but Lakshamana and the whole Ramayani revolves around the truthful activities of Lakshamana (Vidyarthi, 1976). One of the most distinct tribal versions of Ramayana is the Adiya Ramayana. Sita is a woman who hails from Pulpally in Wayanad and belongs to the Adiya tribe. Lanka is not a kingdom across the ocean but is located near a river.

Episodes from various textual versions of the *Ramayana*, such as those of Valmiki, Tulsi, Adhyatama, Ananda, Kritivasa, Adbhuta and Kampan, are also found in oral traditions, where bards creatively incorporate them into their own storytelling. The debate over the priority of oral or written versions is ultimately pointless. Often, due to a lack of knowledge about the original source, communities consider these episodes to be exclusive to their own traditions. It is clear that these episodes are interpreted uniquely in different narratives, resulting in significant variations in how they are presented and resolved across different traditions.

In a Malayalam tribal version, Hanuman chooses to sit at Rama's feet to offer blessings when Rama sneezes, symbolising Rama's human vulnerabilities. In Assam, Sita is portrayed as a skilled weaver, in tune with the expertise of hill women weavers. Among tribal puppet shows, some worship Ravana, believing he cannot be defeated—a legend suggests that Rama only vanquished Ravana's shadow, not the actual demon king.

During the puppetry performance, Rama is cursed three times for killing Ravana: Brahma Hatya (killing of a Brahmin), Bhakta Hatya (killing of a devoteea) and Chaya Hatya (killing of a singer). Interestingly, in many tribal traditions, Ravana is revered while Rama is not. The puppet representing Ravana does not require as much manipulation and is often intricately designed. In puppetry, Ravana's virtuous character is portrayed as a heroic figure.

The indigenous tribes residing in the region give the physical and socio-cultural landscape a distinct native identity, which shapes the sacred geography. They connect the *Ramayana* with the local geography and rituals, incorporating songs and narratives from their own traditions. Additionally, the characters in their version of the epic adhere to the moral and ethical codes of their community, making it unique to each tribal group.

In the tribal versions, there are also variations of Buddhism and Jainism. Within the Tai-phake community in the north-east, Rama is regarded as a Bodhisattva. Odisha showcases one of the most captivating tribal dance forms for the *Ramayana*, known as Chau, which has three distinct styles: Mayurbhanj Chhau of Odisha, Purulia Chhau of Bengal and Saraikela Chhau of Jharkhand. The Purulia and Seraikela Chau dances are particularly recognized for their intricate masks and to this day, numerous dance troupes perform the complete *Ramayana* in sessions lasting 28 days.

In central India, the Baiga tribe recounts a fascinating tale where Lakshamana must endure a fire test to demonstrate his purity. Various folk and tribal renditions portray Sita transforming into Kali and defeating Ravana and other evil beings. Similarly, the Mankali tribal dancers from Kerala solely portray the scene where Sita becomes infatuated with the golden deer, Maricha. The Gonds of Madhya Pradesh possess their unique version of the *Ramayana*, showcasing their local customs and intertwined with their oral storytelling. Renowned for their folk painting tradition, the Gonds showcased the complete epic on canvas. The Gond Ramayana has been translated into Hindi and 500 folk songs centred around the theme of Rama have been preserved in Madhya Pradesh with the assistance of Adivasi Kala Parishad in Bhopal.

The IGNCA is currently focussing on the exploration of 'Ram Katha and Folk Performative Traditions in India', which highlights the widespread influence of the Ramayana tradition in India and Southeast Asia. In addition to the famous literary texts found in various regions of the country, IGNCA also explores the widespread presence of Ramakatha in the oral tradition. Ramakatha takes on various forms and artistic expressions, ranging from rituals and festivals to ballad singing, drama, dance-drama, opera, play, shadow puppets and contemporary modern stage performances.

In 1991, the Anthropological Survey of India (ASI) organized a National seminar on the 'Mahabharata in tribal and folk traditions of India' in collaboration with the Indian Institute of Advanced Study and Himachal Kala Sanskriti avam Bhasha Academy. The seminar aimed to address two main objectives. Firstly, it sought to explore the adaptation and recreation of epic traditions in tribal and folk areas, reflecting the perceptions and aspirations of these communities in performing arts and popular literature. Secondly, it aimed to facilitate the exchange of ideas and research findings among scholars who have worked on the 'Mahabharata in the tribal and folk traditions of India'.

In his presentation, K.S. Singh provides an overview of the various folk and tribal versions of the *Mahabharata* found in different regions of India. Additionally, he shares his experiences in Chota-Nagpur and showcases a collection of Munda songs related to the epic and Lord Krishna. On the other hand, J. Handoo examines the *Mahabharata* as a reflection of Indian avunculate society, highlighting the contradictions and conflicts between avunculate and non-avunculate societies. Handoo argues that the *Mahabharata* represents sibling rivalry, while the *Ramayana* promotes positive sibling relationships. Furthermore, Handoo traces the continuity of *Mahabharata's* societal traits in present-day Indian society and identifies several symbols and metaphors that have remained prevalent throughout history.

The *Mahabharata's* characters have long been associated with the Himalayas and today they are revered as folk deities in the places they visited. This connection is understandable, as the Pandavas, known for their practice of polyandry, had a special bond with the Himalayas, which still holds significance in this tradition. The Himalayan communities are unique in their worship of the Kauravas, particularly Duryodhana, as Samsui. One intriguing aspect is the inclusion of a Himalayan deity named Hidimba in the *Mahabharata*, through the process of spousification. Hidimba was married to Bhima and gave birth to the formidable character Ghatotakach. Bali presents the folk versions of the *Mahabharata* in Duggaradesh or Jammu which have a distinct bias in favour of the Pandavas as gods and heroes and the Kauravas are ignored.

B.K. Sharma discusses tribal and folk traditions in different parts of Himachal Pradesh. Neeru Nanda explores interesting aspects of the Mahabharata lore in this region. H.R. Justa focusses on the connection between the Mahabharata heroes and the temples and village gods in Himachal Pradesh. The Himachal chapter also includes information on the martial game Thoda, which is performed by the Khasha people. During the seminar, we witnessed a demonstration of this martial art. Shivananda Nautiyal provides a detailed account of the transformation of Mahabharata's characters in the Garhwal region of Himachal Pradesh, accompanied by folk songs.

The tribal people of Maharashtra, similar to those in central India, venerate the heroes of Mahabharata as their deities and forefathers. The folk songs and dances that revolve around Mahabharata themes show that Maharashtra has been influenced more by the *Ramayana* traditions than by *Mahabharata's*. The Korku tribe identifies themselves as descendants of the Kauravas, while the Korkus of Nimar trace their lineage back to Karkotak Naga, which is linked to the *Mahabharata* and the Puranas. Draupadi is remembered as Krishna's beloved sister and the Pandavas and Krishna are revered as the main deities during dance festivals. The heroes of Mahabharata are considered ancestors alongside Ramayana figures like Meghnath and Ravana, with dancers wearing masks resembling the Mahabharata heroes.

Bhima, the most revered hero in tribal India, is prominently featured in the folk traditions of South Kosala, as highlighted by Mahendra Kumar Mishra. Known for his immense strength, Bhima is closely associated with the tribal communities in South Kosala. He is attributed with introducing various advancements such as brewing, agriculture, crops like paddy, a wind machine and iron implements. Bhima's skills also include taming wild buffaloes and other animals and ensuring the safety of agricultural practices. Additionally, he is revered as a rain god, worshipped during times of drought. Above all, Bhima is celebrated as a cultural hero. The book, 'Mahabharata in the Tribal and Folk Traditions of India', by K.S. Singh contributes to a deeper understanding of the *Mahabharata* traditions in tribal and folk contexts, fostering interest in this area (Singh, 1993).

The *Mahabharata* references various tribes, with Siya Mahadeva appearing as a Kirata to meet Arjun (Elwin, 1961). The term 'Kirata' was historically used for non-Aryan tribes residing in mountainous regions, particularly the Himalayas. In the *Mahabharata*, the Mundas are mentioned as part of the Kaurava army, possibly indicating an aboriginal group. Bose (1967) suggests that non-Brahmanical communities infiltrated Varna society under different names like Andhras, Madras, Savaras, Yavanas, Kiratas, Paundras and others.

To conclude, epics are an essential element of our lives. They can reveal the ultimate meaning of life to us. They are capable of explaining to us what is beyond our comprehension. They contain the answers to a majority of our queries. They are a great source of motivation for us, providing hope when there is despair. They share so many things with us that are ideal for our success. They help us to have a better comprehension of life. They show us how to conduct our lives.

The Indian epics have been a source of inspiration, guidance and cultural identity for the people of India for thousands of years and continue to be a vital part of the country's spiritual and cultural heritage. Overall, the *Ramayana* and the *Mahabharata* have been integral to Indian culture and living, providing a rich source of ethical, moral, spiritual and cultural teachings that continue to shape the lives of people in India and beyond.

Ramkatha, a subject of study in north-eastern India, remains largely unexplored. It takes various forms and is prevalent in the region, yet most of them are unknown to people both within and outside the region. Ramkatha primarily exists in oral tradition and traditional performing arts, many of which are in decline or at risk of disappearing. Unfortunately, numerous such traditions have been lost forever, without any written or documented records. In certain areas, the prominence of Ramkatha-based traditions diminished with the spread and consolidation of Christianity and was further eroded by the weakening ties to mainland culture due to socio-political factors. Urbanisation and globalization have also had negative impacts. Nevertheless, these traditions, rooted in the indigenous soil, are invaluable treasures of the region, serving as a reminder of India's essential unity. Studying and exploring Ramkatha-based traditions in this region could greatly contribute to national integration (Bora, 2018).

The narratives of the *Ramayana* and the *Mahabharata* stand out as some of the most dynamic and influential motifs that resonate throughout India and even further afield. Regardless of boundaries such as space, time, geography and language, these ancient Sanskrit epics have managed to seep into the collective consciousness of every individual in India. While the written renditions in the original Sanskrit and the various regional languages are widely recognized and celebrated, the rich oral traditions and diverse adaptations within the folk and tribal groups have not been as extensively recorded and documented over the centuries. Yet India boasts an incredibly diverse range of vibrant art, craft and painting traditions centred around the iconic stories and characters of the two epics. Each tribal community is known for its own outstanding cultural identity and artistic expressions inspired by these timeless epics. Tribes such as the Bhils, Gonds, Murias, Sauras, Warlis and Rathwas are renowned for their captivating paintings that bring legends to life through distinctive regional styles.

Some of the most celebrated tribal painting traditions include Pithora, Warli, Santhal and Saura, while the folk-art forms of Picchvai, Mata ni Pachedi, Patachitra and Phad also draw heavily from the epic narratives. These unique art forms remain an integral part of the daily lives and spiritual practices of the tribal peoples, keeping the legacies of the *Ramayana* and the *Mahabharata* alive through vibrant visual storytelling. It is crucial that greater awareness is raised and that these significant traditions are thoroughly documented, as they not only showcase the rich socio-cultural aspects of the tribal communities but also serve as a powerful reflection of their ancient civilisation and worldview.

INTEGRATION, ISOLATION AND ASSIMILATION

India's vast and vibrant tribal population is a remarkable embodiment of the country's celebrated unity in diversity. With the second-largest tribal community in the world, India's indigenous groups can boast of a breathtaking array of distinct traditions, cultures and ways of life that have been passed down over generations. From the remote Himalayan villages of Arunachal Pradesh to the sun-drenched tribal hamlets of Tamil Nadu, India's tribal people showcase an astounding diversity in their languages, environmental adaptations, physical attributes and socioeconomic conditions. Each tribal group, whether it be the ornately adorned Naga warriors of the north-east or the nomadic Gujjar herders of the north, possesses a unique cultural heritage that has been shaped by centuries of distinct historical experiences.

Yet despite this incredible heterogeneity, India's tribal communities also face a shared struggle against political marginalization, economic deprivation and cultural prejudice. Numbering in the hundreds of millions, tribal Indians often find themselves under-represented in the halls of power, with limited access to essential services and development opportunities accorded to the country's non-tribal majority. Ongoing battles over land rights, resource extraction and preservation of traditional life-ways pit tribal interests against the encroaching forces of modernization and state control. Nevertheless, India's tribal people remain steadfast in their commitment to their ancestral ways, proudly asserting their identities in the face of these common challenges. In doing so, they continue to enrich the breathtaking tapestry of diversity that lies at the heart of the Indian nation.

The livelihoods of tribal communities across India are remarkably intricate and multifaceted, shaped by a complex interplay of geographic, social, economic, cultural and political factors. These communities have historically relied on the forests and land that have been inextricably linked to their ways of life—with gathering forest materials, subsistence agriculture, animal rearing, crafts and daily wage labour comprising the primary means of sustenance. However, the perceptions and realities of tribal livelihoods can vary greatly, depending on a myriad influences, from the specific community type to the age, gender and educational background of individual members.

Fluctuations in the availability of natural resources, the accessibility of essential services and infrastructure and the broader socioeconomic and political landscape—these all contribute to these livelihoods' diverse though often precarious nature. Despite the modernization and development that has transformed much of India, many tribal communities continue to face significant challenges in securing their existence through their traditional forest-based practices as they strive to maintain their unique cultural identities and adapt to the rapidly changing world around them. The delicate balance between traditional life-means and the demands of the contemporary era remains a defining feature of the multifaceted livelihoods of India's tribal populations.

Since ancient times, as we have seen, tribes in India have coexisted harmoniously with non-tribal communities, preserving their dignity. Throughout history, tribal communities have enjoyed the freedom to utilise the forest and its resources within their habitats, leading to a strong belief that the forests belong to them. The colonial and post-colonial forest laws considered the tribals as destructors of the forests and wildlife. These laws regulated tribals rights over forest produce and forest lands. However, when the British colonizers arrived in India in the eighteenth century, their focus shifted towards trade and commerce, marking the beginning of the colonial era. They observed the economic and cultural differences among the Indian population and categorised them into specific groups based on their habitats and occupations for easier administration. Unfortunately, the British colonial forest administration prioritized revenue generation and exploitation, disregarding the rights and concessions of forest-dwellers, particularly the tribal communities. In the mid-nineteenth century, various regulations were implemented in the name of forest protection, as well as to sustainably produce timber for both revenue and imperial purposes.

These were antagonistic to the welfare of the tribal communities. People from outside began to move into the forests. Then, the conditions of forests and tribal people began to change. The gradual extension of the authority of the British government in these areas and the natural desire of the forest officials to exercise greater control over the use of forest products deeply disturbed the entire tribal economy and sowed the seeds of conflict. This restricted the tribals from using forest resources.

The traditional economy of tribal communities faced challenges and their rights to agricultural lands were compromised. In response, the British government introduced the first tenant law in 1859, but this did not effectively address the issues faced by poor peasants and tribals. Retired Army personnel were permitted to settle on the outskirts of specific tribal areas to prevent conflicts between tribes and settled farmers, leading to a deepening sense of mistrust and suspicion among tribal people towards non-tribal neighbours. Forests, crucial for providing sustainable livelihoods, were now designated as reserved areas, impacting the reliance of many tribal groups on forest resources for food collection.

Shifting cultivation was restricted in the name of conservation of natural forests. It curtailed the tribal rights on forests without providing an alternative livelihood to the tribes. To ostensibly restrict environmental exploitation, the British government designed a policy on forest reservation, known as the First Forest Policy of 1894. It affected the tribal way of life in many respects. Tribals, once the lords of the forests, slowly lost control over their resource, which was controlled forest department. Their traditional right to the forest was no longer recognized and their free movement inside the forest was curtailed. This forceful displacement of tribes from their original habitat pushed them to resort to criminal activities. Subsequently, the British administration labelled them as 'criminal tribes'.

Further, tribal art and crafts were denied incentives, which created a feeling among the tribals that their products were not up to the mark. Due to industrialisation, a large number of tribals were recruited at minimum, exploitative wages in mining and steel companies. The colonial policy of tribal development in India was based on the axis of isolation. The colonial government dealt with the tribals, keeping their own vested interests in mind and ignoring the interests of the tribal communities. They realised the potentiality of tribal areas and hence restricted the entry of outsiders or people from the plains by making the tribal areas partially excluded. The British adopted policies to isolate tribals from the general masses (Xaxa, 1999, p. 1520).

Since the British rulers were also very eager to exploit the vast forest wealth and utilise forest regions for defence and security purposes, improving communication in these areas was important. They took necessary steps to make these areas accessible but at the same time kept the tribals isolated. Dr J.J. Hutton, writing on the impact of British administration in tribal areas, observed: 'Far from being of immediate benefit to the primitive tribes, the establishment of British rule in India did most of them much more harm than good. It may be said that the early days of the British administration did a very great detriment to the economic position of tribes through ignorance and neglect of their rights and customs. Many changes have been caused incidentally by the penetration of tribal countries, the opening up of communication, the protection of forests and the establishment of schools, to say nothing of the openings given in this way to the Christian Mission. Many of the results of these changes have caused acute discomfort to the tribes' (quoted in Tripathi, 1997, p. 115).

The Dhebar Commission similarly noted the detrimental effects of British governance on tribal communities, highlighting that it led to widespread poverty across much of India. The literacy rates among these groups were alarmingly low, with exceptions in a few regions. Many tribal lands were heavily burdened with debts and a significant portion had already been transferred to non-tribal ownership. Their rights to forest resources were increasingly infringed upon, as external entities involved in government and forestry operations continued to exploit them. Although various reforms were proposed, they ultimately proved ineffective. (Tripathi, 1997, p. 115–116). Prof. Ghurye observed that the acute of discomfort was very often so great that it led to apathy, indifference and moral deterioration and even a population decline.

The forest population has relied on the forests for their sustenance. Nevertheless, after gaining independence, a significant portion of this forest was designated as Reserved Forests and Protected Forests, along with Wildlife Sanctuaries and National Parks. As a consequence, tribal communities were marginalized and viewed as trespassers on this land until the enactment of the Forest Rights Act in 2006 (Reddy et al., 2010). Introducing the FRA has been a significant step in relieving tribals, forest dwellings and dependent communities from the weight of illegality. However, the execution of the FRA has been lacking, resulting in limited progress towards livelihood security, improvements in forest governance and the reinforcement of forest conservation (Kumar et al., 2011).

The forest ecosystem, with its intricate web of interdependencies, has long been the foundation of the tribal way of life. From the flowing rivers and streams that quench thirst to the abundant flora and fauna that sustain livelihoods, the entire forest domain represents the mainstay of the tribal economy. This delicate balance, honed over generations, was irretrievably disrupted by the arrival of the British colonial powers. In a calculated move to consolidate control, the colonizers instituted a new system of land ownership, creating a class of zamindars, or landlords and granting them dominion over the tribal territories. Overnight, the indigenous peoples who had for centuries roamed freely and harvested the natural bounty of their ancestral lands found themselves reduced to mere tenants, strangers in their own homes. This egregious usurpation of their fundamental rights fuelled a growing resentment within the tribal communities, a smouldering resentment that would eventually erupt into violent revolutionary movements. As the tribals fought to reclaim their land and their autonomy, the clash between the traditional, community-based model and the imposed colonial hierarchy laid bare the deep-seated tensions that had been simmering beneath the surface. The forest, once the lifeblood of the tribal existence, had now become a battleground, a symbol of the struggle for self-determination in the face of an unjust and oppressive system that sought to subjugate proud and resilient people.

The tribals responded to their exploitation and oppression through revolts and movements. They identified their enemies in the outsiders (dikus) landlords, moneylenders, contractors, missionaries and European government officials. They launched movements against their oppressors in their respective regions. Their agitations against outsiders was in many ways anti-colonial. They revolted against them because of the exploitation they faced in the form of encroachment on and eviction from their land, annulment of their traditional legal and social rights and customs, enhancement of rent, transfer of land to the tiller and the abolition of feudal and semi-feudal form of land ownership.

On the whole, these movements had economic, social and religious overtones. But they were directed against issues related to existence of the tribals. The agitations were launched under the leadership of their respective chiefs. The tribals had to comply with British policies that were detrimental to their interests. The government introduced protective administration in tribal areas. The government thought that the normal laws could not be applied in the tribal areas. The government passed the Scheduled District Act (1874) and categorised the tribal areas as excluded area in the Government of India Act of 1935.

Upon their arrival, the British encountered resistance from tribal communities. The Battle of Plassey in 1757 marked a turning point, leading to the Sanyasi revolt in 1763 and subsequent uprisings in tribal regions of British India. By the late eighteenth century, around 25 revolts had taken place, with 10 being spearheaded by tribal factions. These revolts encompassed events such as the Dhalbhumi revolt (1766–1777), Moamaria revolt (1769–1799), Chakma revolt (1776–1789), Pahadia revolt (1788–1790), Subandia revolt (1792), Silhat revolt (1799), Choad revolt (1798–1799), Chero revolt (1800) and the Ganjam revolt (1800–1805).

By 1818, the East India Company had established control over Rajputana, Madhya Pradesh, Gujarat and Maharashtra. The conflicts involving the Marathas and Pindaris were taking a toll on the local population. Yet, the British administration did not make any efforts to improve the situation of the Bhils and Gonds in the region. As a result, the Bhils in Khandesh, Nimar and southern Rajasthan rebelled continuously, while the Gonds from Saugar Narbada territory revolted against the British in 1857. The British took over Assam in 1822, sparking a prolonged struggle with the tribal communities there. In 1829, the Khasi and Aka tribes rebelled, followed by the Singpho and Khamti tribes. A decade later, in 1848, the Garos, Abors, Nagas and Lushais also rose up in revolt.

The British had captured Odisha in 1765, but their active influence on the region was not noticeable until 1821. In 1835, the colonial rulers faced a revolt by the Khonds tribe. The Koles, Bhumijs, Kharwars and Santhals of Chota-Nagpur in Bihar also launched agitations, showcasing tales of heroism. During the 1860s, various tribesmen initiated revolts, including the Bhils and Bhilalas of Nimar and Khandesh, the Gonds of Saugar Narbada territory, the Andaman tribesmen, the Murias from Bastar, the Binjhwars from Sonakhan and the Sintengs from the Jayantiya ranges of Assam. The tribesmen dwelling in Gudem and Rampa hills near the Godavari river in the eastern part of Madras Presidency rebelled fiercely. The Mundas from Chota-Nagpur region engaged in conflicts with the British for a significant period, first in the Sardari conflict and later in the Munda Revolt led by Birsa Munda, which added to the glory of tribal revolts.

To counter the tribal unrest, British administrators adopted new executive and legislative policies. At first, they tried to tackle the rebellious tribes with arms and bribed some tribal leaders by giving monetary allowance. Retired military officials were encouraged to settle down around the tribal habitation as they were more effective than civil officers in suppressing the agitation. Thus, British policy of administration proved to be disastrous for tribals.

Post-independence, protecting and integrating the tribal people into the mainstream was extremely complex. This was because of the varied conditions under which they lived in different parts of the country and their different languages and distinct cultures. The government adopted a three-pronged policy—isolation, assimilation and integration—to tackle the challenge.

Tribal welfare became the motto of post-independent India. The policy, thus, is derived from constitutional provisions, various acts, plans and programmes. In order to develop the Scheduled Tribes, the central government has been implementing a large number of schemes, programmes and development measures in the Fifth Schedule and Sixth Schedule Areas and other areas where a large proportion of tribal people are present. As far as strategies are concerned, a focussed and special effort was made during the Fifth Five-Year Plan to evolve a strategy for areas with concentration of tribal population. For instance, the union government gave grants-in-aid to states under Article 275 of the Constitution for the purpose of promoting the welfare of the Scheduled Tribes or to raise the level of administration of the Scheduled Areas. The Constitution-makers understood the exploitation faced by tribal communities and their resistance to the colonial rule. As a result, the government established an extensive system of compensatory measures to rectify the centuries of injustice inflicted upon these communities.

After independence, there was a heated debate on the approach to tribal development in India. The debate revolved around the colonial policy of isolation and the nationalistic policy of assimilation and integration. As a consequence, the state's focus shifted towards tribes, leading to a prolonged period of scholarly and administrative endeavours to devise suitable policy measures. The government of India adopted the policy of isolation, assimilation and integration in a slightly modified form. In the partially excluded areas, they undertook welfare measures. The Constituent Assembly recommended the isolation of some areas as tribal and scheduled areas. The government machinery remained confined to scheduled areas and tribals living outside the areas were not duly protected. Constitutional safeguards and including tribes in the Fifth schedule created a gap between the general population and the tribes. In the five-year plans, tribal development also got financial separation.

The isolationist approach, however, is a colonial mindset of divide-and-rule. It existed in the colonial mind much before Verrier Elwin wrote his book on the Baigas. The Inner Line Permit Regulation of 1873, which was extended to the territories of Nagaland, Manipur, Mizoram and Arunachal Pradesh, was nothing but a strategy of the British administration to keep the tribals isolated. During the 1930s, the concept of isolation in academia was introduced by Verrier Elwin, a missionary who later became an anthropologist. In 1936, he documented the 'Baigas' tribe in Chhattisgarh's Bastar district, emphasizing the importance of preserving tribal life and culture to prevent their extinction. This was not purely Elwin's idea. The notion was influenced by the prevailing intellectual environment among Indian anthropologists at the time.

Elwin proposed the concept of establishing national parks or protected areas where the Baigas and their neighbouring communities could live independently and without facing significant challenges. The government approved Elwin's idea, which was reflected in the Government of India Act of 1935. As a result, protected and excluded areas were designated in the tribal-dominated regions of Bastar in Chhattisgarh, with the intention of preventing potential exploitation by outsiders. Elwin believed that the tribe's temporary isolation was necessary for their overall well-being. The British authorities acknowledged that governing specific tribal regions posed greater challenges than other areas, leading them to separate these regions. Whenever tribal uprisings occurred, the British would declare those areas as protected zones and actively promote the conversion of the inhabitants to Christianity within these protected zones.

In 1931, Hutton discussed the decline of tribal political and cultural independence, particularly in the north-east, attributing it to acculturation. He emphasized the importance of preventing these changes to preserve tribal identity, aligning with Elwin's concept of isolation. Indian scholars such as S.C. Roy and D.N. Majumdar also linked tribal issues to excessive exposure to industrial culture. The writings from the 1930s all shared a common perspective on tribal isolation.

Ghurye expressed his disapproval of the policy of isolation, arguing that it was implemented to generate revenue within the protected land area. S.C. Dube also criticised this policy, saying that it was a deliberate strategy by the colonial government to create division between tribal and non-tribal communities. Additionally, Gandhi condemned the British policy of isolation, as he believed that it fostered separatist sentiments. A.V. Thakkar, a renowned social worker, strongly opposed the policy of isolation, arguing that it only served the academic interests of anthropologists. According to Thakkar, the policy allowed anthropologists to uphold the division between tribal and non-tribal communities, enabling them to idealise tribes from an academic standpoint. In response, Thakkar proposed his own approach, which became widely recognized as the social workers' approach or the policy of assimilation.

Thakkar argued that the Britishers and certain scholars, particularly anthropologists, benefited from the policy of isolation. He believed that isolation contradicted the natural process of acculturation, claiming that tribals lacked entrepreneurial skills and held superstitious beliefs, hindering progress and leading to exploitation. Thakkar emphasized the role of social workers in addressing these issues, advocating a greater awareness of the benefits of mainstream society and facilitating acculturation for tribal assimilation.

Elwin expressed his disagreement with Thakkar's idea of assimilation, raising questions about how a social worker could believe that there was nothing positive in a tribal society. He also highlighted that the tribal people, despite their social differences, should not be considered as belonging to a lower social order. Elwin believed that assimilation is not a natural process and criticised social workers for attempting to forcefully convert tribes or impose elements of a dominant culture on them. He argued that this approach disregarded the meaningfulness of the tribal social system and reduced it to a collection of peculiarities. They believed that the true meaning would become apparent only when those peculiarities were discarded.

In 1952, Prime Minister Jawaharlal Nehru criticised the concept of assimilation, stating that it would result in a superficial imitation of a broader culture and the loss of identity. He argued that this would erode the cultural fabric and questioned whether civilised society was truly more advanced and prosperous. Nehru acknowledged that tribal life, with its unique characteristics, was often happier in many aspects than mainstream society, emphasizing the importance of preserving the best aspects of tribal life. This stance marked the initiation of the integration policy.

Later on, Elwin modified his 'national park' theory of keeping the tribals as 'museum specimens' and clarified, 'We do not want to preserve the tribesmen as "museum specimens" but equally we do not want to stop the clock of progress, it is equally important to ensure that such progress is meaningful and respectful. We may not believe in the myth of noble savage but we do not want to create a class of ignoble'. (Quoted in Vidyarthi and Rai, 1985, p. 415). This modification of the 'national park' theory provides the backdrop to the Nehruvian model of tribal development, popularly known as 'panchsheel' or the five pillars of tribal development.

The five fundamental principles are as follows: (i) Tribal should develop along the lines of their own genius and nothing should be imposed upon them; (ii) Respect must be shown for tribal rights on land and forest; (iii) There must be minimum investment of outsiders (non-tribals) in administration and development; (iv) Administration and launching of multiple schemes should be avoided and effects should be made within the framework of their social and cultural institution; and (v) Evaluation of results should not be done on the basis of statistics alone but also by the quality of life. These principles gave importance to tribal pluralism and aimed to integrate the tribal population with the mainstream society. Prof. Many scholars including Ghurye voiced their disapproval of the integration policy, arguing that it was a Western concept that did not fit the Indian context. Nevertheless, despite the criticism, integration has remained a fundamental aspect of the state's approach towards tribes since independence.

With these principles, administration in tribal areas got a new momentum to rebuild a new India. The principle of charity, as recognized by missionaries, was substituted by the spirit of development. The Directive Principles of State Policy on tribal welfare stress that the 'state shall promote with special care the educational and economic interests of the downtrodden communities including Scheduled Tribes'.

The Fifth Schedule confers uncommon powers of governance on Scheduled Areas on the governor of a state. The administration in the north-eastern states was incorporated in the Sixth Schedule. With the newly created administration, tribal development was taken up in different Five-Year plans. A new approach was introduced in the fifth Five-Year plan for the integrated development of tribes, that is, the Tribal Sub-Plan. It was implemented in different states and union territories and established government institutions such as the Anthropological Survey of India (ASI) in 1945 and the Tribal Research Institute (TRI) in 1954. In both of these institutes, trained anthropologists and administrators conducted research on different tribal communities in order to provide information to the state. Virginius Xaxa argues that reservation was extended to STs with a view to integrate them in the so-called mainstream of Indian life (Xaxa, 2001, p. 2768). Our various policies and programmes of tribal development are supposed to have been based on this approach of integrating tribals with the mainstream and brought at par with the rest of the people.

Independent India aimed to integrate tribals into the national mainstream by establishing a tribal welfare department in 1951 to protect and uplift Scheduled Tribes. The creation of the Fifth Schedule (Scheduled Area) and Sixth Schedule (Tribal Area) through Article 244, along with establishing the National Commission for Scheduled Tribes through Article 338, further strengthened the safeguards for scheduled tribes. In 1999, the Ministry of Social Justice and Empowerment was divided to create the Ministry of Tribal Affairs, which now serves as the central agency responsible for policy-making, planning and coordinating development programs for scheduled tribes.

The interaction between tribes and neighbouring agricultural and occupational groups has resulted in the adoption of customs and practices from the outside population and the acquisition of new skills. Tribes like the Munda, Oraon and the Bhil have assimilated various Hindu cultural traits due to their contact with civilised people. Additionally, a significant number of tribals have transitioned to agriculture, which is a more productive system compared to their traditional tribal way of life. The changing socio-economic landscape is gradually transforming the culture of tribes, with the process of acculturation being influenced by both the colonial period and the post-independence era, where developmental programs for the benefit of tribals played a significant role. However, the rate of acculturation varies among different tribal groups.

In contrast to extreme isolation and assimilation, anthropologists, social reformers and policymakers considered integration as the best strategy for the upliftment of tribes in view of their diversity in the country. According to Nirmal Kumar Bose, neither the policy of complete isolation nor of assimilation can solve the problems in tribal areas. As tribal populations are heterogeneous, a policy of complete assimilation will destroy the rich cultural heritage of tribes. On the other hand, integration with the mainstream would discourage separatist tendencies among the tribals and bring them more opportunities. Bose suggests that tribal development policies should aim to integrate tribals with the mainstream. Anthropologists, social reformers and policymakers advocate for integration as the most effective strategy for uplifting diverse tribes rather than extreme isolation or assimilation. Nirmal Kumar Bose argues that neither complete isolation nor assimilation can adequately address the issues faced by tribal populations, given their heterogeneity. Bose emphasizes that a policy of complete assimilation would erode the unique cultural heritage of tribes, while integration would help curb separatist tendencies and provide more development opportunities. Bose recommends that tribal development policies must focus on integrating tribes with mainstream society for long-term progress and inclusivity.

Over the years, numerous outreaching policies and programmes such as anti-exploitative, protective, economic, social, cultural and welfare measures have been adopted by the central and different state governments. All these measures are of two types: (i) Overall planning at the micro-level. (ii) Specific tribal development schemes for the welfare of tribal communities at the macro-level. Despite these initiatives, a universal development for all tribes has not yet been achieved.

Tribals should be encouraged to use their traditional knowledge to meet their needs by recreating their forest ecosystem and forest-based livelihood. The states must make serious efforts to minimise displacement. There should be a rights-based approach to comprehensive rehabilitation for socio-economic reconstitution of victims of development, including for the backlog of displaced people.

Regrettably, a considerable amount of the forested area has been redirected for mining activities, leading to environmental deterioration, deprivation of livelihoods and the uprooting of tribal communities. Since Independence, tribes have faced displacement due to the construction of dams, making India one of the leading nations in dam-building globally. Dams are considered the primary reason for displacement in the country, as they significantly contribute to the number of displaced individuals (Kumar, 2010; Chikkala and Kumar, 2023).

It is in this context that the devastation of the lives of tribal people caused by the loss of access to forests and involuntary displacement from their land, has to be understood. Dispossession takes place both directly by depriving tribal communities of their land, habitat, livelihood, political system, culture, values and identity, as well as indirectly through denials of benefits of development and their rights. With their control over resources diminishing, tribal communities remain the most vulnerable and marginalized community in the country.

Despite the efforts made by governments in post-independence India, tribal development has not been successful in reaching the entire target population. Many tribals still remain outside the scope of both the central and state government administrative machineries. The lack of coordination among different agencies responsible for implementing tribal development schemes is one of the factors contributing to underdevelopment. Numerous schemes related to agriculture, animal husbandry, cottage industry, health, education and family planning are typically implemented through various departments, resulting in overlapping and confusion among the tribal communities.

Work has been done to improve the lives of these groups through education, healthcare and communication to integrate them into mainstream society. On 13 August 2013, a High-level Committee on Socio-Economic, Health and Educational Status of Tribal Communities of India, chaired by Virginius Xaxa and consisting of five other members from various academic disciplines, was established. The panel submitted its report on the Socio-Economic, Health and Educational Status of Tribal Communities of India to the government in 2014. This report is considered as one of the most comprehensive studies on tribal societies in India, offering well-analysed data on various aspects of their social and cultural life.

The report presents an analysis of data on the socioeconomic, health and educational status of tribal communities, followed by a series of recommendations for consideration by the state and the civil society institutions. These recommendations are then consolidated and their feasibility is discussed. One key point highlighted in the report is that while the state has focussed on development issues in tribal areas, it has neglected to protect these communities from exploitation. As a result, many tribal people have been displaced due to development projects, leaving them vulnerable to various forms of oppression (Srivastava, 2018).

In 2006, the Draft National Tribal Policy was formulated in order to address the issues concerning tribal groups, such as lower literacy levels, economic constraints, poor infrastructure, diminishing control over natural resource base, persistent threats of eviction from their habitat, exclusion from mainstream and economy in the distribution of wealth and opportunities and non-empowerment. Its goal was to place the Scheduled Tribes on a progressive and constructive path and make them active partners in nation-building (Draft

National Tribal Policy, 2006, p. 4). It was recommended that the policy would be guided by the existing constitutional Articles including the PESA Act and the Nehruvian Panchsheel.

According to the Draft National Policy, a majority of the Scheduled Tribes still lived below the poverty line, had poor literacy rates, suffered from malnutrition and disease and were vulnerable to displacement. It also acknowledged that the STs in general were repositories of indigenous knowledge and wisdom. The policy also aimed at concretely addressing each of these problems. It listed out measures to preserve and promote tribal cultural heritage (2006, p. 259). The Draft National Tribal Policy was intended to provide direction for the Indian government in addressing tribal issues with the goal of improving the welfare of tribals, but the policy has yet to be officially approved or implemented.

For centuries, tribal communities fiercely protected their autonomy, culture and traditional lifestyles against colonial intrusions. Their resistance to colonial imposition spans a rich history of defiance, firmly rooted in their quest for autonomy and dignity. This struggle has been integral to India's historical narrative, stretching far beyond the colonial era. India's story of independence remains incomplete if we overlook the determined resistance and challenges faced by numerous tribal communities. Ranging from the Chuar Rebellion in 1767 to the uprisings beyond the Munda revolt, these movements arose as reactions to exploitation, loss of land, cultural repression and oppressive regulations enforced by the British colonial regime.

Tribal movements like the Khasi-Garo movement, Mizo movement, Kol movement, etc. are integral chapters in India's history and struggle for independence. Be it the bravery of Gond Maharani Veer Durgavati or the sacrifice of Rani Kamalapati, the country cannot forget the same. The struggle of Veer Maharana Pratap cannot be imagined without the brave Bhils who fought shoulder to shoulder and made sacrifices. There have been many Adivasi heroes who sacrificed their lives in the struggle for freedom. Sadly, the invaluable contributions of tribal communities remain largely unacknowledged. Mainstream historical accounts often sideline the courageous sacrifices made by these indigenous groups, relegating their stories to the margins of the broader freedom movement. The narrative of India's independence, as traditionally presented, inadvertently undermines the resilience and pivotal role of tribal movements in resisting colonial rule.

Much has been written about the conflict between the British imperialists and the Indian society. However, little mention has been made of the role of the peasants, craftsmen and the tribesmen in this struggle. Modern historians have neglected the revolts of Indian tribes. Sumit Sarkar rightly points out, 'The crucial gap leaves the history of political movements and particularly of nationalism in something like a vacuum and tends to make such history essentially a study from the top downwards.'

Now, for the first time in the country after independence, the art and culture of the tribal society and their contribution to the freedom movement and nation-building are being remembered with pride and honoured on a grand scale. This declaration acknowledges the glorious history of tribal communities and recognizes their efforts towards preserving tribal cultural heritage.

MUCH-DELAYED RECOGNITION

The Azadi Ka Amrit Mahotsav is a programme launched by the Indian government to honour and observe 75 years of independence, as well as its citizens' rich history, culture and accomplishments. This Mahotsav aims to protect and integrate janjatis as part of the government of India's initiative to celebrate 75 years of independence and honour the nation's history, culture and achievements. It recognizes the significant role played by the people of India in the country's progress and emphasizes the potential of Atmanirbhar Bharat.

The historic nomination of Droupadi Murmu, a member of the Scheduled Tribes, to the prestigious office of the President of India, marks a significant milestone in the country's democratic journey. For far too long, the highest constitutional position had seen no representation from the marginalized tribal communities that make up a sizeable portion of India's diverse population. Murmu's candidacy shattered this longstanding glass ceiling, paving the way for greater inclusion and diversity at the apex of India's leadership. Her inspiring personal story—rising from humble beginnings in a remote village to the nation's highest office—resonates profoundly with millions of tribal citizens who have long felt underrepresented and overlooked.

The nomination also serves as a powerful symbol of the progress India has made in recognising and elevating the voices and contributions of its tribal communities. Moreover, the concurrent honouring of numerous janjati men and women with the prestigious Padma awards across diverse fields, underscores these communities' rich tapestry of talent and achievement. These accolades celebrate the indomitable spirit, resilience and ingenuity of India's tribal populations, who have steadfastly preserved their unique cultural heritage while also making invaluable contributions to the nation's development. Truly, it is a watershed moment that holds the promise of a more inclusive, equitable and representative India, where citizens from all backgrounds can aspire to the highest echelons of leadership and national recognition.

At the heart of Azadi Ka Amrit Mahotsav are five central themes that capture the essence of India's remarkable progress and collective resolve.

The first theme, honours the indomitable spirit of India's freedom-fighters, both celebrated and unsung, by revisiting the pivotal moments and movements that led to independence. This includes initiatives like the Birsa Munda Jayanti, which throws spotlight on the heroic legacy of the tribal leader who fought tirelessly against colonial oppression. The 'Ideas@75' theme then shifts the focus to the visionary ideas and principles that have guided India's journey, inspiring individuals and shaping the nation's collective destiny.

Complementing this, the 'Resolve@75' theme emphasizes the unwavering determination of the Indian people to forge the future of their motherland, urging everyone to contribute their part towards this shared vision. Building upon this, 'Action@75' highlights the concerted efforts to position India as a global leader in the post-pandemic world, with a focus on policy implementation and commitments aligned with the Prime Minister's vision of inclusive development and national unity (*Sabka Saath, Sabka Vikas, Sabka Vishwas, Sabka Prayas*).

Finally, the 'Achievements@75' theme celebrates the remarkable milestones and collective triumphs of a nation that has flourished for over 75 years, drawing upon a rich history spanning more than 5,000 years.

The government of India has declared 15 November as Janjatiya Gaurav Divas to commemorate the contributions of tribal communities to the nation's history and culture and to inspire the coming generations in the preservation of our cultural heritage and national pride. This day is also observed to honour all the tribal freedom-fighters and to re-energise the efforts for the socio-economic development of the tribal regions. The date is the birth anniversary of Dharti Aba, Bhagwan Birsa Munda, an iconic freedom-fighter and tribal leader of the country. Since 2021, the Janjatiya Gaurav Divas is being celebrated across the country with zeal and enthusiasm.

On 15 November 2023, Narendra Modi made history by being the first Prime Minister to visit Ulihatu village, the birthplace of Bhagwan Birsa. This visit coincided with the nationwide 'Viksit Bharat Sankalp Yatra' launch. The Prime Minister inaugurated IEC (Information, Education and Communication) vans in Khunti, Jharkhand, to mark the beginning of the 'Viksit Bharat Sankalp Yatra'. This yatra commenced from gram panchayats in 68 districts that have significant tribal populations and will eventually cover all village panchayats in the country.

The primary goal of this yatra is to ensure the successful implementation of government flagship schemes by guaranteeing that the benefits of these schemes reach all intended beneficiaries within a specified timeframe. In tribal regions, the focus areas include Sickle Cell testing, promoting awareness and enrolment in Eklavya Model Residential Schools and Scholarship Schemes. Additionally, the livelihoods of tribal communities will be supported through the issuance of Forest Right Titles and the establishment of Van Dhan Vikas Kendra Self Help Groups. More than 200 Gram Panchayats hosted events as part of these initiatives to further the 'Viksit Bharat Sankalp Yatra' objectives.

In addition, the Prime Minister launched the Pradhan Mantri Janjati Adivasi Nyaya Maha Abhiyan (PM JANMAN), with a budget of around Rs. 24,000 crore for the overall development of Particularly Vulnerable Tribal Groups (PVTGs). The mission will be implemented through the convergence of 11 interventions of 9 ministries.

Under the empowerment of the Tribal Communities programme, the government, recognized the need to protect the socio-cultural fabric of tribal communities and underscored their role in nation-building. The framers of the Constitution of India made special provisions for the protection of tribal culture and the development of Scheduled Tribes. These include the conservation of their language, script and other cultural elements, ensuring their educational interests, providing economic safeguards and taking steps for political empowerment.

Apart from the constitutional safeguards providing a more focussed approach to the integrated socio-economic development of the Scheduled Tribes (STs), the programmes and schemes of the Ministry of Tribal Affairs are intended to support and supplement other central ministries, State governments and voluntary organisations and to fill critical gaps in institutions and programmes, taking into account the situation of STs through financial assistance.

In another initiative for tribal empowerment, effective implementation of the Scheduled Tribes and Other Traditional Forest-dwellers Act, 2006 (or FRA, the forests rights Act) has been undertaken. This helps tribals whose rights on ancestral lands and their habitat were not adequately recognized, resulting in historical injustice to them. Under this Act, total community rights given till May 2014 were 23,578, whereas during the period from 2014 to 2023, 86,621 community rights were given across the country. The total extent of land distributed during the period from the inception of FRA to May 2014 was 55.30 lakh acres; during the period from 2014 to June 2023, 122.60 lakh acres were given (this is almost double the figure during the period till May 2014). A total of 177.90 lakh acres of forest land (47.56 lakh acres individual and 130.34 lakh acres community) had been distributed up to 30 June 2023 across the country.

The Eklavya Model Residential Schools (EMRS) have been set up to provide quality education to ST students (Class VI–XII) in remote areas through residential schooling facilities. Currently, more than 1.2 lakh students are enrolled in 401 EMRS. The number of female students (60,815) in EMRSs exceeds that of male students (59,255). Moreover, a total of 38,000 teachers and support staff are being recruited for the Ekalavya Model Residential Schools, which will benefit 3.5 lakh tribal students.

A number of Fellowship and Scholarship Programmes have been launched to provide financial assistance to ST students for studies ranging from pre-matric and post-matric levels and in the pursuit of higher education and studies abroad. Notably, during the last 9 years, a total of 3.15 crore tribal students have received scholarships/fellowships of over Rs. 17,087 crore (April

2014–September 2023). Prioritising the welfare of tribal communities, the budget allocation of the Ministry of Tribal Affairs has been substantially increased from Rs. 4295.94 crore in 2013–2014 to Rs. 12461.88 crore in 2023–2024—an increase of around 190 per cent.

States receive funds under Article 275(1) of the Constitution to support development schemes aimed at tribal welfare. The Pradhan Mantri Vanbandhu Vikas Yojana has established a venture capital fund to encourage entrepreneurship among ST youth, ensuring minimum support price for minor forest produce and offering marketing support for tribal products through the Pradhan Mantri Jan Jatiya Vikas Mission. The mission has sanctioned 3,958 Van Dhan Vikas Kendra (VDVK) with a disbursed amount of Rs. 398.49 crore, benefiting 183,412 tribal individuals. Financial assistance is also extended to voluntary organisations engaged in education, health and livelihood projects that target the Scheduled Tribes.

The government has taken several measures to facilitate the inclusion of tribals in mainstream economic activity and incentivise the promotion and export of tribal products. As India moves ahead with its strategy for India@75 and focusses on turning the development process into a mass movement, the Tribal Co-operative Marketing Development Federation of India (TRIFED) is working at the grassroots level. With the focus on 'Vocal for Local' and building an Atmanirbhar Bharat, TRIFED has undertaken several activities while re-dedicating its efforts towards tribal empowerment. In collaboration with the Ministry of External Affairs, TRIFED plans to set up an Atmanirbhar Bharat corner in 100 Indian missions/embassies across the world.

Catalogues and brochures that showcase the richness and variety of tribal products have also been shared with the missions and embassies for display. Diplomats from a large number of countries and delegates of international organisations participated at the international conclave at Aadi Mahotsav in 2021. With the Prime Minister's call for 'Atmanirbhar Bharat', aligned with the slogan of 'Be Vocal for Local, Buy Tribal', the goal of *Sabka Saath, Sabka Vikas* will be closer to realisation. TRIFED will partner with NITI Aayog to implement the Van Dhan Yojana in the districts that have been identified as aspirational districts by NITI Aayog.

TRIFED aids in retail marketing to enhance the livelihood of tribal communities in India. An allocation of Rs. 288 crore has been set aside in the annual budget estimate for the fiscal year 2023–2024 to support initiatives through this agency, particularly focussing on self-help groups and producer enterprises. The central sector scheme, 'Marketing and Logistics Development for Promotion of Tribal Products from north-eastern Region (PTP-NER)' was inaugurated under TRIFED to benefit Scheduled Tribes in the region. It was launched in Manipur on 18 April 2023. As part of the celebration of India's 75 years of independence, TRIFED introduced 75 new tribal products to the existing Tribes India catalogue, expanding the range of offerings.

In addition, 75 products of tribal origin have been earmarked for Geographical Indication (GI) tagging, representing 20 Indian states. About 37 out of 75 identified GI tribal products are from 8 states in the north-east; 7 from Jharkhand; and 6 products from Madhya Pradesh have also been identified for GI Tagging. TRIFED remains committed to the Atmanirbhar Bharat mission by supporting tribal incomes and livelihoods through various initiatives. As part of this effort, the agency procures and markets tribal art and craft items through its Tribes India retail network, both online and offline, to showcase the craftsmanship of tribal artisans and boost their livelihoods.

The Pradhan Mantri Adi Adarsh Gram Yojana (PMAAGY) is designed to enhance infrastructure and livelihood opportunities in villages with a substantial tribal population. A total of 36,428 villages with at least 50 per cent tribal population and 500 Scheduled Tribes have been selected to receive basic infrastructure support under this initiative and these include villages in the aspirational districts identified by NITI Aayog. Among the such districts, 86 are common, with 10,509 villages falling under the coverage of PMAAGY for infrastructure development and livelihood enhancement.

Through the National Health Mission, the Ministry of Health and Family Welfare has developed a comprehensive guideline to control and prevent Haemoglobinopathies, including the sickle cell disease. This guideline has been shared with all the states. The government has been actively working towards eradicating sickle cell disease, which primarily affects the tribal population in central, western and southern India. The Prime Minister launched the Sickle Cell Anaemia Elimination Mission on 1 July 2023 in Madhya Pradesh. The mission aims to provide affordable and accessible care to all patients of this disease, improve the quality of care and reduce the prevalence of the disease. This will be achieved through awareness campaigns, universal screening of 7 crore people aged 0–40 years in 278 affected districts and counselling efforts by both central ministries and state governments.

The Mission has screened a total of 5.86 million individuals. Adivasi communities have been prioritized in health schemes like Mission Indradhanush, which focusses on complete immunisation for children and pregnant women, as well as providing free COVID-19 vaccines. The Nikshay Mitra initiative provides extra support in diagnosis, nutrition and vocational assistance to tribal groups undergoing tuberculosis treatment.

In addition to the schemes administered by the Ministry of Tribal Affairs, the welfare of tribal communities is also prioritized through initiatives under other government ministries. These span different sectors and domains, such as housing and road connectivity through the Pradhan Mantri Awas Yojana and the Pradhan Mantri Gram Sadak Yojana, respectively. Financial empowerment is also promoted through initiatives like the Jan Dhan accounts, self-help groups and the MUDRA Yojana. Initiatives such as the Swachh

Bharat Mission, Gobardhan Scheme and Pradhan Mantri Matru Vandana Yojana have been highlighted by Prime Minister Modi as additional schemes that benefit tribal communities; he mentioned them during his address on Janjatiya Gaurav Divas 2022. The nation is moving with the energy of 'Panch Pran' to realise the dreams of Bhagwan Birsa Munda and crores of janjatiya brave-hearts.

India's tribal communities are being honoured and celebrated through the approval of 10 Tribal Freedom Fighters' Museums in states where the tribals fought against the British. Prime Minister Modi has urged the development of Mangarh Dham in Rajasthan's Banswara district, a significant site where 1,500 Bhil freedom-fighters were killed in 1913 by the British. The Mangarh Dham project will be a collaborative effort between the governments of Rajasthan, Gujarat, Madhya Pradesh and Maharashtra, serving as a national memorial to showcase the legacy and cultural heritage of tribal communities.

The government's primary focus has been on the holistic development of Scheduled Tribes (STs) and various initiatives have been implemented under the Development Action Plan for Scheduled Tribes (DAPST) by the ministries/departments concerned, resulting in significant enhancements in the socio-economic status of STs. For example, the literacy rate for these tribes has improved from 59 per cent (Census 2011) to 71.6 per cent (as per Periodic Labour Force Survey, July 2020–June 2021), thus bringing down the gap between overall and ST literacy from 14 per cent between 2001 and 2011 to 7.5 per cent during 2011–2021. The gross enrolment ratio (GER) at upper primary school level has improved from 91.3 per cent (2013–2014) to 98 per cent (2021–2022); GER for ST students at secondary level (Std. IX–X) has increased from 70.2 per cent (2013–2014) to 78.1 per cent (2021–2022); GER for ST students at senior secondary level (Std. XI–XII) has increased from 35.4 per cent (2013–2014) to 52.0 per cent (2021–2022); and GER for ST students at higher education level has increased from 13.7 per cent (2014–2015) to 18.9 per cent (2020–2021).

The government has implemented various initiatives and measures to integrate tribal communities into mainstream society while also respecting their cultures, traditions and way of life. The Ministry of Tribal Affairs is taking several steps to preserve, protect and promote the unique cultures of tribal communities.

The colonial education system brought significant changes to the curriculum and teaching methods in colonized nations, with a strong focus on English as the medium of instruction. This had resulted in a decline in interest in local languages. Science and technology were prioritized in the colonial curriculum, while traditional arts and cultural knowledge were often overlooked. Today, education's internationalisation is closely linked to English-medium instruction and publication in English journals, creating challenges for local authors and researchers. The Westernised/colonial education system's emphasis on standardised approaches has negatively impacted traditional and indigenous knowledge systems, favouring homogenisation over diversity.

APPRECIATING TRADITIONAL KNOWLEDGE SYSTEMS

Tribal communities living historically in the proximity of these natural ecosystems, develop over a period of time specific knowledge on the ecosystem and environmental resources that are later called as traditional knowledge or traditional ecological knowledge (TEK). The tribal communities' harmonious relationship with nature is reflected in a range of traditional practices that embody their culture, agricultural practices, ethno-medicinal uses of plants, religious beliefs, rituals, festivals, customs and traditions. Through their traditional practices and knowledge, tribals help in the conservation of the environment and biodiversity.

Traditional ecological knowledge has its roots in the practices of ancient hunter-gatherers, although the term itself gained prominence in the 1980s. Today, it represents a holistic understanding of the relationship between humans and their ecosystems, making it valuable across various disciplines such as agriculture, pharmacology, ethnobotany and natural resource sustainability. In light of the current environmental crisis, including ecosystem degradation and climate change, traditional ecological knowledge is increasingly recognized as a vital resource for addressing the challenges posed by shifting global environmental conditions. It promotes principles of coexistence and sustainability, offering a wealth of localised knowledge that has been honed over generations. This knowledge is instrumental in shaping practices for decision-making in areas such as agriculture, pastoralism, food preparation, healthcare and natural resource management (Kala, 2022).

In India, many indigenous communities continue to rely on various means of livelihood to this day. For example, agriculture has been a longstanding practice in the mountainous regions of Kerala. The Mavilan tribe, that reside in the Kannur and Kasaragod districts, engage in traditional slash-and-burn farming (known as Kumari cultivation) alongside other agricultural activities such as crop diversity, plant protection and harvesting techniques. They possess knowledge about different varieties of rice and can classify seeds based on their characteristics (Suresh, 2010). This understanding has contributed to the enhancement and cultivation of rice crops. The nutritional needs of tribal communities are met by relying on wild edible plants and various forest resources. Leafy plants, in particular, are crucial for food security and significantly impact the socio-economic well-being of the indigenous and traditional populations in Chhattisgarh, as highlighted by Kumari and Solanki (2019).

Shifting cultivation, also known as Podu or Jhum cultivation, is a traditional farming method practised by various tribes in India, such as the Konda Reddi, Kolam, Dongria Kondh and the Kuki. It involves clearing forest land, burning vegetation for soil enrichment and rotating cultivation sites to maintain soil fertility. The tribes have a deep understanding of crop rotation and grow a variety of crops, including rice, maize, vegetables and medicinal plants. This sustainable farming practice not only meets their dietary needs but also contributes to the overall health of the forest ecosystem. Additionally, communal cultivation activities promote social cohesion and preserve cultural traditions through rituals that honour the land and nature.

The Dongria Kondh are renowned for their sustainable agro-forestry practice called 'Podu cultivation', on the Niyamgiri hills. They utilise mixed cropping and integrate forest resources to adapt to the hilly terrain ecosystem. This shifting cultivation involves clearing small forest patches for crops such as millets, pulses and cash crops while relying on the forests for fuelwood and medicinal plants. The Dongria Kondh also prioritize crop rotation as a collective effort to maintain soil fertility and promote social cohesion, guided by their traditional knowledge and cultural significance.

The Apatani Cultural Landscape in UNESCO is renowned for its sustainable agriculture practices, particularly terrace farming. By transforming the steep slopes of the Ziro Valley into terraced fields, the Apatani people effectively prevent erosion, conserve water and optimise land usage. Their agricultural methods involve cultivating a variety of crops, including rice, millet, maize, soybeans and vegetables, that not only enhance soil fertility but also improve its resilience. Additionally, integrating fish farming with rice cultivation serves the dual purpose of increasing protein production and controlling pests. Through the collective stewardship facilitated by the traditional institutions like the 'Bulyan' system, the Apatani community ensures sustainable resource management, preserves biodiversity and successfully adapts to environmental changes. These institutions enable the collective management of land, water and forests, further contributing to the sustainability of their agricultural practices.

Likewise, local communities of Maldah district of West Bengal depend on wild edible plants to fulfil their food needs and earn their livelihood. A large population lives in areas adjacent to the forests, thus playing a role in their conservation (Chowdhury and Mukherjee, 2012). Indigenous knowledge is cultivated through ongoing practice, experimentation, innovation and adaptation. Similarly, various agricultural and farming practices have evolved over generations, contributing to the sustenance and conservation of the environment (Hanazaki et al., 2020).

The indigenous Soliga community in Karnataka heavily depends on non-timber forest produce (NTFPs) sourced from the Biligiri Rangaswamy Temple

Tiger Reserve and its surroundings. They employ sustainable harvesting methods to protect forest resources and uphold the ecological equilibrium of the area. NTFPs like honey, wild edibles, medicinal plants, fibers, resins, spices and crafting materials play a vital role in their diet, health, traditions and economy. The Soligas excel in beekeeping and foraging for wild edibles and possess extensive knowledge of medicinal plants. They use forest resources to create traditional medicines, crafts and flavourings, which not only support their livelihoods but also safeguard their cultural legacy and bonds with the land.

Throughout human history, plants have been utilised for their healing properties, serving as remedies for a wide range of ailments and diseases (Marques et al., 2021). The ancient practice of Ayurveda, known as the 'science of life', is deeply rooted in the medicinal uses of plants, which emphasizes the significance of preventive medicine. These medicinal practices were intricately woven into the fabric of people's culture, rituals, customs and ceremonies, serving as a means to encourage adherence to these practices and maintain good health. The utilisation of various parts of plants in wound-healing, the preparation of decoctions and traditional therapies have been well-documented in ancient texts and continue to be practised today. Within tribal communities, local traditional healers or medicine men play a vital role in preserving traditional knowledge and biodiversity by practicing treatment and healing methods (Gupta, 2021).

Exploring ethno-medicine is a significant aspect of the Traditional Knowledge Systems (TKS). In their research, Kumar (2006) and Yesodharan and Sujana (2007) focussed on studying the ethno-medical practices of the Kolams of Andhra Pradesh and Malamalasar tribes in Kerala. Their findings revealed that these tribes rely on medicinal plants to treat various ailments, including cuts, snakebites, headaches, dysentery, jaundice and other diseases. However, the research also highlighted the potential risk of losing this valuable ethno-medical knowledge due to a lack of documentation.

Tribal healers, frequently referred to as traditional or indigenous healers, hold a crucial position in the healthcare systems of numerous Indian tribes. For instance, the Gond community, predominantly located in central India, has traditional healers called Bhagats. These practitioners are well-versed in herbal medicine, rituals and spiritual methods designed to address physical, mental and spiritual issues within their communities. Research conducted in 2018 by IGNCA on healers in the north-east underlined significant insights regarding their strengths and the challenges they face (Reddy et al., 2022).

Research conducted by Ota and Reddy (2023) highlights the significance of community-based healing practices. It is essential to recognize that various tribes throughout India possess distinct healing traditions, which are typically transmitted orally across generations. These practices often adopt a holistic perspective, merging herbal remedies with spiritual and cultural components to enhance overall well-being. The volumes emphasize the importance of preserving traditional knowledge and the necessity for documentation, integration and support systems for herbal healers. 'I have been advocating to parliamentarians and members of the Rajya Sabha for the establishment of "healers huts" in each panchayat, with assistance from local and state resources' (Ota and Reddy, 2023).

In their research on the involvement of women in preserving indigenous biodiversity among the Adi tribes of Arunachal Pradesh, Singh et al. (2013) highlight the significant contribution of elderly women who possess valuable knowledge and expertise in the preparation of traditional food. These women have played a crucial role in the utilisation and conservation of biodiversity, with 34 out of the 55 species they used having ethno-medical significance.

Various plants, including those that yield spices, are utilised by the Tangkhul Tribe in Ukhrul District, Manipur, for treating a wide range of diseases and health issues (Salam and Jamir, 2016; Shimray and Lungleng, 2017). In the West Medinipur district of West Bengal, tribal communities near the Kakrajhore forest rely on ethno-medicinal plants like Smilex ovalifolia, Emblica officinalis and others to create medicinal treatments (Biswas et al., 2017). The Kani tribals in Thodu hills of Kerala, India, use Plumbago zeylanica and Ocimum tenuiflorum, among other plants, for first aid and to address common ailments such as cough, cold, fever, headache and poisonous bites (Xavier et al., 2014).

Various indigenous communities have historically valued the animals they raised and domesticated, ensuring their survival over time. An example is the Todas of Nilgiris, who consider their buffaloes as a crucial aspect of their socio-religious identity, highlighting the significance of animal husbandry in their culture (Kumar et al., 2006). Many medicinal plants have been reported to be used to treat various human and livestock diseases and thus conserved by tribal people.

For example, in 2004, Kamal K. Misra and K. Anil Kumar conducted a study on the Konda Reddi tribe in Andhra Pradesh. They extensively documented the tribe's utilisation of medicinal plants to treat various ailments in domestic animals. These ailments include contagious ecthyma (notigadlu or muthipundlu) or mouth diseases, foot rot (kadlagadlu), enterotoxemia type of diseases (chitukuvyadi), blue tongue (nilinaluka), smallpox (ammoru), ephemeral fever (kurma), tuberculosis (shakyarogam), trypanosomiasis (jomma), pneumonia (domma), haemorrhagic septicemia (kantivapu), black quarter (yerrachippi), rinderpest (musaravyadi), etc. These diseases are treated with plant-based therapeutic knowledge from the tribals. Ethno-medicinal practices have been a longstanding tradition which is deeply ingrained in the lives of local communities due to their trust in herbal remedies and lack of access to modern healthcare facilities.

The Jarawa and Nicobarese tribes have preserved their ancestral traditions by engaging in hunting, gathering and fishing in the Bay of Bengal. Their fishing practices are in harmony with nature due to their extensive knowledge of fishing species and seasonal patterns. They prioritize sustainable methods to protect natural resources and the ecosystem, while also ensuring their own livelihood. These methods, such as the use of nets, spears and hooks along the coastlines, have been passed down the generations and provide a diverse range of marine resources that fulfil a significant portion of their dietary needs. Their deep understanding of local ecosystems and fish migration patterns demonstrates their adaptation to the marine environment.

The ancient practice of 'Halma' by the Bhil and Bhilala tribal communities in Jhabua district of Madhya Pradesh has been instrumental in addressing water scarcity issues. This indigenous tradition showcases the technological expertise of the Bhil community and contributes to sustainable development. Through the construction of small earthen dams, the Halma system ensures a consistent water supply for agriculture by recharging groundwater aquifers. Community-led efforts in maintaining these dams highlight the importance of social solidarity and community participation in managing ecological resources effectively. The Halma system promotes sustainability by reducing reliance on unpredictable rainfall patterns and mitigating the impact of droughts, all while respecting cultural values and minimising environmental harm.

The Changpa community in Ladakh and Jammu & Kashmir follows a semi-nomadic pastoral lifestyle, depending on yak herding for sustenance. They migrate seasonally with their animals, moving to higher altitudes during summer and lower regions in winter. Yaks play a crucial role in their daily lives, providing essential resources like milk, meat, wool and hides. The Changpas have inherited traditional knowledge of animal husbandry, transmitted orally through generations and reside in portable tents crafted from yak hair or goat wool. Their pastoral traditions are deeply intertwined with their cultural heritage, honoured through ceremonies and festivities. Despite challenges such as climate change, land degradation, shrinking grazing areas due to development and competition with wildlife, the Changpas exhibit resilience in maintaining their way of life.

The shifting climate is impacting important cultural and community resources, species, habitats, individuals and assets. These changes are expected to be significant, potentially altering the ways of life of indigenous communities. Throughout history, tribes have preserved their cultural practices, showing great resilience amidst evolving environmental and social circumstances. For example, Pakho Khet, a traditional agroforestry method practised by the Lepchas and Bhutias in Sikkim, involves integrating crop cultivation with trees and shrubs to stabilise the soil. This technique improves water management by capturing and retaining water, crucial in areas with seasonal water fluctuations like Sikkim. Moreover, it supports soil health and biodiversity and utilises traditional knowledge to adapt to changing climate conditions and enhance agricultural resilience.

India's tribal house architecture is a testament to the diverse traditional building styles and techniques used by indigenous communities throughout the country. The use of locally sourced materials like bamboo, wood, mud, thatch and palm leaves promotes environmental sustainability and provides insulation and structural strength. These architectural designs are deeply rooted in the respective regions' cultural, social and environmental aspects, reflecting the tribal ways of life and beliefs. The preservation of indigenous knowledge and heritage is a key aspect of traditional tribal architecture in India, offering valuable insights into sustainable construction practices, community living and cultural identity. Therefore, studying and preserving these architectural styles is of utmost importance.

For instance, the Nyishi tribes in Arunachal Pradesh practise communal living in the Longhouse, where multiple families reside together, sharing resources and responsibilities for extended periods. This arrangement fosters unity and efficiency and reduces environmental impact by minimising the need for individual households. Traditionally constructed on high platforms or bamboo stilts, with wooden and bamboo walls and thatched roofs, the Longhouse maximises resource utilisation and living space while embodying Nyishi values of sustainability, harmony with nature, conservation and community cooperation.

Tribal artefacts too are derived from raw materials from nearby forests or natural resources. These products are uniquely designed and are finding wide attention globally. Crafts differ from tribe to tribe and depend upon the availability of raw materials. Some of the very famous and exquisite Indian tribal crafts are metal crafts, tribal textiles, tribal paintings, tribal jewellery, pottery, cane and bamboo products, etc.

Tribal crafts encompass handmade artefacts created by indigenous communities, using raw materials sourced from nearby forests or natural resources. Tribal artisans from Chhattisgarh, Bihar, Odisha and West Bengal are renowned for their metal crafts, specifically the Bell Metal Art or Dhokra Art. Additionally, Indian tribes have crafted diverse handlooms, incorporating drawings inspired by their rich history and culture. These handlooms have vibrant and striking colours derived from natural ingredients.

Indigenous artworks serve as a reflection of tribal culture, showcasing their artistic flair and uncomplicated lifestyle. Renowned tribal art in India include Warli, Gond, Pithora and palm-leaf paintings. Tribal adornments signify their social standing and authority, with items like necklaces, bracelets and anklets crafted from locally sourced materials. Tribes residing in forested regions, particularly near cane and bamboo forests, utilise natural resources to create a variety of everyday items such as baskets, hats and vessels. Additionally, tribal communities exhibit their craftsmanship through pottery, with the Longpi pottery from Manipur being a well-known example reserved for affluent tribal members.

The communities residing in the hills and forests possess a profound tradition of art and crafts that frequently embodies their cultural heritage and relationship with nature. For instance, the Warli tribe, predominantly located in Maharashtra, is renowned for its distinctive painting style, which features geometric shapes and stick-figure representations of everyday life and rituals. Unfortunately, their artistic expressions and cultural legacy are often exploited by outsiders— who purchase them at throwaway rates and sell them elsewhere for huge profits, while the artistes persist in a state of poverty.

Numerous tribes, such as the Gond and the Bhil, are skilled in the art of bamboo craftsmanship, producing a variety of items including baskets, mats and musical instruments through traditional methods. The Dhokra tribe, which is dispersed throughout central and eastern India, is known for its metal casting techniques. The tribe's artisans create detailed and artistic figurines, jewellery and functional objects using the lost wax casting process. Pattachitra, a traditional painting technique, is practised by several tribes in Odisha, featuring intricate designs on fabric that illustrate mythological narratives, nature and everyday life. The Banjara tribe is recognized for its colourful and ornate embroidery, utilising vibrant hues and mirror embellishments to enhance textiles, garments and accessories.

Tribal textiles are known for their unique representation of cultural identity and traditions, with specific costumes for various ceremonies and events, reflecting age and social status within the community. Several Indian tribes have a rich tradition of textile-weaving, creating unique fabrics with distinctive designs. Here are a few examples: Various tribes in Odisha, such as the Sambalpuri and the Kotpad weavers, are known for their intricate Ikat weaving. They use tie-dye techniques to create vibrant patterns on silk and cotton fabrics. The Santiniketan tribes in West Bengal practise Kantha embroidery, which involves hand-stitching decorative motifs on sarees and other textiles, that tells stories passed on through generations.

Across the north-east, in Manipur, Assam and Naga, tribes are skilled in weaving traditional skirts and shawls with unique patterns and symbols. They have distinct weaving styles and motifs, making their textiles culturally significant. The tribal communities in Kutch, Gujarat, are known for Bhujodi weaving. They produce handwoven textiles, including shawls and blankets, using traditional techniques. The Toda tribe in the Nilgiri Hills of Tamil Nadu practises intricate embroidery on shawls and garments. They use geometric patterns and bright colours in their textile art. These examples highlight the diversity and skill of Indian tribes in the realm of textile weaving, showcasing their unique cultural expressions through fabric (Charusmita Gupta in Ota and Reddy, 2023).

These and numerous other artistic expressions not only highlight the ingenuity of the indigenous communities residing in India's forests and hills, but also serve an essential function in safeguarding their cultural heritage and traditions. While these art forms are highly sought after, both nationally and internationally, the tribes receive only minimal financial compensation, as the profits are predominantly appropriated by intermediaries and commercial entities.

Indigenous communities worldwide have faced a daunting array of obstacles in their efforts to safeguard and preserve their traditional knowledge and cultural practices. Foremost among these challenges has been the devastating impact of colonisation, which has resulted in the dispossession of ancestral lands and territories that were the very foundation of indigenous ways of life. The suppression of native languages, religious customs and time-honoured traditions has further eroded the ability of these communities to pass down their knowledge and wisdom from one generation to the next. Assimilation policies implemented by dominant cultures have also placed immense pressure on the indigenous peoples to abandon their distinct cultural identities in favour of conformity with the mainstream. Additionally, the continued economic exploitation and extraction of resources from indigenous lands, often without their free, prior and informed consent, has undermined their ability to maintain sustainable livelihoods in harmony with the natural environment.

Despite these daunting challenges, indigenous communities have demonstrated remarkable resilience in preserving and transmitting their invaluable traditional knowledge. This knowledge, honed over centuries of close observation and intimate connection with the land, holds tremendous potential to inform solutions to the pressing environmental crises the world faces today. From traditional agricultural practices that promote biodiversity and soil health, to holistic approaches to healthcare and pharmacology, the rich endowment of traditional knowledge possessed by indigenous groups represents a vital resource that has long been undervalued and marginalized by dominant, Western-centric systems of knowledge production.

Recognising the central role that indigenous knowledge can play in sustainable development, environmental conservation and the improvement of community wellbeing—particularly for the most vulnerable populations—is, therefore, of the utmost importance. By safeguarding, incorporating and actively promoting the preservation of traditional knowledge, they will have the opportunity to not only honour cultural diversity but to discover innovative pathways towards a more harmonious and ecologically balanced future.

The Tribal Knowledge System today embodies the collective wisdom, practical experience and adaptations passed down through generations or oral tradition (Trafzer et al., 2008; Anil Kumar, 2012). The absence of written documentation should not devalue the significance of the Indian Knowledge System.

The dismissal of tribal practices and knowledge as primitive or backward is a problem that arises from the way they are portrayed in significant ethnographies and books on tribes. To address this issue, we must reevaluate these texts and restructure them within the context of tribal culture, utilising methodologies like conceptual distortions or knowledge concept clusters. This transformative task requires collaboration among anthropologists, sociologists, social workers and educationists from various fields (Claerhout, 2014). It is essential for researchers to identify the taking place of hybridisation and distinguish between the TKS and Western culture during the initial documentation process. Additionally, the preservation of the local environment and culture is crucial as climate change, deforestation and land loss not only affects the tribes' sustenance but also leads to the devaluation of their knowledge systems.

Safeguarding the intellectual property owner and the intellectual property itself is crucial. Malagi and Malagi (2022) propose strategies like safeguarding plant species of indigenous communities under the Protection of Plant Varieties and Farmers Rights Act, 2001 and Biological Diversity Act, 2002 and enhancing awareness about these laws among Indigenous groups. Consolidating tribal philosophy amidst diversity and differences poses a challenge, yet a unified belief system can be formed. According to Kala (2022), these principles have the potential to shape environmental and cultural preservation strategies.

President Droupadi Murmu's remarks underscored the vital importance of integrating the rich, time-honoured knowledge systems of India's tribal communities into the country's broader intellectual and educational frameworks. As the nation's first tribal president, Murmu has brought a unique and invaluable perspective to the table, highlighting the immense value that Indigenous wisdom can contribute towards transforming India into a true 'knowledge superpower'. The existing Indian Knowledge System is a key focus area of the landmark National Education Policy, has historically been dominated by scholarly work produced under colonial rule—a body of knowledge that, while significant, has often failed to adequately capture and reflect the nuanced, community-based understandings held by tribal populations across the subcontinent.

Under Murmu's leadership, the union government, in partnership with the National Commission for Scheduled Tribes (NCST), is now spearheading a critical initiative to 're-document' these indigenous cultures, social practices and knowledge systems. This vital undertaking aims to give voice and visibility to the rich intellectual heritage that has long been marginalized or overlooked, bringing it to the forefront as an integral component of India's overarching knowledge ecosystem. By weaving tribal epistemologies into the Indian Knowledge System, India can unlock a wellspring of place-based, holistic wisdom that has the power to revolutionise fields ranging from sustainable resource management to traditional medicine. Ultimately, Murmu's vision is to create a more inclusive, representative and future-ready knowledge architecture that draws upon India's unparalleled diversity, thus empowering the nation to truly fulfil its potential as a global leader in innovation and discovery.

The National Commission for Scheduled Tribes (NCST) has launched an important new initiative aimed at empowering India's indigenous and tribal communities to take the lead in researching and documenting their own rich cultural heritage and societal practices. As NCST chairperson Harsh Chouhan explained, the goal is to motivate sociologists, anthropologists and other scholars from within these tribal communities to directly study and record the nuances of their own traditions, customs and historical legacies. This represents a significant shift away from the colonial-era research approaches that have long dominated the study of India's tribal populations, which were often characterized by an outsider's perspective and a failure to truly capture these communities' authentic lived experiences and perspectives.

By placing the research and documentation efforts in the hands of the tribal scholars themselves, this new initiative intends to generate a far richer, more insightful and more culturally grounded understanding of tribal societies, identities and the critical issues surrounding tribal rights and self-determination. The government hopes that this grassroots, community-driven research will provide invaluable new insights to inform more effective policymaking and better protect India's diverse indigenous populations' unique cultural heritage and political autonomy. Overall, this is an important step towards decolonising the study of tribal communities and centring their own voices, experiences and visions for the future.

The Union Ministry of Tribal Affairs is implementing a special scheme called the Conservation-cum-Development Plan (CCD), meant for 75 identified Particularly Vulnerable Tribal Groups (PVTG) in the country. Under this centrally-sponsored scheme, grants are given to states and union territories inhabited by the particularly vulnerable tribal groups to ensure that, along with development interventions, the culture of such communities is also preserved, protected and promoted. The Tribal Affairs Ministry allocates annual budgetary provisions to the states/UTs where the PVTGs inhabit. Twenty seven Tribal Research Institutes (TRI) have been set up across the country with an objective to act as a think tank and become repository of information on tribal communities. Under the scheme, 'Support to TRIs', the ministry provides funds to these institutes for undertaking studies, conducting research, providing training, fostering capacity-building initiatives and documentation on the life and culture of tribal communities, including tribes of the Northeast.

TRIs have conducted documentation (audio-video, photos and documentation in written and published form) on indigenous knowledge systems practices, cultures and customs of the tribal communities. The details of such projects/studies are available on a digital repository (https://repository.tribal.gov.in/) developed by the Ministry of Tribal Affairs. The photos and videos of such practices based on studies undertaken by TRIs can be seen at the Audio video tribal Repository (https://tribal.nic.in/repository/). These repositories can also be accessed through the Ministry's website (https://tribal.nic.in/) and Performance Dashboard (https://dashboard.tribal.gov.in/), which provides link to these web applications. The ultimate goal of establishing TRIs as a central knowledge hub, dedicated to promoting holistic tribal development.

Over the past few decades, concerted efforts have been made by the government and various organisations to protect and better integrate the forest-and hill-dwelling communities within the broader social fabric of the country. These marginalized groups, who have for centuries lived in isolation and faced significant challenges in accessing basic amenities and opportunities enjoyed by the general populace, are now slowly being brought into the mainstream. Landmark legislations such as the Forest Rights Act have empowered these communities, granting them legal rights over the land and resources they have traditionally depended on for their livelihoods.

Additionally, targeted welfare schemes, improved access to healthcare and education and greater representation in local governance have all contributed to enhancing the socioeconomic status of these historically disadvantaged groups. However, the road ahead is still long and arduous. Deeply entrenched prejudices, lack of infrastructure in remote areas and the disruption of traditional ways of life pose significant hurdles that must be overcome. Bridging the vast economic and social divide between the forest/hill dwellers and the urban mainstream will require a multi-pronged, sustained approach involving sensitive policy-making, robust implementation and a fundamental shift in societal attitudes. Only then can these vibrant, resilient communities be truly integrated and empowered to thrive alongside their fellow citizens, their unique cultures and knowledge systems celebrated as an integral part of the country's rich diversity.

A CIVILISATIONAL APPROACH

Decolonising Indian anthropology provides an opportunity to examine the field without the influence of colonial biases. This approach enables a deeper understanding of the intricate relationships among the forest, hill and plains populations. Emphasizing indigenous knowledge is essential for achieving sustainable development. Colonial narratives have frequently disregarded the historical and economic interconnections among various groups, leading to a distorted view of isolated societies. In reality, these communities were interdependent, engaging in trade, resource sharing and common cultural practices.

The neglect of these relationships served the colonial strategy of division. It is imperative to centre indigenous knowledge in anthropological research, as their insights are crucial for a comprehensive understanding of Indian society. Oral histories and folklore serve as significant informational resources, offering perspectives from indigenous communities about their past. These narratives preserve vital cultural knowledge, historical events and social structures, providing insights often overlooked in written records. We must acknowledge and honour these oral traditions as valid historical sources. The robust economic, social and cultural connections among different communities must be recognized to foster equitable and sustainable development.

India is considered one of the oldest continuing civilisations in the world and home to nearly 1.4 billion people. It's known for its cultural diversity and plurality. It is beyond the scope of one discipline to capture all the diversity, which is found in every dimension of life, in every population, in all geographies, in the environment, in modes of livelihood—and above all, in its cultures. India represents a variety of historical migrations that have resulted in racial, ethnic and religious diversity. The populations are concentrated in different regions, speak diverse languages and have a distinct way of life that sets them apart from each other. The ecological and physiographic variations of different regions of India explain its richness and diversity.

The complexity of Indian society and culture has long been a challenge for scholars of anthropology and sociology due to its diverse religious beliefs, languages and caste groups spread across different regions. India, being older than most Western civilisations, has its own scholars and knowledge sources that were often overlooked due to the Western notion of its own superiority and Orientalism. The scientific study of Indian society through anthropology, which began during the British colonisation period, struggled to comprehend the intricacies of governance in the Indian provinces.

The British had no choice but to hire anthropologists to conduct a scientific study, which would assist administrators in finding solutions to their governance issues. Additionally, the fact that India was a British colony provided an advantage for British anthropologists who came to the Indian sub-continent to test prevailing theories. These theories required empirical evidence to either support or refute them, or to develop alternative theoretical foundations. Scholars approached their studies from various theoretical perspectives based on their interests and research areas.

Those who were interested in understanding the origins of caste or to explain the diverse culture of the tribes and different communities approached their study from the 'evolutionary perspective'. Those who wanted to understand the role of history in understanding the present, approached it from the 'historical perspective'. Those who were concerned with understanding the purpose of certain social institutions or customs pivoted their study from the 'structural-functionalism perspective'. Those who wished to understand the communities and suggest measures to change the way they function approached it through a 'Marxist perspective'. Those who wanted to study the society in its totality and to establish their connection with the other units of the system, approached it with a 'civilisational perspective.' Those who wanted to understand the power structure of the gender relations adopted the 'gender perspective'. Those who wanted to understand the lower castes and their role in the society and to understand their plight approached their study through the 'subaltern perspective'. There have been other perspectives that anthropologists employed based, on the requirement of the study and their personal inclinations.

Anthropology has established itself as a strong academic discipline by employing replicable and testable approaches to study Indian society and its culture, enabling the validation or refutation of previous research findings. British anthropologists in the past were intrigued by the concept of studying 'other' and 'simple' communities in order to find practical solutions or evidence for the 'complex' problems they faced in their own societies. They approached their field studies from an evolutionary perspective, influenced by the prevailing academic discussions of the time. India and other colonies were seen as 'infants of the society' due to the dominance of evolutionary theories.

Scholars sought out 'primitive' or 'simple' societies in the hope of understanding their social institutions, with the belief that this knowledge could shed light on the complexities of their own societies. They viewed the colonies and non-Western societies as being in the early stages of evolution, with the hypothesis that these societies would eventually become more complex over time. The evolutionary lens through which Indian society and culture were studied had the potential to undermine their independent significance, as it primarily focussed on comparing them to Western societies. This perspective further bolstered Western superiority and the notion that non-Western societies were merely backwards and straightforward.

Understanding the historical texts and drawing interpretations based on these historical sources gave rise to the orientalist and Indological approaches in studying Indian society and culture. With the British taking up the administrative role more vigorously, they faced problems in understanding its diverse and variant social institutions and cultures. Some of the British officers thought by depending on the written records and the scriptures that are native to India they could throw some light to bring uniformity to the diverse cultures and social institutions. They heavily depended on the travellers accounts to understand India from a historical perspective. The acceptance of the Scripture as historical evidence gave the impression that Indian society is static and uniform in nature, whereas empirically, India provides a contrary view. This particular criticism against the use of the Scriptures as the historical evidence had led to the rise of importance on the empiricism and collecting of first hand data by the Anthropologists in India.

Later scholars, with a keen interest in studying Indian society and culture, shifted their focus away from relying heavily on scriptures. Instead, they sought to comprehend the intricate historical processes that shaped Indian society. Consequently, they concluded that the present society and culture are the outcomes of lengthy and intricate processes. Oommen (1998) identified seven significant historical processes that have profoundly influenced contemporary Indian society and culture.

(i) The Aryan 'advent', (ii) Rise of Indian protestant religions–Jainism, Buddhism and Sikhism—against certain Hindu religious practices and the subsequent revival of Hinduism, (iii) The coming of non-Indic religions as immigrant religions and their impact on the native religions and the people, (iv) Muslim 'conquests', (v) Western colonialism, (vi) Indian independence movement and (vii) partition of the Indian sub-continent. Indian society and its culture were deeply influenced by these seven historical processes, leaving a lasting impact on various aspects including religion, caste, land tenure, architecture, the concept of nation and nationalism, economy, politics and demography.

Anthropologist L.H. Morgan classified societies into Savagery, Barbarism and Civilisation, in his work, *Ancient Society* (1877), suggesting that non-Western societies were primarily in the Savagery and Barbarism stages, while Western societies were in the Civilisation stage. This raises the question of what exactly constitutes civilisation. Pre-historians and archaeologists classify sites as either 'civilisations' or 'primitive' based on their material findings. However, this approach faced significant criticism when applied to existing societies and cultures, as it implied the superiority or inferiority of specific cultures and societies. Academic discussions during that time influenced young anthropologists to abandon the practice of categorising societies as primitive (simple) or civilisations (complex) and instead encouraged them to view them as cultures with equal value in their own unique ways.

Numerous scholars attempted to comprehend cultures through the lens of civilisational perspective after receiving training from this particular school of thought. This perspective aims to analyse every aspect of society and culture in relation to one another, forming an intricate network that offers a holistic understanding rather than studying individual components in isolation.

Since the time of postulation of evolutionary theory, anthropologists are familiar with the term 'civilisation', but it was the pioneering work of Robert Redfield of Chicago University, United States of America, whose efforts brought movement in the history and development of anthropology by the introduction of the study of civilisation. According to him, civilisation has two main dimensions, namely folk and urban. He studied folk-villages and urban centres and made an effort to understand the patterns and processes of interaction between them. Hence, he developed the concepts of folk society, urban society and folk-urban continuum. Since then, the study of a village as a unit of rural civilisation and urban centre as a unit of urban civilisation came into existence. In the development of a civilisation, religion holds an important place and in order to understand the role of religion in the development of civilisation, Robert Redfield developed the concept of Great and Little traditions as he defines civilisations as a complex whole of great and little traditions.

According to him, the Great tradition refers to the formal literate tradition of a civilisation, which is regulated by the elites of the society, while the Little tradition refers to the formal illiterate tradition of rural people living within a civilisation. He also introduced the term 'cultural specialist', who mediates between the two traditions (Robert Redfield, 1953, 1956). Many anthropologists of America such as Oscar Lewis, Mc Kim Marriott, Milton Singer and Mandel Baum, supported Redfield's theory and added upon the study of civilisation as proposed by Redfield. Redfield and his followers visited India and studied Indian villages in order to understand the Indian civilisation. It was he who initiated the point in the history of dimensions and of civilisation in anthropology. It is because of this reason that he is known as the founder of the civilisational school of study of anthropological thought.

His followers, such as Marriott, Singer, Lewis, etc., are also known as Redfieldians or Civilisationists. Robert Redfield was well aware of the fact that civilisation began with writing, urban life and civil government to control the area. But he also observed that the history of world was witness to the phenomenon that man had achieved the stage of civilisation nearly 5,000 years before today. Why the, he wondered, were certain cultural groups in the stage of primitive, some in the stage of advanced and some in between the two. Observing these facts, he came to the conclusion that civilisations has many dimensions such as folk and urban, on the basis of residence and Great traditions and Little traditions, on the basis of written and oral traditions. In India, the dimensions of civilisation are tribal, rural and urban. Redfield believed that both folk and urban civilisations were not in isolation, but rather interdependent and interactive. It was on this idea that he developed the concept of folk-urban continuum in order to understand the processes of interaction between folk and urban, the two aspects of the civilisation.

In order to understand the interaction between folk and urban civilisation, he divided the traditions into two parts, oral and written. The oral tradition is the property of folk-people, whereas written tradition belongs to the urban people. The folk-people with oral traditions are termed as Little traditions and the urban people with written traditions have been designated as Great traditions by Robert Redfield. He believed that civilisation 'is a complex structure of the Great and Little traditions'. The civilisational perspective believes that every aspect of society and culture are interlinked and interdependent; one has to study them in their totality to understand the societies and cultures better.

Cohn (1971) points to four broad approaches/directions that can be used to understand Indian civilisation. They are: Catalogue approach; Cultural Essence approach; Cultural Communication approach; and Approaching India as a Type.

The Cataloguing of Traits approach entails recording traits, institutions and qualities presumed to be essentially Indian. The variations and deviations that India may represent are examined in terms of mean or mode statistical measures. India and its population reflect diversity, which may be explicable in terms of geographical, ecological, regional, class or religious differences. However, the emphasis of the approach is to list out traits or qualities that are distinctly Indian or contribute to Indianness. This, of course, is primarily based on assuming the notion of what it means to be Indian and these can vary from scholar to scholar.

The Reading of Cultural Essence approach entails the discovery of essential style and process—the cultural essences truly representative of Indian civilisation since its inception, but not trait or content. The cultural essence reflects India in its true spirit, which the country has imbibed over the years in the wake of historical and various other exigencies. It indicates that India is not statistically measurable. Rather, its essence may be understood in terms of concepts like 'unity in diversity', 'tolerance and brotherhood' and 'respect for the spiritual and divine'. The concept of ethos is essentially abstract and deductive in nature. It again is highly subjective as a concept.

The Cultural Communication approach entails focussing on the ways and processes through which the content of the civilisational system are transmitted and communicated through different levels of society. It draws attention towards the structural integration of Indian civilisation. The works of social anthropologists McKim Marriott (1955) and Robert Redfield (1956) provide a significant basis for understanding the unity and interdependence of various parts of a civilisational entity. Marriott highlights cultural synthesis and interaction between Great tradition and Little tradition, while focussing on festivals celebrated in a small north Indian village, Kishangarhi in Uttar Pradesh. Similarly, Redfield's analysis reflects constant interaction and communication between great tradition and little tradition in the form of the folk-urban continuum, which stands for a symbiotic and interdependent relationship between the two.

The Analysing Indian Civilisation as a Type approach is predominantly popular with comparative sociologists. According to this method, Indian civilisation is seen as a distinct type in juxtaposition with other societies and cultures. The emphasis is to view Indian society as a traditional unit, which is experiencing processes—such as modernization—that illustrate cultural, social and historical principles. The aim is, however, not to read distinct values or aspects that are unique to India's structure but to typify on the basis of what the structure has in common with other societies and cultures and then to examine the variations. For example, India may be seen as a 'type' in being a village society or an agrarian society, as this allows comparisons with other societies and cultures that may display a similarity in terms of the presence of a rural life and community. However, to view India as a caste society would be a futile exercise as the concept/phenomenon of caste is unique to India. This rules out the possibility of making cross-cultural/societal comparisons. The unique is thus 'scientifically incomprehensible' in view of this approach (Cohn, 1971).

McKim Marriott, in his essay, 'Little Communities in an Indigenous Civilisation', based on his fieldwork in the Kishan Garhi village in Uttar Pradesh, tried to provide us a civilisational perspective. He elaborated by saying that the village Kishan Garhi reflected the Indian universe (i) through certain aspects of its social structure and (ii) through parts of its religious culture. Marriott, in furthering his arguments, analyses the village social structure, that is, the village as an isolable whole and yet at the same time its connectedness to the other villages and the state through its economy, marriage and kinship, social relationships and politics. In analysing the religious culture, Marriott also argues how the village has unique religious pantheons and customs (parochialisation) of its own, yet it also seeks connection and tries to universalise its religious practices. Trying to imitate the social structure of the state and king by the dominant caste by establishing the jajmani system the village provides enough evidence that it stands alone. Yet, it is a component that is connected with the more extensive network to its outside society revealing the larger picture of how it is a civilisation that one needs to understand. His work proposes the twin concepts of Universalisation and Parochialisation to explain the cultural exchange between the Great and the Little traditions in India.

Singer Milton through his work, 'The Great Tradition in a Metropolitan Centre: Madras' (1958) seeks to argue how the culture of Madras, that can be categorised as a Great tradition, still resembles or seeks connection with the Little, The continual flow of cultural connection between these two makes it a whole, making it a civilisation. He analyses the cultural performances of the Little traditions such as Bhajans and the ritual customs which were adopted in a manner that the people could still participate but with certain modifications and variations to the versions of the Little traditions. Milton also analyses how the cultural performances such as music and dance are elevated to the greater tradition yet firmly grounded with the roots of the little tradition.

In his methodological study in India, Singer (1955) applies some of Redfield's views to the study of Indian civilisation. He examines Redfield's concept of 'cultural specialists' in Indian situations and formulates some other concepts 'cultural media', 'cultural performances' and 'cultural stages'. He makes a distinction between the unit of cogitation and the unit of observation. He calls such units of observation as prayers, rituals, recitations, rites and ceremonies and cultural performances. He terms 'cultural stages' as a place where cultural performances occur. They may occur in the home or in a temple or in any other sacred or secular place under a separate priesthood. He further suggests that concepts like Great and Little traditions or 'social organisation of traditions' can be formulated at more abstract levels.

On the basis of this methodological approach, Singer suggests four hypotheses regarding the civilisation of India, which may be stated as follows:

(1) That the Great tradition is in cultural continuity with the Little tradition to be found in diverse regions, villages and castes. (2) That this cultural continuity was the product and cause of a common cultural consciousness shared by most Indians and expressed in essential similarities of mental outlook and ethos. (3) That this common cultural consciousness has been formed in India with the help of certain processes and factors which also play an important role in other primary civilisations, that is, sacred books and sacred objects as fixed points of worship, a special class of literati (Brahmans) who have the authority to recite and interpret the sacred scriptures, professional story-tellers, a geography of sacred centres (temples, pilgrimage places, shrines, etc. and leading personalities who, by their identification with the Great tradition and with the masses, mediate the one to the other. (4) That the cultural continuity is so great that even the acceptance of modernising and 'progress' ideologies result in the 'traditionalizing' of apparently modern innovations.

The growth of Indian anthropology was greatly influenced by the American social (cultural) anthropologists who took up village and caste studies along with studies on the dimensions of Indian civilisation. Robert Redfield and Milton Singer were deeply concerned with the theoretical and methodological problems of studying a civilisation. M.N. Srinivas put forth the concept of Sanskritisation as the process which represents actual or aspired for cultural mobility within the framework of the established great tradition and stratification system of caste.

McKim Marriott stressed the importance of studying the religion of a little community to understand the processes of universalisation and parochialisation which operate in Indian civilisation. Globalization is yet another process which is all about connectivity, of increasing interdependence of world society into a single whole. Cultural globalization creates a global culture based on the values of multiculturism and democracy. Culture as a particularistic and localised phenomenon is fast becoming outdated with the increasing penetration of external elements of non-integrated traits accumulated through the process of globalization.

Renowned anthropologists and sociologists such as Morris E Opler, Oscar Lewis and David G. Mandelbaum and their students came to India from the US to study Indian society and culture. Many of these scholars did fieldwork in the villages of and tested their hypotheses on the village studies. Opler came to India in 1951 and did acceptable research in the village of Senapur in Uttar Pradesh. Along with Indian anthropologist R.D. Singh, he developed a concept of unity and extension of Indian villages. The two scholars explained how, in a village, unity and extension prevails. During celebrations, community rituals, marriages, or deaths, etc., the entire village shows cohesion and strong bonds of unity. The village follows the rule of exogamy in marriage. They marry their children outside the group; hence the sign of extended relationships can be traced. This shows the inter-relationship among distant villages. Also for trade purpose, people go out from the village and maintain business relations with the other villages and people.

Not only in these issues, there are many other factors which also show the extension of Indian villages, such as in education, procurement of medical facility, pilgrimages and to get connected with urban markets. The villagers establish contacts with the outside world, thereby showing the extended relations.

Oscar Lewis travelled to India in 1951, where he conducted his research in the village of Rampur, Uttar Pradesh. He vividly portrayed the essence of Indian village life, emphasizing the profound sense of community that exists within these settings. The connections in such villages extend beyond mere interpersonal relationships; they encompass the bond between individuals and their environment, including their land, homes, livestock and flora. This intricate web of relationships forms the foundational structure of an Indian village. Lewis further elaborated on the various connections that individuals maintain, including their ties to the land, to one another, to religious institutions, to political entities and to economic activities.

Western researchers who arrived in India after independence primarily focussed on studying caste, village dynamics and Indian civilisation through the lens of a high-caste Hindu structure, reinforcing the models proposed by Bose and Srinivas. Unfortunately, the emergence of a secular and national anthropology in India was stifled, leading to the Hinduisation and Westernisation of Indian anthropology. Indian anthropologists, obsessed with caste issues, overlooked the necessity of adopting a secular and indigenous perspective for the advancement of a national anthropology and nation-building.

N.K. Bose in his book, *Hindu Samajer Gadan* (Structure of Hindu Society, 1949), explained various social processes that shaped the Indian social structure: such as the impact of British rule, social movements in the medieval period in relation to Islam. He observed that classical Varna Jati system would not be suitable for modern India though some of its components and ideas may have functional significance. The cultural history of Indian civilisation exhibits unity in diversities. Various diversified groups are bound together by the Indian system of Jajmani, in which each caste works for the other in accordance to hereditary positions and occupations. Bose has thrown light upon characteristic traits of a civilisation, but he did not adequately distinguish the concept of civilisation from that of culture.

For Bose the study of civilisation is essentially a study of innermost, that is, matters of the mind responding to changing life-experiences of people. According to him, Indian civilisation differed from European civilisation in the basic sense that the former advocated cultural pluralism while the latter was based on war experience, leading to a spirit of nationalism. In his book, quoted earlier, Bose gives a civilisational view of Indian society. He has divided it into three parts. The first mainly belongs to the domain of ethnography, where he presents material based on his own fieldwork, primarily done among tribal communities. The second part is predominantly Indological, where he presents an account of the theory and practice of Hindu social life. The third part deals with social history.

Bose shows that the influence of Aryan or Brahminical civilisation has been greater in both extent and depth among the Mundas and the Oraons than among the Juangs or the Savaras. It is through influences of this kind that tribal communities become increasingly articulated with the wider society. The process was described as 'the Hindu Method of Tribal Absorption'. According to the author, it enabled marginal communities to become a part of Hindu society without requiring them to abandon all their particular customs. It is interesting to note that Hindu castes like Ahir, Lohar and Midha also join the tribal people in their celebrations, it is difficult to distinguish between them. As an anthropologist, Bose was interested not merely in revealing a certain pattern of culture but also in discovering the theory behind the pattern. The theory was an indispensable aid in understanding how the society actually worked.

Bose was deeply interested in the study of architecture, Indian civilisation and the caste system. During his lifetime at Puri in Odisha, he came in contact with a temple architect who initiated him in the traditional canons of Odiya architecture. He learnt from the field that a student of civilisation will have to integrate information from various levels—the text as well as the product of arts. He had an abiding interest in the material culture of the tribal people and wrote with professional skill on the technology of shifting cultivation and on various crafts such as oil-pressing, pottery and weaving.

Nirmal Kumar Bose was a prominent advocate of Hindu anthropology. In his 1929 textbook, *Cultural Anthropology*, he made a unique effort to demonstrate that ancient Hindus classified human desires and needs into economic (artha), sexual (kama) and spiritual (moksha), similar to later functional anthropologists in the West. He believed that the Hindus, like Western anthropologists, had their own understanding of human nature and behaviour that had existed for a long time. Later, Bose introduced the theory of 'Hindu Method of Tribal Absorption' in Indian anthropology, which effectively influenced subsequent generations of Indian anthropologists. This idea was initially presented in a paper at the Indian Science Congress in 1941, based on Bose's field trips among the Juang tribal community in the Pal Lahara region of Odisha.

Another scholar, D.N. Majumdar, was exposed to the teachings and writings of colonial anthropologists their theoretical contribution shaped and influenced future studies among the tribal communities in India. Majumdar ventured into new arenas of research in Indian anthropology, such as village (rural) studies, urban studies, industrialisation and modernization and its impact on the cultural change, cultural transition among the tribals and village communities. With the approach of functionalism and Ruth Benedict's 'culture pattern', he started to analyse the transforming communities with a blend of both the theories.

L.P. Vidyarthi, with his work, 'Sacred Complex as a Dimension of the Indian Civilisation', analyses the Gaya pilgrimage centre as a defining factor for Indian civilisation. He studied the sacred city of Gaya and described in detail three analytical concepts. He analyses Gaya's Sacred Geography (which has both the aspects of little and greater traditions), Sacred Performances and Sacred Specialists. These three concepts are collectively called the Sacred Complex. This reflected a level of continuity, compromise and combination between the Great and the Little traditions. The Sacred Specialists of a place, with their distinctive style of life, transmit certain elements of the Great tradition to the rural population of India. Through his study, Vidyarthi establishes that how the pilgrims who come from every corner of the India bring something that is part of the little tradition and carry something back with them that is part of the Greater tradition, making Gaya a key dimension of Indian civilisation.

In furthering the analysis of sacred complex, Vidyarthi, in collaboration with B.N. Saraswati and M, Jha, studied Kashi. They tried to understand the (i) cult of Thirthas (ii) cult of Viswanath (iii) cult of Ganga (iv) cult of Smasan and offered an analysis of how these could be understood as dimensions of civilisation and its characteristics. With his analysis, Vidyarthi proved that it was not necessary that scholars should restrict themselves to tribal, rural and urban dimensions and their interchangeability, but could understand Sacred Complex such as Gaya and Kashi and offer dimensionality in studying Indian civilisation as a whole.

Another prised contribution that he put forward is the Nature-Man-Spirit complex, while carrying out his research among the Maler community of a hill tribe in Bihar. During his research, he found that the Maler worldview revolves around the nature they live in and depends on the environment they make use of for economic, religious and social reasons. Nature is imbedded inseparably in the lives of Maler. Their points of reference, their metaphors and their associations revolve around the nature they are connected with. His research also proved how man plays the role of centrality in this whole complex. He analyses their social structure and kinship and tries to see the process of socialisation and personality formations that are deeply rooted in the culture of the Malers. Their belief in the spirit of ancestors and their understanding of continued communication and seeking guidance from those who are not physically present, reflect the complexity of the thought process of the tribes.

Vidyarthi, with his landmark anthropological concepts of Sacred Complex of Gaya and Kashi and Nature-Man-Spirit Complex, developed a theoretical base for studying Indian civilisation and this attracted the attention of a number of scholars who were encouraged to work on the concepts. Several anthropologists have examined the Sacred Complex of classical civilisations in India, with studies conducted by M. Jha in Janakpur (1971), V.S. Upadhyaya in Dwarika (1974), Vidyarthi, Saraswati and Jha in Kashi (1978) and V.P. Sharma in Ayodhya (1973, 1984). These studies highlight the significant roles of Sacred Specialists in upholding tradition and facilitating evolution in the core of major traditions.

The evolutionary approach is not suitable for analysing India; instead, the historical approach is more appropriate. The historical approach rejects the idea that tribes represent different stages in cultural evolution and cannot be placed in a linear sequence of development. In India, tribes have coexisted with civilisations and other social groups since ancient times. Archaeological evidence from Daojali-Hading indicates that tribal communities in the Garo Hills were cultivating crops during the Neolithic period, alongside what are now considered 'non-tribal' communities. This suggests that, in the past, both tribes and non-tribes were at similar stages of development, challenging the notion of a linear evolutionary progression in Indian society.

In India, the distinction between tribes and non-tribes is not based on cultural evolution stages, but rather on interactions. Scholars like N.K. Bose, S.C. Dube and F.G. Bailey have studied tribes historically due to the colonial influence on the evolutionary approach. Unlike in Australia and Africa, where there are clear differences between local communities and civilisations, in India, civilisation has existed from the start, with tribes constantly interacting with it.

The impact of G.S. Ghurye, Radcliffe Brown and Evans Pritchard on M.N. Srinivas is clearly reflected in Srinivas's perspectives on individualism, society and culture. He emphasized the need to develop indigenous concepts to understand the Indian social reality. His central ideas related mainly with structural-functionalism, villages in India, the caste system and social mobility. His work presents holistic and profound understanding of society of that time. He has studied issues relating to national integration, dowry, bride wealth, the effect of industrialisation on villages, urban communities, hospitals, gender issues, etc. Srinivas has done prolific research to study regional culture of South India and propounded various concepts to understand caste mobility and social change in Indian society. These concepts are Sanskritisation, Westernisation, secularisation and the dominant caste and concept of vertical and horizontal caste solidarity. He viewed village as a vertical entity that consisted of several horizontal layers—each of which was a caste.

Sanskritisation brought changes within the framework of Indian tradition, whereas Westernisation was a change resulting from the contact of British socio-economic and cultural innovations. Westernisation is a process which includes all cultural changes and institutional reforms inflicted upon Indian society as it came in political and cultural proximity with British rule and governance. The changes occurred in various attributes of Indian society, namely, technology, institutions, ideology and beliefs. Westernisation incorporates scientific approach, individualism, egalitarianism, rationalism and liberalism, rise of nationalism, establishment of technological and educational institutions and new political culture and leadership in the nation. It has assigned some flexibility to the earlier rigid caste system, promoted disintegration of joint family and induced several social reform activities. The abolition of the practice of sati is a prominent example of the impact of Westernisation.

Srinivas believed that village studies were the best way to learn about Indian society, culture and civilisation. They signified a transition in social anthropology's emphasis from tribal studies to studies of peasants' lifestyles, social movements and societal change. Srinivas made a significant contribution to the realistic understanding of villages. At the outset, he busted the myths that surrounded villages in India. The Select Committee on the Affairs of the East Indian Company's Fifth Report treated the village as a little republic; a stagnant, passive and unchanging entity. Srinivas countered this overly simplistic view by bringing out the reality. He shed light on inequality, disease and illiteracy as also village resources. Srinivas made the point that, rather than being egalitarian, villages were driven by hierarchy and influence of politics. He drew attention to the gap between lived reality in villages and perceived or imagined reality in the minds of policymakers.

S.C. Dube, in the early 1950, developed a keen interest in village studies, especially studies of those villages that had a multi-caste social structure. He returned to India to study a village in Hyderabad, called Shamirpet. He studied the interrelationships of Hindus and Muslims to understand jati relationships that existed between communities. Dube, as part of his field research, also studied the impact of community development planning on villages. In his book, *Indian Village* (1955), he undertakes a thorough study of Shamirpet. The book presents adequate information on historical, geographical and political background as well as social, economic and religious practices of village in India.

Dube's aim has been to present a clear picture of an Indian village life and he has basically used the structural–functional approach. He stated that economic system of rural India was based on occupational mobility, interdependence and caste's functional specialisation. He emphasized that caste ranking in villages mainly relied on rituals and not on an economic system. Family ceremonies, village ceremonies and communal festivals are the major types of religious services and festivals which are observed in the village. Also, the Muslims and the Hindus freely interacted with each other during festivals.

The dominance of American schools has influenced the position of Indian anthropology, which has been largely colonial. Professor Bose believed that by immersing themselves in the study of Indian civilisation, Indian social scientists could establish their own areas of expertise and contribute to the development of theoretical and methodological issues in the study of humanity. Surajit Sinha believes that despite the various trends, Indian anthropologists have not given sufficient consideration to developing a distinct research methodology for studying the distinctive cultural patterns and processes of the sub-continent. However, there are some exceptions: such as Bose, Das, Chattopadhyay, Karvey and Vidyarthi (Sinha, 1978).

Saraswati, Baidyanath (1979), in the book, *Pottery-making Cultures and Indian Civilisation*, shows how India gave a vital space to pottery in history and that is the reason why that period was called the Ceramic age. Pottery-making in the Neolithic age helped anthropologists a lot in studying the lifestyle of people living in that era. There are many communities and tribes which practise pottery and are totally dependent on pottery art for their financial requirements.

Surajit Sinha (1926–2002) expressed unique and critical perspectives on Indian anthropology, which have been overlooked by many anthropologists in India. Sinha's published works in 1970 and 1980 highlighted his belief that Indian anthropology—because of training under colonial anthropologists—continued to mimic Western approaches even after independence, challenging the widely accepted theory of Hindu method of tribal absorption advocated by his mentor Nirmal Kumar Bose. There is a standard critique of Indian anthropology advanced by some of the Indian anthropologists. The critics say that Indian anthropology is the product of a colonial tradition and that Indian anthropologists for various reasons followed their colonial masters in one way or the other (Abhijit Guha, 2019).

On the reverse side of the critiques, there also existed a view that an Indian form of anthropology could be discerned in many ancient Indian texts and scriptures before the advent of a colonial anthropology that was introduced by European scholars, administrators and missionaries in the Indian subcontinent. As early as 1938, Jogendra Chandra Ghosh in his interesting article, *Hindu Anthropology*, published in the Anthropological Papers (New series) no. 5 of the University of Calcutta, tried to show that before sixth-century BCE, the Hindus innovated various measurements on human body and its parts, which in European terms may be called Anthropometry, an important branch of Physical Anthropology. Ghosh began his article by saying that anthropology was one of the modern progressive sciences. Anthropometry and Ethnology were the two important branches of this science.

He offered some facts to show that the Hindus had their Anthropometry and Ethnology from a very early period. Ghosh further pointed out that the earliest record of those anthropometric measurements was found in Susruta-Samhita, a medical treatise written by the ancient Hindus. He also held that the ancient Hindus had their own notion of Ethnology and its first expression was found in the *Rigveda*, in which 'races' were classified on the basis of their skin colour. Suffice it to say that Ghosh was hinting at the fact that 'racial theory' became a major theme in later day Western anthropology (Abhijit Guha, 2019).

Indian anthropology has been subject to criticism from both colonial and Hindu perspectives. However, these critiques have overlooked the materialistic, socially committed, secular and nationalist aspects of Indian anthropology. Prior to and after independence, Indian anthropology was flourishing under the guidance of exceptional anthropologists. Unfortunately, instead of studying the socially committed works of these later anthropologists, critics have chosen to focus solely on criticising the pioneers. This failure to recognize and honour the nationalist predecessors has led Indian anthropologists to rely heavily on the wisdom of Western scholars.

Surajit Sinha had a negative perspective on the growth of Indian anthropology after independence, considering it as a mere imitation of Western anthropology. He failed to recognize the nationalist trends within Indian anthropology, despite acknowledging the independent ideas of some of his teachers. Sinha never conducted a comprehensive historical review of Indian anthropology, which would have revealed the presence of early scholars who attempted to establish a nationalist tradition in the field. Therefore, there is a pressing need for a new discourse that explores the nationalist trend in Indian anthropology within the discipline of New Indian Social History (Abhijit Guha, 2019).

India's rich social history is best understood through a civilisational lens that examines the intricate interconnections between the diverse geographic regions and cultural spheres that have coexisted and interacted across the subcontinent for millennia. A key aspect of this civilisational framework is the dynamic relationship between the hill-forest regions and the expansive plains that have long shaped the contours of Indian society. The hill and forest areas, often inhabited by tribal and indigenous communities, have historically maintained a symbiotic yet complex rapport with the settled agrarian populations of the plains. This mutually dependent yet sometimes fraught dynamic has given rise to exchanging goods, ideas and social customs, forging an indelible bond between these distinct ecological zones. The hill tribes, with their intimate knowledge of the forest resources and specialised livelihood practices, have provided the plains dwellers with vital forest produce, labour and cultural influences, while also serving as conduits for the diffusion of Sanskritic and other mainstream religious and philosophical traditions into the hinterlands.

Conversely, the agricultural surpluses, technologies and administrative structures of the plains-based kingdoms and empires have profoundly impacted the social, economic and political organisation of the hill and forest communities, leading to a constant process of cultural synthesis and transformation. This civilisational framework, which recognizes the Hill-Forest-Plains continuum as a crucial axis of Indian social history, allows us to appreciate the composite and ever-evolving nature of the subcontinent's diverse cultural heritage.

CHAPTER 5

Discarding Colonial Anthropology

Anthropology originated from the colonial expansion of Europe, shaping the dynamics between anthropologists and the communities they observed. This historical context influenced the methodologies and concepts within the discipline, such as the perception of the anthropologist as an 'objective outsider', leading ironically to potential biases and exploitation in research. The Imperial culture was considered superior to that of indigenous cultures, especially those of Asia and Africa. The colonizers strongly believed that they knew the 'others' and they defined who those 'others' were. This assumption led them to colonise countries and annexe them as their own.

The decolonisation of previously colonized populations has challenged the conventional position of anthropologists, leading to a standoff between anthropologists and the communities they once observed. The postcolonial period necessitates a re-evaluation of the roles of anthropologists and the adoption of more pertinent methodologies and concepts. To explore alternative approaches, one must focus attention on the 'native ethnography'.

Anthropologists working in India and Africa were mostly associated with governments that worked from 'outside'. The integrity of such anthropologists is being questioned today by people in Asia, Africa and Latin America, as well as by ethnic minorities in North America, which is pushing scholars to examine themselves critically and reevaluate some of their presumptions. The following questions can be posed: Is anthropology a truly universal discipline? Can it be utilised for explicit self-study and self-knowledge by all people? Is it able to meet the challenge of the oppressed people who seek solutions to their problems? Is it useful only in providing information about powerless people to those in power? Is it to remain an adjunct to Western exploitation and manipulation of Third World people?

According to Lewis (1973), this perspective contends that, given its contentious colonial past, anthropology owes a duty to the cultures it has previously studied—mostly wrongly. It should not be limited to the West in its knowledge acquisition of non-Western and non-White populations.

Anthropology and other social sciences ought to create a framework that accommodates people's interests in theory and practice in order to serve everyone's needs.

The post-colonial period has witnessed a perplexing patron-client relationship, which is distinct from the colonial connections. Indian anthropologists, in their attempt to analyse this relationship, have uncritically adopted models from the Western context, disregarding the perils of their applicability in India and their underlying ideological assumptions. Such unproductive imitation has rendered the subject almost irrelevant. Moreover, the borrowed theories tend to be selective, primarily serving the purpose of maintaining the existing system. The shift observed since 1960 in Indian anthropology can be attributed to the replacement of British scholars with those who have had a greater Western-oriented approach. The support from various Western foundations, the training of Indian anthropologists in Western universities and the widespread distribution of Western anthropological literature at affordable prices have facilitated this transformation. The creative thinking of the new generation of anthropologists has remained insignificant.

A DISCIPLINE OF THE MASTERS

The anthropology of India has its origin in British colonialism. The discipline of anthropology, like any other social science, is historically and socially conditioned. It emerged during the colonial period to meet the administrative needs of the expanding colonial regime. The administrative problems that arose in the expansion and consolidation of the colonial rule shed light on the fact that the rulers had scarce data on the colonized people. The intellectual climate of Western Europe and the political and economic conditions then favoured the development of social sciences, particularly anthropology and sociology. The intellectual environment in Western Europe, coupled with the prevailing political and economic circumstances, fostered the growth of social sciences, including anthropology and sociology.

The development of sociology and anthropology in India can be traced back to the dynamic between the ruling colonizers and the colonized population. British administrators recognized the importance of understanding Indian culture for effective governance, leading to the early collection of data on customs and social structures by figures such as Henry Verelst in 1769. Subsequently, British officials and missionaries were posted in different parts of the country, which produced knowledge on local societies and cultures to acquaint the colonial government to facilitate the smooth functioning and implementation of laws. The purpose of official anthropology was to contribute to scientific knowledge and strengthen and improve British rule.

The anthropologist's work was pursued in the interest of the colonizers in terms of the concepts and theories they developed as well as the roles they played. Indian society, as seen by the Britishers, was a 'traditional' society—an antithetical 'other' of modern European society. The society was made up of separate religious communities; castes were a distinct social group, with the tribal population at the periphery. The terms 'tribe', 'aborigine', 'savage' and 'barbarian' have been used. The study material of social anthropology presents a definition that prompts one to consider it as a product of fiction created by the dominant culture.

The discipline of anthropology, along with many other disciplines, was one of the sites where these articulations took shape. In the Indian system, being part of a tribe signifies being separate from the state and civilisation, rather than reaching a specific level and living alongside the state and civilisation. Tribal studies in India, or the study relating to the multi-dimension of tribes in India, started during the late British period, particularly after the 1930s. From 1930 to 1950, only British scholars undertook such studies. The British attributed the 'backwardness' and the 'inferiority' of the tribes to the habitation structure and isolation of the people, who were shy of joining the mainstream society. In his classic work, *The People of India*, Rilsey summarized his views on the origin and classification of the Indian races based on his historical speculations and anthropometric research. His contemporaries and subsequent writers criticised Risley for focussing so much on the racial basis of caste and stressing anthropometric measurements. Anthropologists in India are defined by the roles of the coloniser, outsider and the 'objective' observer.

In the colonial period, there was a policy of isolating the tribes. As isolationists, the British in position declared certain contiguous and thickly populated tribal belts as 'Excluded and Partially Excluded' areas. The policy of isolation was supported by the then-separatist anthropologists who advocated for tribal reserves. For them, broadly speaking, isolation referred to a phenomenon where a group of people or communities was disconnected from other communities and resided in remote pockets with their own distinct ways of life. It could be in a relative form, complete or partial. Subscribing to isolation, Elwin in 1939 suggested the establishment of the 'National Park' theory (Mann, 1993).

After the country gained independence, Indian anthropologists acknowledged that anthropology in India was predominantly a replica of Western practices, with only a handful of exceptional studies conducted by some of the pioneering researchers. In addition, there was a notable absence of research on the history of Indian anthropology within the field itself. Interestingly, foreign and Western anthropologists who have studied various aspects of Indian society and culture have shown minimal enthusiasm for documenting the history of Indian anthropology.

Some Indian anthropologists have critiqued Indian anthropology, claiming colonial traditions heavily influence it. They argue that Indian anthropologists have, for different reasons, emulated their colonial predecessors to some extent. In 1971, Surajit Sinha, a renowned Indian anthropologist, highlighted in his article published in the Journal of the Indian Anthropological Society that despite significant advancements in research and professional expertise in social and cultural anthropology over the past century, Indian anthropologists continued to rely heavily on Western and colonial traditions. Sinha further explored this colonial dependence in a chapter titled, 'India: A Western Apprentice', in the book *Anthropology: Ancestors and Heirs*, edited by Marxist anthropologist Stanley Diamond and published by Mouton in 1980. In this chapter, Sinha discussed the process of assimilating various aspects of Western anthropological traditions, concluding on a pessimistic note. Amitabha Basu and Suhas Biswas, both professors at the prestigious Indian Statistical Institute in Kolkata, critiqued Indian anthropology in their article titled, 'Is Indian Anthropology Dead/Dying'. Published in the Journal of the Indian Anthropological Society, they questioned the social relevance of the subject in the post-colonial era, suggesting that it was either dead or dying (Basu and Biswas, 1980).

Interestingly, other commentators, such as Balakrishnan (1980) disagreed with Basu and Biswas, arguing that anthropology in India remained valuable for the ruling and privileged classes, but may not be as useful for the masses. Renowned social anthropologist and sociologist André Béteille highlighted in a 1997 article in the Sociological Bulletin that Indian sociologists tended to overlook the work of their predecessors and lack innovation in their research. In an article titled 'How Egalitarian Is Indian Sociology?', Vivek Kumar highlighted the presence of a caste bias within the field of Indian sociology and social anthropology. Biswanath Debnath criticised Indian anthropologists for not developing their own tradition and instead imitating colonial practices by studying small tribal communities in his article in the Economic and Political Weekly. Similarly, almost the same kind of voice on the purported neo-colonial bias in Indian anthropology was heard in the writings of J.J. Roy-Burman in 2011 (Abhijit Guha, 2019).

It is evident from the above discussion that many anthropologists should have made efforts to study forest and hill people from a historical and civilisational approach. Anthropology faced criticism for its colonial nature, particularly due to its Eurocentric perspective and its association with colonisation through the concept of social evolution, which defined 'civilisation' as synonymous with the Western world. It can be argued that the Indian university curriculum is still in the hangover of this colonial modernity. At this point, literature produced by outsiders, such as colonial anthropologists, historians and writers who rely on existing exhaustive reviews, definitions and terms, may not be acceptable to the native people. It is imperative to reject the writings of colonial anthropologists at this juncture. This calls for an urgent rewriting, reviving and decolonising the history of forest and hill people in India from civilisational and native perspectives, which ultimately ends with deconstructing tribes/tribals in India. In this context, there is a need to promote a new Indian social history as one possible alternative.

This analysis presents a critical examination of dominant narratives from a post-colonial and oppositional perspective within the framework of cultural studies.

The civilisational approach is significant because it can give recognition and value to individuals who have been marginalized or ignored by dominant discourses. This research method involves challenging colonial historiography and creating a new narrative that accurately represents the history of the people. The imbalance is corrected by reassessing and rewriting history with a focus on individuals' nature, role and function.

NEEDED A REVISED CURRICULUM

The focus of social anthropology in the colonial period was primarily on teaching and learning about basic topics like social institutions, tribes, castes, religious and ethnic communities, community development, applied and action anthropology and methodology. However, there was minimal emphasis on socio-cultural history and civilisation, with students not being encouraged to explore the social history and civilisation of Indian societies from their own viewpoints.

Anthropologists must abandon their value neutrality and cease their resistance to significant, large-scale changes. They should adopt a historical and contextual approach to study traditional, regional and national communities. Participant observation and case study methods are not the final methodological judgements in anthropology, those should not determine the scope of anthropological research. The task is formidable, but let there be attempts to make the subject socially relevant.

The academic effort to study and deliberate on tribes in India is marred by a singular dominant interpretation. Besides, it is hugely influenced by the Western imagination of tribes and tribal life. For example, 'isolation' is one of the defining features of tribal life in the Western world, which has been imposed by academicians in India without looking at the indigenous reality. The policy implications of a wrong understanding have been colossal. The development has often been looked at as anti-tribal in post-independent India. A course-correction—setting the narrative right for protecting tribal identity and ensuring development—is needed of the hour. It has enormous implications for national security and the development of the nation.

Shedding the colonial identity and formulating a post-colonial identity for the discipline depends much on how the subject is taught in colleges and universities. The University Grants Commission, the apex body for regulating higher education, established the Curriculum Development Committees (CDC) for developing curricula in different disciplines, including anthropology, in 1998. The committee report does not specifically dwell on the colonial base of the discipline and ways to overcome it by appropriately revising the curricula and textbooks. There was no mention of phasing out outdated textbooks and preparing textbooks with a contemporary focus.

Indian Knowledge Systems (IKS) is an attempt to revive the acknowledgement of Indian knowledge, such as arts, crafts, literature, tradition and other forms lost in the intergenerational transfer process. The National Education Policy (NEP)-2020 had laid the foundation for IKS and aimed to integrate it into curricula at all levels of education. This endeavour is to erase all traces of servitude created by the Western education system and elevate the pride in India's heritage and legacy among students (UGC, 2022).

In this backdrop, the need is to provide requisite training to students and carry out research relevant to contemporary society. Curricula should reflect the dynamic changes in society and books prescribed should relate to national, regional and local issues. Learners need to be sensitised about the conditions and objectives of knowledge construction during the colonial period and later. Alternative material based on current practices in the discipline and society becomes more relevant. Books written by Indian scholars should receive the importance they deserve. More textbooks by Indian authors need to be commissioned as alternatives to books by foreign authors. Opportunities are available in the form of Indian Council of Social Science Research (ICSSR) study methodology courses and capacity-building programmes, UGC Human Resource Development Centres and induction programmes for newly recruited faculty. All these agencies and opportunities should give priority to decolonisation and non-Western and indigenous perspectives.

There are many important areas to be considered for inclusion in the curricula of Indian anthropology departments for decolonising and making them more contemporary. Is it possible to draft a vision and mission statement for anthropologists encompassing such areas? There can be multiple versions, but clarity on the vision and mission for the discipline is important to give focus to its scope. What are the institutional structures for the execution or operationalization of the vision of the discipline? Professional associations, research journals and departments of universities and colleges can play a role in this regard.

CRAFTING A NEW PERSPECTIVE

Many researchers are increasingly scrutinising established anthropologists, questioning many of their borrowed theoretical and methodological presumptions. The applicability of these presumptions to the urgent problems the nation faces is the subject of a contentious debate. This rising chorus of dissent is becoming a powerful intellectual force and demands a departure from conventional anthropological theories and research projects. The scathing criticism of present ideas and models draws attention to how inadequate modern anthropological methods are in tackling societal issues and comprehending new developments. The need to adjust to the changing social context drives the need for new viewpoints and methodologies in anthropology, which are made possible by the revelation of these flaws.

Various testimonies from different disciplines, such as literary, epigraphic, historic and linguistic, along with comparative civilisational and historical evidence, clearly indicate that in order to study and understand the relationships between the people of the plains and the people of the forests in India, it is necessary to break the barriers of individual disciplines. Only through an interdisciplinary approach can a comprehensive and integrated view emerge. A multidisciplinary approach is essential to truly grasp the deep integration between the Indian plainsman and the forester. To comprehend the extent of knowledge required to explore and grasp the intricate connection between forests and plains, as well as the diverse communities inhabiting these regions, one must appreciate the wide range of disciplines involved. A multi-disciplined approach is, indeed, the only way forward.

In order to conduct a review or contemplate a change in mindset and behaviour, national educational organisations must undergo a significant psychological transformation. This is the initial step in reevaluating and altering the Western anthropological perspective on the indigenous communities residing in the forests and hills of India.

The following assumptions must be brought into the teaching-learning syllabus in the universities and other national institutions:

- Course curriculum and syllabus that are found to have Western concepts/perspectives taught at the Indian educational institutions (colleges, universities, other institutions) must be updated to reflect the ground reality from an Indian perspective.
- There must be a revival of Indian narratives on traditional communities residing in forests, plains and hills. Community insider writings must be encouraged.
- Research on the understanding of Janjatiya Samuh should be carried out on three important aspects: 'Asmita' (identity), 'Astitava' (existence) and 'Vikas' (development).
- Efforts must be made to understand and devise characteristics of janjatis from their own definitions.
- We must look at the janjatis from the standpoint of their worldview and the relationship between other jatis and the state.
- We should understand the origin stories, folklore, spiritual aspects, worldview(s), philosophy, lifestyle and continuity of the Janjati Samuh of India in their own ecological setting(s).

- There is an urgent need to document oral histories/stories of janjati communities and references to janjati communities in ancient Indian texts/classical literature and vernacular texts.
- An understanding of the common rituals, customs and traditional cultural practices between Indian civilisation and janjati communities must be promoted.
- Collating, collecting and analysing the existing literature with a focus on understanding local wisdom, knowledge and practices should be done.
- A detailed catalogue of reference materials, which reflect the Indian narratives on the janjati community, must be prepared.
- A review of the colonial concepts, names or labels imposed on the janjati communities of India should be undertaken.
- There is a need to understand the 'social capital' of the Janjati Samuh with specific reference to the community-driven practices.
- Critical analysis of the working/relevance of Schedule-V and Schedule-VI areas mentioned in the Constitution of India ought to be carried out.
- The traditional dispute resolution practices of the janjatis of India should be understood in the proper perspective.
- Elaborate research is required on different approaches to the study of Indian civilisation.
- India is a religious nation and further research must be done at pilgrimage sites spread around the nation, where religious festivals are held.
- There is a need to change the whole narrative of janjatis in Indian anthropology.
- Syllabus on community language, literature and folklore must be incorporated.
- The languages of the forest and hill people are treated as 'unscheduled languages'. In the wake of a change in the educational scenario, many of the tribal languages are facing the threat of extinction. The loss of language may adversely affect tribal culture, especially their folklore. This should be taken note of and action implemented.
- The preservation and documentation of tribal languages is the main objective. It is crucial to promote education in the native language at the primary level. Additionally, there will be a focus on promoting books and other publications in tribal languages.
- The curricula for meta skill upgradation are to include aspects of tribal games and sports.
- A new methodology is needed to study the forest and hill people's narratives. Therefore, to move away from the colonial constructs/

narratives and their perspectives or framework, the new methodology shall include the following approaches in understanding the Janjati Samuh of India:

1. Indological approach
2. Civilisational approach
3. Historical approach
4. Cultural relativistic approach
5. Autoethnograpical approach
6. Phenomenological approach
7. Ethno-methodological approach.

- Tribal communities have accumulated extensive knowledge in adapting to various environmental challenges by residing in diverse terrains such as hills, forests, coastal areas and deserts. Their expertise is evident in their innovative water harvesting methods, traditional irrigation systems, construction of cane bridges, desert survival skills and utilisation of forest resources for medicinal purposes. It is crucial to document and safeguard their invaluable wisdom to prevent its loss due to modernization and the passage of time. This can be done by establishing a centre to train tribal youth in areas of traditional wisdom, by organising exhibits at appropriate places and by transferring such knowledge to non-tribal regions.

Over time, indigenous communities—which are renowned for their independence and self-sufficiency—have developed a distinctive therapeutic practice using locally obtained herbs and natural resources. They have developed their own systems of diagnosis and treatment that incorporate faith-based healing, spiritual energy and taboo beliefs. Tribal groups exhibit notable variations in their health state and healthcare service utilisation, which can be attributed to cultural customs, exposure to diverse societies and the degree of adaptability. Against this background, it is to promote the traditional health care system and also a synthesis of the Indian systems of medicine like Ayurveda and Siddha with the tribal system.

- Validate identified tribal remedies (folk claims) used in different tribal areas.
- Encourage, document and patent tribals' traditional medicines.
- Promote cultivation of medicinal plants related value addition strategies through imparting training to youth.
- Promote the formation of a strong force of tribal village health guides through regular training-cum-orientation courses.
- Formulate area-specific strategies to improve access to and utilisation of health services.

The Janjatis (Scheduled Tribes) of India have their own specific origin stories (jati puranas), their own deities and their own rituals and festivals. These, taken together, reflect the core strengths, commitments and beliefs of the tribals. They also have their own glorious histories that include several revered heroes, saints and kings. They often have their own dialects. They are the carriers of specific and valuable skills and technologies. Individual janjatis are associated with specific parts of India and their places of origin or habitation have specific geomorphological features, such as rivers, vegetation and animals. The janjatis have strong associations with these. For them, all of these have a special sanctity. They revere the hills, rivers, water bodies, vegetation and animals of their specific geography and undertake pilgrimages to pay their respects to these sacred entities. This reverence for the land and its specific flora and fauna arises from a deep sense of oneness with nature and all beings, which is also expressed in their stories and songs.

The geography they hold as sacred is often endowed with extraordinary beauty, richness and grandeur. These several geographies, histories and traditions are important component parts and manifestations of the civilisational heritage of India. In order to create a corpus of authentic literature on the special attributes of the individual janjatis of India, our educational and research institutions must take up this as one of their priority areas of study and research. The following actions can be taken up:

- Special cell for the study of art, culture, specific stories, histories and geographies.
- Such a study must aim to accurately and meticulously document the life narratives of the heroes, saints and monarchs belonging to different ianajati communities.
- Research and documentation on tangible and intangible heritage.
- Research proposals on crafts, art, culture, folk art, folk dance, folk songs, folk paintings, folk literature, etc.
- Research on rituals, beliefs, tribal fairs and festivals.
- Tribal artists can be empowered through training at the 'Aatmanirbhar Bharat Centre for Design' (ABCD) project to safeguard and enhance tribal art and craft. ABCD is committed to fostering innovation in crafts, providing sustainable partnerships and establishing market connections to support craftsmen. The project focusses on promoting 'Vocal for Local' and 'Make in India' initiatives to elevate creative manufacturing as a vital component of the Indian economy. Efforts are concentrated on promoting Indian handicrafts and handlooms as a sustainable income source for artisans and a unique option for global consumers.
- Scheduled Tribes are known for their knowledge and wisdom of their ethnic origin. There is, however, no legal and/or institutional framework to safeguard their intellectual property rights.

- Therefore, the aim must be to make legal and institutional arrangements to protect their intellectual property rights and curtail the rights of corporations and other agencies to access and exploit their resource base.
- Particularly vulnerable tribal groups have not benefited from developmental activities. They face continuous threats of eviction from their homes and lands. They live with food insecurity and a host of diseases like sickle cell anaemia and malaria.
- Teaching shall be in the tribals' mother tongue/dialect.
- Considering PTGs' poverty, school-going children shall be provided incentives.
- Emphasis shall be laid on vocational education and training.
- PTGs shall enjoy the 'right to land'. Any form of land alienation shall be prevented and landless PTGs will be given priority in land assignment.
- A new, socio-economically advanced category of ST, which some scholars term as 'Tribal Elites', has come into existence. Unfortunately, the government of India continues to classify the community as an ST, based on the criteria of the late 1960s, which is considered irrelevant in today's context. We suggest a need to review ST's classification process, as not all STs are in a disadvantaged position. The benefits should go to the sections of weaker ST communities. The government's attempt to introduce a creamy layer (even though unsuccessful) by streamlining the procedure and changing community classification criteria must be seriously considered. Unfortunately, sections of the political class, mainly on account of vote bank politics and political intervention from tribal elites, have been overlooking this critical issue of national interest.
- Identification of tribal groups with 'primitive traits' shall be done away with on a priority basis.
- Opportunities shall be provided for tribals to interact with outside cultures.
- Encourage NGOs in tribal development activities. They can play an important role in the opening of residential and non-residential schools, hostels, dispensaries, hospitals and vocational training centres, promotion of awareness programmes and capacity building.
- Their geographical isolation shall be minimised through the development of roads, transport and means of communication and the provision of concessional travel facilities.
- Existing Tribal Research Institutes located in different parts of the country should be further strengthened for carrying out purposeful research and evaluation studies and working towards the preservation of the rich tribal cultural heritage. It also envisages the establishment of a national-level research institution.

- The Ministry of Tribal Affairs should work to create a repository of data on tribal literature in all aspects.

REVISITING TRIBAL POLICY

Tribal policies can be seen in two broad periods: first, in the colonial period; and second, in the post-colonial period. In the colonial period, there was a policy of isolating the tribes. In the post-independence period, the integration model of tribal development became the focus. Various conventional programmes were initiated in tribal areas so as to meet the constitutional commitments and bring about social and economic change among the tribal people. In the early 1990s, there was a shift in the economic policy of the government of India with the introduction of economic liberalisation, which impacted the majority of the tribal groups adversely.

The Eleventh Five-Year Plan did not make a special plan for STs. It rather continued the existing schemes and programmes of the previous plans that were directed at the socio-economic development of the tribal population through an 'area-based approach'. This plan laid emphasis on poverty eradication in rural and tribal areas, which focussed on sustainable development, education, employment, access to forest resources, agricultural production and subsidies.

The Draft of the National Tribal Policy was released for the first time in February 2004 and its revised version came in July 2006. The draft National Tribal Policy tried to address issues concerning lower educational levels, poverty, poor infrastructure, diminishing control over natural resource base, persistent threats of eviction from their habitat, exclusion from mainstream economy in distribution of wealth and opportunities and non-empowerment; and also to place Scheduled Tribes on a progressive and constructive path to make them active partners in nation building.

In the current situation, a clearance to the final draft of the National Tribal Policy was pending at the time of writing. The draft observed at the outset that it was for the first time in the history of tribal administration that the government of India was formulating a National Policy on the Scheduled Tribes. The policy aims to provide an overarching strategy, philosophy and developmental plan for tribal communities. While the first version was abysmally short and unfocussed, the second one is detailed, covering almost all the matters that concern tribal communities. Whereas the first version suggested that 'assimilation' was best for tribal persons, in the second, the objective of the development plans is to 'mainstream' the tribal people, so that they are integrated with the wider world. In fact, since the second half of the twentieth century, the main approach to tribal communities has been that of 'integration', developed after Verrier Elwin's work on NEFA, which had a foreword by Jawaharlal Nehru. It was popularly known as the 'Tribal panchsheel'. In his paper, Srivastava gives a detailed appraisal of the draft and the points to be taken up for further discussion and improvement. One of the issues that the draft raises pertains to the scheduling and de-scheduling of communities and it needs to be given serious thought.

In fact, the Adivasi Resource Centre has submitted that the government should formulate and outline a set of new criteria for scheduling tribes from the point of view of their deprivation and exclusion, whether economic, political, or social. The cultural and individual traits of the people are not to be taken into consideration. Further, the right to self-determination, whether one should retain or rebuild one's cultural or political identity, should be given the status of a fundamental right. The people should be the masters of their destiny (Srivastava, 2013). The National Policy is designed to tackle each of these issues effectively. Additionally, it outlines specific actions to safeguard and enhance the cultural heritage of tribal communities. In order to safeguard them and ensure their full integration into Indian society, a National Policy for Janjtis is desperately needed.

THE WAY FORWARD

A screening of the model syllabi provided by the University Grants Commission (UGC) for the faculty development programmes for IKS shows that the UGC has tried to imbibe multidisciplinary streams to develop insights into our knowledge systems. However, the Tribal Knowledge System (TKS) is missing from their purview. The President of India has also emphasized the need to integrate the TKS into IKS. Similar to the components of the Indian Knowledge System, the TKS has suffered from stereotypes, external influences and a lack of documentation. The tribals' simple life and constant interaction with nature and its resources provide vital insights into sustainable and cohesive living. The following aspects of the tribal knowledge system and its importance need to be incorporated into the syllabus of educational institutions.

- It is imperative to change the narratives of janajatis (new discourse in search of Indian social history).
- It is essential to update the curriculum of the janajati course in universities and other educational institutions and the curriculum must focus on:
    - Janjati history and civilisation.
    - Janjati unsung heroes and ecological warriors.
    - Janjati Traditional Knowledge System (Livelihoods, traditional food and healthcare, astronomy, navigation, ecological understanding, natural resource management and conservation practices).
    - Janjati traditional agriculture, horticulture and kitchen garden practices.

- Janati cultural dimension of biodiversity conservation and climate resilience.
- Janjati habitation and traditional architecture (housing and other structures).
- Janjati performing arts and crafts.
- Janjati textiles (regional and local attire).
- Janjati visual art.
- Janjati celebrations (fairs and festivals, oral traditions, folklore, dance and music, traditional sports, etc.).
- Janjati language and literature (in regional and local languages).
- Janjati governance practices.
- Janjati philosophy (worldview, symbiotic relationship with nature, spirituality).
- Janjati identity, existence and development.
- The study of the curriculum mentioned requires the application of a new methodology.
- In order to implement the aforementioned changes, workshops and seminars at universities and national institutions should be organized.
- It would be useful to undertake research in unexplored domains.

The involvement of national institutions and the ministries concerned is indispensable in order to implement the aforementioned modifications and ensure their widespread dissemination.

CHAPTER 6

Conclusion

The book "Decolonising Indian Anthropology: A Civilisational Approach to the Inter-Relationship among Forests, Hills and Plains People," critically examines the historical misrepresentation of India's tribal communities by Western anthropologists. This misrepresentation was heavily influenced by a colonial mindset, which viewed these communities as the 'other,' perpetuating stereotypes and inaccuracies that have long affected the understanding of India's diverse cultural landscape.

The discussion in the book follows meetings and discussions between the Vivekananda International Foundation (VIF) and the Indira Gandhi National Centre for the Arts (IGNCA) teams held based on a paper titled 'Need for an Indian Civilisation Approach to Study India's Forest and Hill People', authored by Swaminathan Gurumurthy, chairman of the VIF (attached as Annexure 'A'). The paper argued for a civilisational approach to the study of the inter-relations between the peoples of the plains and the forest and hills of India. The content of that paper and the outcome of discussions based on it are summarized here:

- *Western Anthropology as the study of the other—savage, uncivilised people terms, which are now moderated as tribal and indigenous*

Anthropology as an academic subject originated in the civilised colonists' efforts to understand 'the other' people. Western anthropology, out of which Modern anthropology evolved in the twentieth century, was originally the study by the colonizers of the 'other'—the colonized people—who first labelled the tribes as 'savages', 'barbaric', 'semi-barbaric' and 'primitive'. This was later moderated to 'tribal' and 'indigenous'. Notwithstanding the change in terminology, Western anthropology continues to be the study of the 'other'.

- *Origins of Western anthropology*

What was the trigger for the colonial anthropological thought? Everywhere, the colonists found that the colonized had no evolved language—an evolved language was considered a test of a civilisation. This belief provided the basis for the colonists to deem and study the 'other' as uncivilised. It provided a justification to the colonists to easily classify the original Americans and Africans as the 'other'. However, India, which they thought also belonged to the same category, challenged their understanding as they learned more about its history and culture. For over 350 years, after Vasco da Gama began colonizing India in the late fifteenth century, the colonists applied the same rationale to India that they had used in America and Africa. They regarded all Indians as the 'other' till they encountered the greatest challenge to their idea of anthropology, which had presumed the 'other', that is, the less civilised, as the subject of study.

- *First challenge to Western anthropology in India—Monier Williams' discovery of Sanskrit*

The challenge came when Monier Williams discovered the Sanskrit language in the second half of the nineteenth century and described it as a wonderful language that was more perfect than Greek, more copious than Latin and more refined than either.

In the early 2000s, Thomas McEvilley wrote in his magnum opus titled 'The Shape of Ancient Thought', on the origin of Indian and Greek civilisations, that Monier Williams proved that 'the language of the colonized Indian people was the language of the colonial masters themselves'.

The discovery of Sanskrit, along with ancient Indian literature, history and the ways of life of India, disrupted the project of the colonizers. The discovery did not align with the established colonial view that colonized people were less civilised than others and that colonized people needed the discipline of anthropology.

The colonists, who had to continue to keep their subjects subjugated with a feeling of inferiority, quickly re-theorized that the Sanskrit language evolved from the Greek. They labelled and owned it as an Indo-Aryan language. Consequently, they theorized that the Indian people were the 'other people', civilised by the Aryans who had invaded India.

After three decades of study of Indian and Greek literature and civilisation, which culminated in his book, *The Shape of Ancient Thought* [2001], Thomas McEvilley, concluded that the Greek philosophy (of Plato, Socrates and others) had no basic research laboratory in Greece and that it was only from ancient India that the Greek philosophy had borrowed its foundational premises.

Over 250 years before Thomas McEvilly, Edward Pockoke traced the origin of Greek civilisation to India in his book, *India in Greece*, which was first published in 1830 but never saw the light of day during the colonial rule in India.

Their work almost killed the foundational premises of Western anthropology, namely, that colonists are the civilised people and Indians are the 'other', uncivilised or less civilised people. This ought to have put a full stop to the practice of applying the colonial anthropological principle to India. However, even after the findings of Edward Pockoke and Monier Williams, the colonists refused to give up on their pet theme of colonial anthropological approach to Indians.

The theory of the superior Aryans civilizing the natives of India expounded post Monier Williams, soon met with another big challenge, when the Harappa civilisation was uncovered. In the initial findings of Harappan symbols, there was no Vedic civilisational trace—though later, thanks to the work of an internationally acknowledged Indus-Saraswati Valley expert and Vedic-literate epigraphist, linguist and archeologist, Iravatham Mahadevan, it is now accepted or at least not disputed that the Indus Valley was an amalgam of Vedic and pre-Vedic civilisations.

- *Dangerous Aryan-Dravidian divide to justify the forest-plains divide*

A century of illiterate and deliberately distorted interpretation of the Indus Valley civilisation led to the more dangerous and divisive colonial view that the nomadic and pastoral Aryans invaded India and destroyed the rich Dravidian civilisation—even though this premise made the earlier view of superior Aryans civilizing the native Indians stand on its head.

Thus, the Indus discovery legitimized one more bias, a racial basis dividing India, namely that the Indus civilisation was pre-Aryan. Therefore, India was continuously colonized by some race or the other and it had no particular indigenous identity.

All this was, as Thomas McEvilly had said, only an attempt to justify the colonial rule over the colonized Indian people. As mentioned, the later discoveries of Iravatham Mahadevan from 1978 established that there was a confluence of the Vedic and Indus civilisations. However, the discourse and narrative of the Indus civilisation, being pre-Vedic, still holds the field, thanks to the colonial hangover. Just as the narrative—although thoroughly discredited—that the Aryans had come from outside, remains embedded in the minds of certain historians.

All of this meant twists and turns in the colonial perceptions of India from time to time, whose sole purpose was, as McEvilley said, to maintain the colonial superiority over Indian civilisation as a reason to justify the colonial rule over them.

- *Faked forest and plains divide in India*

The outcome of the contortions in colonial theories on India was that, unlike in the Americas and Africa, the Indian colonists at least accepted that the plains people of India are not the 'other' people but as their own, like —as Indo-Aryans, belonging to their own racial stock. This led to the racial division of Indian people as civilised Aryans and the native Dravidians—who were driven into forests and hills by the invading Aryans —being regarded as the other people. There was no way that Western anthropologists were going to abandon their 'other people' theory.

The discovery of the Indus civilisation led to the revised theory of civilised plains people and backwards forest people, to smuggle in and justify the colonial anthropology that divides the Indian people into two anthropological groups: the plains people and the forests and hills people. This was a fake and even dishonest attempt, but it succeeded because it was driven by a colonial power.

This misleading and polarizing narrative overlooks the reality that the people of the plains, forests and hills were differentiated by their lifestyles, which were well-suited to their respective geographic ecosystems. Despite these differences, they shared a common literary, social, cultural and religious exchange that was unique compared to other regions of the world, whether colonized or not.

Anthropology, which was the colonial instrument to study the colonized people—savages—as the 'other' people, turned into the study of the forests and hills people in India, which was founded on the colonial Western view that forests are antithetic to civilisation and are therefore backward and those living in forests and hills are uncivilised.

- *Ancient Indian view: Forest as a place of enlightenment and modern science view that the Upanishads, the books of the forests, contain modern scientific ideas*

The Western construct completely contradicted the ancient Indian view that forests are the place of contemplation and enlightenment for humans seeking higher knowledge. The *Upanishads*, which speak of one universal consciousness as the origin of the universe, are known as the book of forests—which emanated from forests.

Many Nobel laureates have said that the answers to the unanswered or unanswerable questions of modern science are to be found in the *Upanishads*, which constitute the knowledge gathered in the forests. From Einstein's theory of relativity, the developments in quantum science have travelled through Stephen Hawking's Big Bang theory and now to Roger Penrose's theory of quantum consciousness beyond computable physics as the origin of the universe and matter. They all point to the book of forests, the *Upanishads*, as the book of science. Thus, the mightiest philosophic thoughts rooted in what the Nobel laureates hail as scientific have been generated in the forests of India.

- *Uninterrupted forest-plains civilisational and social intercourse from ancient times*

There is undoubtedly a paradigm difference between colonial anthropology, which regards forests as backwards and the ancient Indian view, which regards forests as places of enlightenment and scientific engagement with nature. In the Indian civilisation, the plains people have moved to the forest for the pursuit of higher knowledge—known as *Vanaprastha* — and the forest people have migrated to the plains.

There was continuous civilisational intercourse between the forest and the plains. This is illustrated by Indian philosophy, Vedic literature and the several *Puranas*, principally the *Ramayana* and the *Mahabharata*. In *Ramayana*, Lord Rama embraces Guha, the Monkey King and the tribal lady Sabari as his equal. In fact, Rama, the *Ramayana* says, ignored the Vedic *rishis* to give importance to Sabari and happily ate the fruit that she had earlier tasted. He considered her superior to the learned Vedic pandits. The Western concept that forest and hills people are less civilised was alien to Indic civilisation. This was because, in Indian civilisation, the idea of who was civilised and who was not was founded on the quality of evolution of the human mind and not where one lived—forests, hills, plains, or in huts or mansions. Indeed, the worth of a person was not decided on his or her material evolution.

In India, those living in forests and in plains had a common history, social and cultural interface, unlike in any other part of the world. The forest-plains civilisational relations have been highlighted in the UN Debar Commission Report in the early 1960s on the forest and hill people. The forest-plains social and civilisational intercourse was disrupted by the colonists by segregating the forest people as the 'other' based on their anthropology, thus creating an artificial divide. The pictures from the colonial period of most people from the plains would look as if they were also the forest people.

By intensely studying historiographies across the world, noted historian Sebastian Conrad finds no single enlightenment or modernity of which the West is the origin and source, as the West would like the Rest to believe. Conrad says that recent interventions provide a welcome reminder that the image of non-Western societies as stagnating and immobile is wide off the mark. The West did not have a monopoly on cultural transformations and intellectual conflicts. Such an archaeology of independent seeds of the modern is frequently connected to the larger project to revise the modernization theory and to replace it with the paradigm of early, alternative and multiple modernities.

Admitting that the eighteenth-century philosophical movement in Europe, the Enlightenment's global impact was not energized solely by the ideas of Parisian philosophies, Conrad says that rather it was the work of historical actors around the world—in places such as Cairo, Calcutta and Shanghai, who invoked the term and what they saw as its most important claims, for their own specific purposes. The challenge of the Rest extended from Egypt to India to China to the Koreas.

- *The forest-plains divide in India today is not civilisational, but a colonial physical divide which has become a development divide*

The segregation of the forest people by a 'reserved areas policy' of the colonial state based on the Western anthropological approach created a development and evolutionary divide between the people of the forests and the plains in India. This divide was later—and is even now—used to justify the study of the artificially segregated people who had lagged behind as the 'other' people, resulting in a chasm between the so-called tribals and the rest of the Indian society. Only a civilisational approach can uncover and undo this mischief.

Another aspect that needs to be considered is that the colonial view, which posits that the Western Enlightenment is the sole origin of modernity and the foundation of Western anthropology, is no longer valid. The emerging opinion in the West itself seems to question the old claim as the single source of enlightenment for the whole world.

- *The foundation of Western anthropology was knocked out by multiple modernity theories. The story that the Western Enlightenment is the sole source of modernity holds no water*

In a seminal essay titled, 'Enlightenment in Global History: A Historiographical Critique' (The American Historical Review October 2012), Conrad, who holds the Chair in Modern History at Freie Universität Berlin and is the author of many books, including his latest, *What is Global History*, says that the rest of the world does not share the view that the West is the geographical origin and intellectual source of enlightenment and modernity. He also points out that there are multiple enlightenments and modernities in different parts of the world. Conrad writes:

The Enlightenment has historically occupied a crucial role in the narratives of world history, symbolizing the dawn of modernity and continuing to do so in contemporary discourse. However, traditional interpretations have often relied on a Eurocentric framework, reinforcing the notion that Europe has been the sole catalyst for global interactions. Recently, historians have begun to contest this perspective, leading to the emergence of a global history approach that transcends the fixation on the European roots of the Enlightenment (Conrad S: 2012).

The dominant readings are based on narratives of uniqueness and diffusion. The assumption that the Enlightenment was a specifically European phenomenon remains one of the foundational premises of Western modernity and the modern West. The Enlightenment appears as an original and autonomous product of Europe, deeply embedded in the cultural traditions of the Occident. According to this master narrative, the Renaissance, humanism and the Reformation "gave a new impetus to intellectual and scientific development that, a little more than three and a half centuries later, flowered in the Scientific Revolution and then in the Enlightenment of the eighteenth century" (Tony E Huff: 2010). The results of these efforts included the world of the individual, human rights, rationalization and what Max Weber famously called the "disenchantment of the world" (Max Weber: 1919). Over the course of the nineteenth century, or so the received wisdom says, these ingredients of the modern were then exported to the rest of the world. As William McNeill exulted in his *Rise of the West*, "We and all the world of the twentieth century, are peculiarly the creatures and heirs of a handful of geniuses of early modern Europe" (William H. McNeill: 1963). This interpretation is no longer tenable. Scholars are now challenging the Eurocentric account of the birth of the modern world Conrad S 2012).

• *Enlightenment and civilisation, as being interchangeable*

Enlightenment and civilisation, Conrad observes, have been interchangeably used and enlightenment has been equated even to social evolution. In this sense, civilisational continuity includes changes within continuity, which is an internalized modernization process. Only when a society is frozen, as happened in the West, which the West itself admits to as the Dark Ages, does the process of change, that is, enlightenment, look like a distinct and dated event. The social evolution implicit in the civilisational continuity of other nations is the basis of a challenge to the claim of the West as the sole geographic origin and exclusive intellectual source of enlightenment and modernity for all peoples on the planet.

This summary is the foundation of the present project of Civilisational Approach to the Inter-Relationship among Forests, Hills and Plains People, which seeks to decolonise the contemporary and totally inappropriate Anthropology in India.

The initial paper of the VIF Chairman, on the basis of which the discussions took place, resulting in the summary above, is attached as Annexure A.

The present book is an outcome of the approach papers of the VIF Chairman and the discussions. Based on the summary that has been set out above, the paper argues for a re-evaluation of tribal narratives from an Indian civilisational perspective, rejecting the Western construct that portrays forest and hill people as backwards. The paper highlights the need to revive Indian narratives on traditional communities, emphasizing the civilisational, social, cultural and historic interconnectedness of these communities with the plains people, the likes of which have existed nowhere else in the world between the two peoples. The colonial concept of 'tribe' was imposed by Western anthropologists and was based on an evolutionary approach that viewed tribal communities as less developed or primitive. This perspective led to the artificial segregation of the forest people by the policy of reserving the forests for the so-called tribals. Over centuries, this led to evolutionary and development gaps between the forest and plains people, which later came to be viewed as the anthropological divide.

This caused the marginalization and misrepresentation of these groups, often portraying them as isolated and static entities. The authors call for discarding the colonial concept of 'tribe' and adopting a new research methodology that is free from Western biases. Even in the United Nations' view, the term 'indigenous people' is inappropriate to the forest and hill people of Asia. What else can be the overarching expression of all the people of the forests and hills of India? The term 'Janjati' is significant in this context of India as it represents an attempt to move away from the colonial concept of 'tribe', which is laden with negative connotations and implies a sense of otherness and primitivism. 'Janjatis' is a more inclusive and respectful term that acknowledges the historical, cultural and social contributions of these communities to Indian civilisation. The book suggests using terms such as 'Jana' or 'Janjatis' to refer to communities, which align with the Indian cultural and historical context.

The book also discusses the impact of colonial policies on tribal communities, such as the 'divide and rule' strategy and the subsequent challenges faced by these communities in post-independence India. It calls for a re-evaluation of the constitutional categories of Scheduled Tribes and the need for terminological dignity for these communities.

The influence of the Indian epics, the *Ramayana* and the *Mahabharata*, on Indian tribal and folk traditions is explored in this paper. The focus is on their impact on the spiritual, religious and cultural aspects. These epics have served as a source of inspiration for literature, art and performance, fostering a sense of national identity and unity. The tribal communities, an integral part of Indian society, have also been influenced by these epics, incorporating their own customs and beliefs into their versions of the epics. The document highlights the interaction between tribal societies and the dominant Hindu tradition, with tribes adopting Hindu religious practices and contributing to the cultural unity of Indian civilisation through various performances and festivals.

The authors advocate extensive research to uncover the social capital of traditional communities and to establish their Indian narrative through an objective interpretation of empirical data. They propose a civilisational approach to understanding the historical, cultural and social dimensions of these communities, which have been integral to Indian culture and civilisation.

In conclusion, the book emphasizes the urgent need for a paradigm shift in the study of Indian tribal communities, advocating a decolonised approach that recognizes the inherent dignity and civilisational contributions of these groups. It calls for a reimagining of Indian social history that integrates the narratives of forest and hill communities into the broader Indian story, fostering a sense of national pride and unity.

In the background of how the colonial rule has conducted the discourses and built the narratives to undermine the Indian civilisation and particularly in the context of the relations between the forest and hills communities, the book puts forth several suggestions and recommendations for studying and understanding forest and hill communities in India, with a focus on adopting an Indian civilisational perspective.

- Move away from the colonial mindset of studying the forest and plains people as being different from the plains and look at the common links and civilisational relations between the forest and plains people—from ancient Indian literature to the medieval times when the forest and plains' people worked together to fight invasion.
- Integrate quantum science and quantum scientists' view, namely, that the book of forests—the *Upanishads*—are scientific books, which would mean that the forest was not backwards in the Indian civilisation and the forest was a place of enlightenment, in the study of forest and plains people.
- Integrate the Indian civilisational view that being 'civilised' does not depend on where one lived—forests or plains or in huts or concrete buildings—or what dress one wore—but it meant human values. This view has been completely kept out of Western anthropology.
- Recall and incorporate Indian traditions of forests as the origin of enlightenment and totally dismiss the Western view that forests are the habitat of barbarians.
- Revive and incorporate the common bases of Indian forest and plains people from the *Puranas* to the historic period.
- Recall and bring in the role of the people of the forests and the plains fighting together against invaders and colonialists.
- Adopt the multiple modernity theory and discard the idea of the West being the single source of modernity and the foundation of contemporary anthropology.

To achieve these clear objectives, the following approach is suggested:

- Discarding Western narratives, theories and terms and substituting them with Indian terminologies and narratives. There is an immediate need to review existing literature from an Indian perspective, using new research methods that are free from Western approaches.
- Indulging in extensive research. Extensive and intensive research should be carried out across India to bring out the inherent and embedded 'social capital' of traditional communities.
- Adopting a civilisational approach: The civilisational approach should be adopted to understand the hill, forest and plains communities of India, focussing on aspects of co-existence and continuity among people in a specific geographical setting. It suggests adopting a civilisational approach that recognizes the historical continuity and coexistence of communities in India, rather than the evolutionary approach often used by Western social scientists. This approach emphasizes the interconnectedness of communities and their contributions to Indian civilisation.

- Decolonising anthropology: This document calls for a shift away from the colonial and Western-centric perspectives that have dominated anthropological studies. It advocates a reevaluation of the discipline's approach to studying tribal communities, rejecting the labels of 'savage', 'barbaric', 'primitive' and 'indigenous' that have been imposed by Western anthropologists. It is necessary to move away from colonial constructs and their perspectives or frameworks, which have resulted in scientific colonialism and academic dependency.
- Giving greater attention to oral histories and alternative archives: Emphasize the importance of alternative archives, such as oral narratives, to overcome the deficiency of the colonial archive and offer insights into the lived history of Adivasi communities.
- Offering terminological dignity: The names and labels imposed on Janjati communities by colonial reports should be reviewed to accord terminological dignity to these communities.
- Promoting insider perspectives: Prioritize insider narratives from the Janjatiya Samuh members and encourage scholars from these communities to conduct in-depth studies on their own cultures.
- Taking a holistic view: Adopt an Indian holistic view that recognizes the art, craft, celebrations and oral traditions of the community as participatory and essential to understanding their narrative.
- Engaging in critical analysis of legal frameworks: Critically analyse the working and relevance of Schedule-V and Schedule-VI areas mentioned in the Constitution of India.
- Understanding and appreciating traditional practices: Get a better grasp of the traditional dispute resolution practices of the Janjati Samuh of India.
- Emphasizing social capital: The document highlights the importance of conducting extensive research to uncover the social capital of traditional communities, which has been overlooked or misrepresented in Western narratives.
- Preserving oral histories and traditional knowledge systems: This calls for the preservation and documentation of tribal languages, oral narratives and traditional knowledge systems, all of which are at the risk of being lost in the race for modernization and globalization.
- Integrating tribal communities into national narratives: The document aims to bring together and interweave the narratives of forest and hill communities into a broader Indian story, thus fostering a sense of national pride and unity.
- Conducting interdisciplinary research: There is a need to encourage interdisciplinary research to further an understanding of the socio-economic, political and cultural interactions between hill and forest communities and the plains. It suggests collaboration among different

disciplines to reevaluate ethnographies and translate them within the context of tribal culture.

- Protecting and integrating: Janjati communities have to be integrated within the broader social fabric of the country through legislation, community participation, welfare schemes and improved access to healthcare, education and governance.
- Initiating educational reforms: It is important to update our educational curricula in order to reflect Indian realities and encourage community-insider writings. The curriculum in anthropology and other social sciences must be revised to include more culturally-sensitive and context-specific methodologies. Incorporating community languages, literature and folklore into the syllabus, as well as promoting research that is free from Western bias, is required.
- Adopting Indological and cultural relativistic approaches: The document recommends incorporating Indological and cultural relativistic approaches to understand tribal communities within their own cultural and historical contexts, rather than through Western frameworks.
- Resetting research priorities: Focus research on understanding the identity (Asmita), existence (Astitav) and development (Vikas) of Janjati communities from local and regional languages.
- Using a contextual and historical approach: Anthropologists should adopt a historical and contextual approach to study traditional, regional and national communities. This would avoid the pitfalls of a lopsided understanding of the subject.
- Ensuring cultural Continuity: It is important to understand the cultural continuity between the larger, great traditions of Indian civilisation and the individual traditions of regional and local communities.
- Recognising policy implications: The policy implications of understanding tribal communities for national security and development need to be appreciated more. The document recognizes the need for policy changes that protect tribal identity and ensure development and the implications these have for national security and the country's development.

The recommendations are intended to enhance one's comprehension of India's traditional communities through a culturally sensitive, inclusive and historically grounded approach—a comprehension that recognizes the contributions of these communities to the Indian civilisational ethos. The objective is to present a more accurate and respectful portrayal of tribal communities by acknowledging their cultural richness and historical significance in Indian society through the rejection of the Western prism view.

ANNEXURE A

Need for an Indian Civilisational Approach to Study India's Forest and Hill People

S. GURUMURTHY

INTRODUCTION – RISING GLOBAL CIVILISATIONAL CONSCIOUSNESS

Asia's economic and geopolitical rise in the last decade is powering a civilisational consciousness across the world, which was previously dominated by the political and economic ideologies of the post-World War II period. Even Communist China, which had sworn to destroy its own civilisational consciousness during the Cultural Revolution in the 1960-70s, is now recalling and talking about its antiquitous civilisation of thousands of years not only with pride, but also as a guide for the future.

A neo-Confucian China is now seen as emerging from the ashes of pure Communist ideology. This rising new civilisational consciousness is perceived to have the potential to cause a paradigm shift in the global order and relations. As the rising civilisational consciousness of individual nations weakens Western universalism, it is forcing the diffusion of global power and, in turn, this diffusion of power is leading the rise of civilisational consciousness of individual nations.

This rise of civilisational consciousness around the world has also raised deeper questions about whether the West and its "Age of Enlightenment", which the Euro-centric world once assumed as the singular source of modernity, are the only sources of modernity. The West as the single source of modernity also had negated any new civilisational approach as anti-Modern. The world is beginning to recognise that there are multiple sources of modernity and that each nation is evolving its own modernity. For example, there is Japanese modernity, Chinese modernity and Indian modernity.

The originally West-centric UN in whose dictionary the term diversity never featured throughout the last century too has begun to recognise this diversity of cultures. The Cultural Diversity Convention [2001] recognises the cultural diversities of the world. The UN, which mandated the rest of the world to adopt the Western anthropology of modernity through the Measures for the Development of Underdeveloped Economies in 1951, for their development, gradually retraced its position and recommended a culture-led development model for all in the Millennium Development Goals in 2015. Undoubtedly, the world is in the midst of a new civilisational revolution.

INDIA'S RISING CIVILISATIONAL CONSCIOUSNESS

India is no exception to this global trend. Ancient India has been a civilisation since time immemorial. It was no surprise that the Indian freedom movement itself was civilisational. In his foundational treatise, "Hind Swaraj", Mahatma Gandhi defined India's struggle against the British as civlisational. His chosen successor, Jawaharlal Nehru, also said in his article on the freedom movement in the Foreign Affairs magazine in 1938, that India's battle for freedom was cultural. Yet shockingly, the millennial civilisational consciousness that drove the freedom movement went underground post freedom in the euphoric economic, secular and ideological politics of that time, which worked against the civilisational impulses of all nations, including India. The sudden disappearance of Indian civilisational consciousness impacted various aspects of national life and even national security. It is only as late as the final decades of the previous century that pre-independence Indian civilisational consciousness once again began to manifest. This coincided later with the rise of global civilisational consciousness. A rising Indian civilisational consciousness has undoubtedly begun informing different aspects of national life.

YET NO CIVILISATIONAL APPROACH FOR THE FOREST AND HILL PEOPLE OF INDIA

But in one important and critical area of national life, the relation between the forest and hill people and the people of the plains, there hasn't been a perceptible effort to undertake a civilisational approach.

India's forest and hill communities constitute a fifth of the country's population, yet, even after 75 years of attaining freedom, the Indian establishment is still blind and continues to ignore the reality about these communities. It is shocking to see the western colonial anthropological approach and their methods of dealing with forest and hill communities in colonised countries, continuing to dominate the Indian establishment narrative and public discourse and still uncritically remaining institutionalised in India.

A few testimonies from India's past, dating not just centuries, but thousands of years back, on the relationship between the forest and the plains, and peoples' of both, will irrefutably settle the differences that exist between Indian reality and the Western approach. And, that would be adequate to show how wrong, or even ridiculous, is the adoption of the Western approach to the forest and hill people of India.

One, the Western colonists' approach to the forest and hill people was that of them being savages, which led to their total elimination and genocide in the Americas, Europe and Oceania. The small number that survived this genocide are labelled as an indigenous people and presented as curios by the West. While that is a fact of Western history and geography, it is not so in the case of Africa and Asia, where no one was exterminated by anyone, including by the colonisers. And yet, this labelling of those small number of peoples and communities leftover after colonial genocide as "indigenous" by colonial explorers in the Americas, Europe and Oceania, is mechanical applied to the people of the forests and the hills in other parts of the world, particularly India. This has resulted in an artificial dividing line being drawn in India, in particular, distinguishing the forest people from their millennial civilisational and cultural cousins in the plains.

Two, in the Americas, Europe and Oceania, there was nothing in common between the forest people exterminated during the colonial exploration and the colonisers who occupied their land and called it plains. But Bharat was a total contrast. In Bharat, there has been a common and continuous cultural, civilisational and religious interface and integration lasting over several millennia that transcends all other differences between the people of the forests and hills, and the people of the plains. Such civilisational integration is unknown anywhere else in the world. In 1962, the UN Dhebar Committee on People of Forests, labelled as a study of tribals, had cited the Ramayana, Mahabharata and ancient texts to show that there was no dividing line between forest and plains. The Committee said that because of the continuous migration between the forests and the plains, it has been difficult to distinguish between who is from the forest and who is from the plains. And yet, government policies and public discourse in India continues to be more in alignment with Western views institutionalised by Verrier Elvin as explained later on.

Three, it would have shocked Western anthropologists who considered the forest and hill people as dark, backward, savages and barbarians, had they known that the forest civilisation in India was considered as a source of higher knowledge and enlightenment. Aranyakas, ancient India's most revered text and part of the Vedas, meaning "The Book of Forests", had its origins in the calm and quietude of the forests and the hills through the contributions of sages and rishis, i.e., India's greatest and most revered sages were themselves forest dwellers!

On the contrary, the people of the plains were known as the consumers of this great enlightenment emanating from the forests. Therefore, in those times, to seek purer knowledge one had to move to the quietude of the forests. Even today, there are many in India, who in the autumn of their lives, give up their material comforts in search of higher spiritual pursuits, leaving the plains and going to the forests. This stage of life is called Vanaprastha, meaning "Journey to the Forest".

The Vayu Purana, which is at least 2000-years-old, says that the father of Bharath (from whom the name of Bharatvarsha for our country originated), handed over the kingdom to his son Bharath and went to the forest for higher seeking!

Four, the Ramayana and Mahabharata, two of the oldest epics of Bharat, are full of episodes of people of the plains, the emperors and the ordinary folk, adopting and relating to the people of forests and hills as brothers. The most revered godly personality in Indian civilisation, Sri Rama, embraced Guha, the boatman as his brother, Hanuman and Sugreeva, the monkey heroes of the Deccan, as his friends, and the revered Sabari, the elderly forest woman of Kerala, as his mother, and as a saint, and even ate the fruit which she had already tasted. When hundreds of great seers were waiting to see Sri Rama, he went straight to Sabari's home. This is the civilisational relationship between the forests and the plains.

Ignoring this millennial civilisational relationship that existed in India, post-Independence Indian establishment studies and public discourses, nose-led by Western scholars and ideas, have attempted to civilisationally divide the foresters and plainsmen, like the colonists did. Regrettably, there has been no systematic thought or attempt to study them from an Indian civilisational perspective. But with the kind of historic, epigraphic and civilisational testimonies tumbling out in the last few decades via different disciplines, the colonial assessment of the role of forests and hills needs total review. A survey of Indian civilisational testimonies will prove that adopting a systematic and comprehensive approach to understanding the forest and hill people of India from an Indian perspective, not so far undertaken, is needed to come to terms with Indian reality.

Such a survey is not only a social, cultural and civilisational imperative, but also strategically important for the nation, its security, peace and harmony. Because the colonial ruler's approach was to divide and not to integrate them with the plains people, it was part of the overall colonial game to separate and disaggregate the people of India as Hindus and Muslims, or as belonging to this caste or that caste, or as belonging to this language group and that language group. Yet, even decades after the nation became free, the Indian academic and establishment has not found the need to revisit this flawed and dangerous colonial approach.

The result is that in the academic, social and political discourse, the approach to the people of the forests and the hills, the tribals, unfortunately continues to be based on the colonial view that they are civilisationally different from the rest of Bharathiyas, very much 'the other people', viz, savage, barbaric and primitive, to be studied by the plains people, who by implication, were seen as more civilised. The original and privileged burden of the colonialists' and their mission to civilise a colonised people, i.e., a fundamentally racist approach, later got transformed into a social science discipline and as anthropology of modernity, for the people of the plains to perceive and treat the hills and forest people as ones to be modernised and civilised.

NEGATION OF INDIAN REALITY AND ITS PHILOSOPHY OF HARMONY IN DIVERSITY

The western anthropological approach, which considers the foresters backward and the plainsmen as forward, is the very negation of the Indian view of them, as related by a higher philosophy of integrated humans as a whole. The ancient Indian philosophical exposition "Isavasyam Idam Sarvam" in the Isavasya Upanishad, translated by Mahatma Gandhi as meaning that "Everything down to the tiniest atom is divine" integrates not only the humans inter se but also humans, animals, and all animate and inanimate things that constitutes the earth. On the integration of the humans Swami Vivekananda said, "Every soul is potentially divine – Amritasya Putrah". These were not just philosophical declarations, but informed practices of a people, ranging from kings to commoners. Let's just take one celebrated and revered example from the epic Ramayana. Rama, a self-exiled prince, related to Guha, the boatman, Sugreeva, Hanuman and the monkey population of forest, and Sabari, the dweller in the hills, as being integral to his own life. The Ramayana is no ordinary piece of literature, but one that is revered throughout Bharat, both plains and forests. Lord Rama is a national symbol of reverence and worship. The Ramayana is so deeply entrenched in the Indian DNA that there are over 300 versions of it that have penetrated the Indian consciousness, including in the minds of the forest and hills people, whether it be in the remote North East, the Mizos, or elsewhere [Rama Katha in Tribal and Folk-Traditions: Introduction by K.S. Singh.pdf].

Many more versions of Ramayana have travelled outside India, to South and South East Asia. The number of people who viewed the "Ramayana" serial 1987 is estimated to have been 650 million, according to the BBC. The episodic messages of Sri Rama in the "Ramayana" and off it, are recited by millions of humans, rich or poor, socially deprived or dwellers living on the banks of rivers, or in the forests or the hills, even today. Sri Rama did not regard the forest and hills people as savages, or barbarians, or even as animists and soulless worshippers devoid of core spiritual knowledge.

This understanding flowed from the higher philosophy expounded in the "Isavasya Upanishad", that not just humans, but creation in its entirety, is divine. This foundational integral approach is totally absent in Western civilisation which saw everything that we saw as interrelated internally, as separate externally. It is this thought and attitude that led to forest and hills people being described as savages, barbaric and primitive.

It is not just that the forest and hills, and the plains people are related and integrated. In ancient Indian civilisational view, the forest was not backward, but a place for contemplation and a source of enlightenment for people coming from the plains. In contrast, the Western perspective saw the forest as dark, backward and devoid of civilisation. The Western view was based on brick andmortar structures, while the Indian view was built on spiritual and human consciousness. That is why there is a paradigm difference between the Western anthropology of modernity and the ancient Indian approach to the forests and the hills, and their respective inhabitants. Unless this fundamental difference between the two approaches is recognised, the Indian civilisational approach to the people of the forests and the hills will never be understood. While there is a need for an Indian civilisational test for every colonial version of Indian history, theory and assessment, the approach to the foresters and hills people of India as related to the plains people, it is inevitable that this realisation would even benefit other branches of knowledge.

DID INDIAN CIVILISATION EVER REGARD ITS FORESTERS AND HILL-MEN AS SAVAGE, BACKWARD, OR AS "THE OTHER" PEOPLE? THE ANSWER IS A BIG 'NO'.

The most critical and primary question for understanding the forest and hill communities is whether they were "savages and barbaric" in the Indian philosophy and practice, as western anthropology thought and taught, which the West later modified as "the other people, tribal, backward", and finally as indigenous people. The answer to this question comes from Indian philosophy that originally included and described all human diversities as one harmonious whole. Western colonial ideology, on the other hand, divided humans as either being civilised, or being savages. The fundamental and shocking difference between the Indian and Western approaches is that while the latter considers the forests as dark and backward, the former celebrated them as sources of enlightenment. In the Indian philosophical view, foresters and hills-men cannot be considered backward, and if by applying the Western view, they are described as such, then all Indians have to be considered backward which is how the colonists regarded the colonised elsewhere. It is, therefore, necessary to now explain how the origin of Indian civilisation was in the forests and the hills, and not in the plains.

In Indian civilisation the plainsmen supported and defended the right of the foresters to remain in the forests and contemplate on the higher reaches of human consciousness and the plainsmen themselves moved to forests to gain higher knowledge. Both plainsmen and foresters were joint developers of Indian civilisation. In that context, the plainsmen appear more as consumers of and less as contributors to the origin and development of Indian civilisation. Therefore, in Indian civilisation, the foresters and the hill people are not "the other people" in relation to the plainsmen, but function as co-partners in its evolution.

FOREST, BACKWARD IN WESTERN ANTHROPOLOGY, IS THE ORIGIN OF KNOWLEDGE IN INDIAN CIVILISATION

Irrefutable textual, historic and civilisational testimonies exist to show that the forest is the primary source of knowledge in Indian civilisation. The etymological meaning of the earliest literature in the Vedas– the Aranyakas, that is the Book of Forests as the Upanishads were known– shows how the forest is the source of true knowledge in Indian civilisation. This is explained in detail later. There are two broad divisions of the Vedas– the Upanishads and the Brahmanas. The Upanishads, which originated in the forests, are called the Aranyakas, or the "Book of Forests". The Aranyakas are regarded as the source of Gnana or source of knowledge. The Brahmanas, which contain the ritualistic part of the Vedas, are observed and practiced by the plains people. It would not be incorrect to say that knowledge generated in the forests through the Upanishads was deployed in the plains. The Bhagavata Purana originated in the forests. Naimisharanya (modern day Nimsar in Uttar Pradesh), where according to the Bhagavata Purana, thousands of rishis assembled to discuss the dawn of Kali Yuga and ways to handle the evil effects and challenges of the future. This is how and why the plainsmen looked up to the foresters for guidance in Indian civilisation. The issue is not whether that happened or not; the message is that in Indian civilisation the forest was the source from which the plains got their guidance and that the foresters were not a backward people.

VEDAS OF THE FOREST AND INDUS VALLEY OF THE PLAINS — THE SOURCES OF INDIA'S PAST

There are two ancient Indian civilisational testimonies- the Vedas and the Indus Valley. It is undisputed that the Indus Valley and the Vedas constitute the very beginning of Indian civilisation. The Vedas originated in the forests representing the higher consciousness of Indian foresters, while the Indus Valley Civilisation manifests the development of India's plainsmen. There have been and still there are, disputes whether the Indus Valley predates the Vedas, or has a mix of the Vedas. It is necessary to analyse both the Vedas and the Indus Valley to understand the origins and nature of Indian civilisation.

Originally, the Western view that followed the discovery of Sanskrit, was that cultured Aryans White people who conquered and civilised India. [See: The Shape of Ancient Thought by Thomas McEvilly]. This entire theory turned on its head after the Indus Valley discoveries of nomadic and pastoral Aryans invading and destroying that civilisation. The Aryan invasion theory, which was groundless, was gradually given up and replaced by the Aryan migration theory. The migration ridiculed the theory that the Aryans invaded destroyed the Indus Civilisation, but changed the narrative to Aryans over powering Dravidians. And now the Aryan-Dravidian racial divide itself is suspect and has changed into linguistic difference. Originally the Vedas were considered mythological as the Saraswati River mentioned in the Vedas was considered non existent and imaginary. Slowly the theory gaining ground is that the Saraswati River, which is mentioned in the Vedas, thought of as imaginary and therefore, the Vedas itself, did indeed exist and that the most probable reason for the destruction of the Indus Civilisation was the drying up of the Saraswati due to natural causes. There are satellite imageries and hydrological studies which tend to support the view that the Saraswati which existed could have been diverted by natural calamities, or earthquakes, into the Sutlej, or the Yamuna and the Ganga. One thing that emerges as a certainty is that that the theory river, which described river as a myth, is now untenable [See Saraswati: The River that Disappeared by K.S. Valdiya published by ISRO]. Consequently, like the Saraswati, which was considered a theory, the description of the Vedas as a myth, too has become an outdated theory. While the existence of the Saraswati River establishes that the Vedas are not a myth, subsequent researches by renowned scholars like Iravatham Mahadevan show that the Rig Vedic "Soma Ritual" is depicted in the seals of the Indus Valley as sacred ritual and filter [See The Cult Object on Unicorn Seals: A Sacred Filter (1983) by Iravatham Mahadevan]. When Mahadevan wrote his research paper, the theory of Aryan-Dravidian divide was almost undisputed. Further pioneering research by him also pointed to a possible convergence between Vedic texts of the forests and the Indus Civilisation of the plains

Likewise, Western scholars had originally theorised that the Indus Valley Civilisation was an extension of the Babylonian Civilisation. But that also changed when they conceded that the Indus Civilisation had evolved independently, unconnected with any other [See V Gordon Childe New Light on the Most Ancient East]. Now with both Western theories becoming untenable, it is clear that the Indus Valley of the plains and the Vedas of the forests were real and constituted the twin sources of the Indian civilisation of that time. It could well be that the Indus Valley constitutes the civilisation of the Indian plains and the Vedas, the Aranyakas and the endless continuum of sacred texts that followed them, constitute the soul of that civilisation. Now a brief account of how the Indus civilisation has been accepted as home grown in India.

INDUS VALLEY- THOROUGHLY INDIAN, NOT A DERIVATIVE OF ANY OTHER CONTEMPORARY CIVILISATION

It is now an undisputed fact that the Indus Valley Civilisation was an autogenous evolution and not a derivative of any of its contemporaries. The

Encyclopaedia Britannica says that the civilisation is thoroughly Indian in origin, independent in evolution and unconnected with either the Babylonian or the Egyptian Civilisations. It says that the elements of Indus civilisation are present in the contemporary Indian way of life. To quote historian V. Gordon Childe:

> *"While the Indus (or Harappan) civilisation may be considered the culmination of a long process indigenous to the Indus valley, a number of parallels exist between developments on the Indus River and the rise of civilisation in Mesopotamia. It is striking to compare the Indus with this better-known and more fully documented region and to see how closely the two coincide with respect to the emergence of cities and of such major concomitants of civilisation as writing, standardised weights and measures, and monumental architecture. Yet nearly all the earlier writers have sensed the Indian-ness of the civilisation, even when they were largely unable to articulate it.*
>
> *India confronts Egypt and Babylonia by the 3rd millennium with a thoroughly individual and independent civilisation of her own, technically the peer of the rest. And plainly it is deeply rooted in Indian soil. The Indus Civilisation represents a very perfect adjustment of human life to a specific environment. And it has endured; it is already specifically Indian and forms the basis of modern Indian culture." (New Light on the Most Ancient East, 4th ed., 1952).*
>
> *The force of Childe's words can be appreciated even without an examination of the Indus valley script found on seals; the attention paid to domestic bathrooms, the drains, and the Great Bath at Mohenjo-daro can all be compared to elements in the later Indian civilisation. The bullock carts with a framed canopy, called ikkas, and boats are little changed to this day. The absence of pins and the love of bangles and of elaborate nose ornaments are all peculiarly South Asian. The religion of the Indus also is replete with suggestions of traits known from later India. The significance of the bull, the tiger, and the elephant; the composite animals; the seated yogi god of the seals; the tree spirits and the objects resembling the Shiva linga (a phallus symbolic of the god Shiva) of later times—all these are suggestive of enduring forms in later Indian civilisation*
>
> [https://www.britannica.com/place/India/The-Indus-civilisation]

That the Indus Valley Civilisation was home grown and grew autogenously, is critical to the study of the civilisation of the Indian people which includes all people of India.

Now a brief account of how the Vedas, the soul of the Indian civilisation, emanated from the forests and foresters.

THE VEDAS EMANATED FROM THE FORESTS AND FORESTERS

That in the Indian paradigm, the forests and the hills, and their inhabitants, were not backward, and were in fact, the light of Indian civilisation, is self-evident from the very source of knowledge in Indian civilisation– the Vedic text – was forests. The ancient Vedic texts, not less than 4000-years-old, are divided into two parts. One, Aranyaka [etymologically derived from "Forest"] regarded as the Book of Forests and the other, Brahmanas, regarded as the Book of Villages; that is the Plains. The Indira Gandhi Centre for Arts, Ministry of Culture, Government of India, says that in the Indian civilisation, it is from the forests that the people of the plains sought enlightenment. To quote:

> *The term Aranyaka is derived from the word 'Aranya' meaning 'forest'. The Aranyaka texts are so-called because 'they were works to be read in the forest'....it has to be understood that Vedic rituals [Yanjas] are intended to confer not only material benefits but also mental purity by constant discipline. Having obtained purity [by Yajnas] one must seek the solitude of forests for further concentration and meditation,.the Aranyakas containing explanations of the rituals and allegorical speculations thereon are meant for Vanprasthas, who renounce family life residing in the forests for tapas and other religious activities. Winternitz calls them as "forest texts" to be studied by forest hermits. Or the reason might be that these texts were propounded by the Rishis who resided in the forests and thought upon the secrets of the Yajnas. Aranyakas describe the actions of life and also the acquisition of knowledge.*

Vedanta emanated from the Aranyaka [Upanishads]. If the high Vedic text is identified with the forests, can anyone say that the foresters are savages, barbaric, or backward?

It is also necessary to consider whether the Vedas are relevant any more, or are they merely a proud heritage and just a treasure of the past only to be exhumed to study Indian civilisation and the relation between the forest and hill people? No. There is abundant scientific testimony to support the view that the light which the Vedas contain has the potential to answer many unanswered questions of contemporary science.

NOBEL SCIENCE LAUREATES ON VEDAS AS ANSWERS TO QUESTIONS OF MODERN SCIENCE

From the testimonies of global scientists and scholars, it would appear that the Vedas are no ordinary literature, and the Vedanta is no ordinary knowledge. They are probably the only ancient texts whose validity today is acknowledged and celebrated by the high minds of the West and East, as containing the clue to answering modern scientific questions. The Vedas and the Upanishads in particular, are regarded as containing the highest scientific truths by the world's leading scientists and intellectuals, many of them Nobel Laureates, and as revealing the most advanced scientific knowledge.

Here are acknowledging comments of some Nobel scientists on the Indian philosophy, Vedas and Upanishads as containing answers to the questions of contemporary science.

> *After the conversations about Indian philosophy, some of the ideas of Quantum Physics that had seemed so crazy suddenly made much more sense.* Werner Heisenberg (1901-76), One of the greatest physicists and co-founder of Quantum Physics, a Nobel Prize Winner.
>
> *Some blood transfusion from the East to the West is must to save Western science from spiritual anaemia. Vedanta teaches that consciousness is singular, all happenings are played out in one universal consciousness and there is no multiplicity of selves* Erwin Schrodinger (1887-1961), Austrian physicist, known as the Father of Quantum Physics, a Nobel Prize winner for his invention of Wave Mechanics.
>
> *In all world there is no kind of framework within which we can find consciousness in the plural. This is simply something we construct because of the temporal plurality of individuals, but it is a false construction. The only solution to this conflict insofar as any is available to us at all lies in the ancient wisdom of the Upanishads.*Erwin Schroedinger (1887-1961), one of the greatest physicists of 20th century, who was awarded the Nobel Prize for his invention of Wave Mechanics
>
> *I go into the Upanishads to ask questions.* Niels Bohr (1885-1962), a Danish nuclear physicist who developed the 'Bohr Model of the Atom'. A Nobel Prize winner for physics in 1922 for his Theory of Atomic Structure.
>
> *The Vedanta and the Sankhya hold the key to the laws of mind and thought process which are co-related to the Quantum Field, i.e. the operation and distribution of particles at atomic and molecular levels:* - Brian David Josephson (1940), a Welsh physicist and the youngest Nobel Laureate.
>
> *Indian students should value their religious culture and, of course, the classical Indian culture bears importantly on the meaning of life and values. I would not separate the two. To separate science and Indian culture would be harmful. I don't think it is practical to keep scientific and spiritual culture separate*

- Charles H. Townes (1915-2015), an American Nobel Prize winning scientist, who worked extensively during World War II designing radar bombing systems and invented the microwave spectroscopy.

Robert Oppenheimer (1904-67), another great scientist, said: "Modern physics is exemplification and refinement of the old Hindu system". He further stated "The greatest privilege this century may claim over all previous centuries is the Vedas", adding that the, "Most terrifying scientific achievements of the West were the mystical experience of the Bhagavad Gita".

David J. Bohm (1917-1992) said: "Brahman is scientific consciousness".

[The vastest knowledge of today cannot transcend the Indian rishis", said Alfred North Whitehead (1861-1947).

"To the Indian Rishis the 'Divine Play' was the evolution of the Cosmos", said Austrian-born American author, physicist, systems theorist and deep ecologist Fritjof Capra (1939).

"Hinduism is dedicated to the idea that the Cosmos itself undergoes an immense, indeed an infinite, number of deaths and rebirths. It is the only religion in which the time scales correspond to those of modern scientific cosmology", said Dr. Carl Sagan (1934-96).

"Deepest thinking of India made its way to Greece", said John Archibald Wheeler [1911-2008].

"The motion of stars calculated by Indian thinkers 4500 years (ago) vary not even a minute from modern tables", said French astronomer, mathematician, freemason, and political leader Jean Sylvain Bailly (1736-1793). "Hindu astronomy was the source of knowledge for all world civilisations", he added.

The Editors of Encyclopedia Britannica said that the "atomic structure of matter is mentioned in the Hindu treatises Vaisesika and Nyaya".

Emmelin Pluneret said: that the Vedas contain an account of the dimension of Earth, Sun, Moon, Planets, and Galaxies".

Many great philosophers, thinkers, writers and poets of the world have described Ancient India in a number of ways.

India is the cradle of the human race" [Mark Twain 1835-1910],

"Indian literature is the profoundest thought"(Georg Wilhelm Friedrich Hegel 1770-1831),

"Vedas contain profoundest power, unfathomable peace" [Ralph Waldo Emerson (1803-1882),

"Upanishads are the products of the highest wisdom"(Arthur Schopenhauer 1788-1860),

"The Veda was the most precious gift for which the West had ever been indebted to the East" (Voltaire 1694-1778),

"India is the mother of philosophy to maths, the mother of all us"(Will Durant 1885-1981),

"The only way to salvation for mankind is the Indian Way" [Arnold Toynbee],

"To the philosophers of India, however, the Theory of Relativity' is no new discovery" adding that if the West applies the Theory of Relativity to make atom bombs, India applies it to create a new state of consciousness" [Alan Watts (1915-1973),

"India is a country to be searched for knowledge" (Friedrich Hegel 1770-1831).

"In comparison with (the) Gita, modern literature is puny and trivial" (Henry David Thoreau 1817-62),

"Facts established by today's science all are known to the seers who founded the Vedas"(Ella Wheeler Wilcox 1850-1919),

"The Vedas fill a gap which no literary work in any other language could fill"(Friedrich Max Müller 1823-1900),

"Vedas still represent eternal truth in the purest form ever written"(Paul William Roberts 1950-2019),

"Whatever be the scientific discoveries, none can dispute the eternal truths propounded by the Upanishads"(Paul Deussen 1845-1919),

"The loftiest philosophy of the Europeans appears like a feeble spark before the Vedanta"(August Wilhelm Schlegel 1767-1845),

What great scientists, Nobel Laureates and other great men and women of the world have read, understood and celebrated as sources of high knowledge unavailable except in India emanated from forests and hills of India, authored by the foresters and hills-men!

IF VEDAS EMANATED FROM FORESTS, INDIAN FORESTERS CANNOT BE BACKWARD

If Vedas which contained the most advanced scientific truths which great scientists and thinkers acknowledge had emanated from Indian forests, can the Indian foresters be regarded as backward? Obviously not. Against this background, it is ridiculous that, carbon copying the Western Anthropology of Modernity, the Indian discourse regards the forests and hills as backward and the rishis who were forest dwellers as savages and semi-barbaric, and their descendants, the forest dwellers, to be uncivilised. Contrary to Western Anthropology, which dismisses the forest as the home for savages and the barbaric, in Indian spiritual and civilisational traditions, the forests have been and are still the source of contemplation, meditation, enlightenment and higher knowledge.

PARADIGM DIFFERENCE BETWEEN THE INDIAN AND WESTERN VIEW OF FORESTS

In any attempt to study India's forest and hills people, it has to be clearly told and understood s that there is a paradigm difference between the history, civilisation and background of the traditional Indian forest communities and their contemporary counterparts in the West, whom Western anthropologists understood and labelled as savages first, barbaric next, primitive later and tribal even later, and now as an indigenous people.

To summarise, there are four reasons why there is a paradigm difference between the two perspectives – the Western and the Indian – about the forest and hills people:

One, the Western narrative is founded on the basis that the forests and the hills, and the people residing in it, are backward and that the people of the plains are advanced. But the Indian reality is that the forests are the places of contemplation and the very origin of highest knowledge – the Aranyakas of the Vedas [Book of Forests], which contained the highest wisdom, according to the great men of the world, including Nobel Laureates.

Two, the Western narrative is almost entirely an outcome of colonial history, which distinguished between the original occupants of colonised territories and those who invaded them, but the Indian reality is different as no one invaded or occupied the territories of the original occupants.

Three, in the Western narrative, the people of the forests and the hills are totally separate in history, culture and faith. The Indian reality is that the people of the forests and the hills have a strong to broadly common and shared history, culture and faiths with the people of the plains.

Four, the Western narrative justified the forced segregation or separation of the forest and hills people and disconnected the Indian foresters from their plainsmen cousins. In direct contrast to this forced separation, the Indian history shows continuous migration between the forests and the plains, and according to the UN Dhebar Commission, which admitted that there was such two-way migration between the forests and the plains, and therefore, it is difficult to say which were the homes of the people of the forests and which were the homes of the hill people.

WESTERN PARADIGM AND VERRIER ELVIN

But in a bizarre imitation totally inappropriate to the Indian context, the Indian establishment, before and after independence, applied Western anthropological assumptions to the forest and hill people of India. Shaped by the western anthropological thought, the Indian establishment, saw the forest and hills people as savages and barbaric like the West did till at least Independence. Post- Independence, while the Western notion diluted, confusion prevailed over how to perceive them, but the dominant view was to continue with western concepts.

The post-Independent Indian establishment was guided by a Westerner Dr. Verrier Elvin who, though not a trained anthropologist, started off as one. A Christian evangelist, he came under the influence of Mahatma Gandhi, gave up his priesthood but not his faith, married a couple of forest dwelling girls and spent over three decades with foresters in different parts of Bharat. He became the anthropological adviser to the government post Independence. He became the missionary of what he liked to call 'Mr. Nehru's Gospel for tribes'. He shaped the policy of the Government of India on foresters and hillmen. His ideas and work on the forest dwelling people became the Bible for the government for which he won the Sahitya Academy Award. He was also a recipient of the Padma Bhushan (India's third highest civilian honour) in 1961. Elvin observed and spent considerable time with forest dwellers unfortunately not from the original Indian civilisational perspective which integrated with the plainsmen. He could not fathom them as a community that had been forcibly separated by the colonists from the plainsmen and kept isolated in Reserved Forests under British colonial rule, which in turn, led to a deep development-related divide between the plains and forests, making the people of these dwellings vastly different to each other to the naked eye [See infra Blind import of Western Anthropology caused development Divide]. As he did not know the Indian civilisational paradigm he could not see a totally different paradigm operated in Bharat.

Because of his association with Mahatma Gandhi who had been highly critical of the Western civilisation, Elvin did not accept, and, therefore, could not apply the Western Anthropology of Modernity which regarded the forest people as savages to be civilised in its entirety. He valued their culture, but wanted their culture preserved without interference from their civilisational cousins in the plains, without understanding the millennial commonality between the plainsmen and foresters. He did not understand that it would not be preserved when the forest people were allowed to be converted in which he was deeply involved. His position on the forest people in principle was the same as the Western – that is they are the "other people" for the plains people. His solution was to keep them isolated forever like the colonists did. He was a Trisanku – neither was he a modern Westerner to destroy their culture and modernise them, nor a Bharatiya, to renew the cultural common links between the plainsmen and foresters and maintain their culture.

Verrier Elvin was therefore convinced that their culture needs to be preserved without integrating with plainsmen. This was definitely contrary to the modern Western anthropological solution that they must be contracted out of their societies and modernised. Closely looked at, it would be clear that Elvin's solution of complete isolation was far more dangerous to national integration and national security than the Western model of anthropologically modernising them. It was also in total conflict with the millennia of civilisational interaction between the forest and plains people in India.

Verrier Elvin was also confused in his understanding of the Indian foresters and the hillmen of India as compared to their counterparts in the West. The confusion was the result of a gap in his understanding of the foresters' position in Indian civilisation and their contemporary status caused by long years and decades of isolation from the plainsmen imposed by the colonists. Elvin did not have the opportunity to study the Vedas, the Puranas and the philosophic traditions of India relating to the foresters and hillmen. He did not have the overarching civilisational bonds between the foresters and plainsmen in India. He was obviously misled by the bewildering and conflicting diversity of the Indian peoples both in the plains and in the forests. In those times there were debates about whether the people of the plains, who were bafflingly diverse themselves, constituted a nation or not. The plains people too were as bewilderingly diverse as the people of the forests. And yet the entire freedom movement succeeded and the subsequent history of India proved that underneath the puzzling diversity was an underlying unity which did not stop at the plains but extended deep into the forests of India. Had he studied and done a civilisational analysis of India, he would probably have acquired a proper understanding of the nation's civilisational unity and harmony underneath the baffling diversities. He would have been shocked to know that in the Indian perspective forests are not backward and that the forest people are not backward.

WESTERN ANTHROPOLOGY CAUSED DEVELOPMENT DIVIDE

The blind import of the Western idea of the forest and hills people as the other people, into India by the colonial regime, in total disregard and negation of their broadly common civilisation, culture, history, mythology and even worship, forced them to isolate the forest people from those living in plains like they did in the other colonised countries. The colonists segregated the foresters by introducing a reserved forest area policy and cutoff the millennial civilisational and cultural intercourse that had existed between the foresters and plainsmen from ancient times. The colonists could not understand that the foresters and plainsmen of India were not different like the colonists and the foresters in the lands they had colonised. Many characteristics of the forest and hills people could be found in the people of the plains in India. For example, if the Indian foresters are animists, the plainsmen are no less so. The names of forest and hill communities are found in the Ramayana and the Mahabharata and the other Puranas. Instead of building on that civilisational integration, the blind application of the Western Anthropology of Modernity allowed the colonists to physically divide the people of the forests from the people of the plains. This physical divide over a couple of centuries of colonial rule, transformed into a developmental divide and eventually became a psychological divide between the plainsmen and foresters during the colonial period itself. Post-Independence, it became a political divide in which external forces intervened and enlarged this into separatism and insurgency that soon turned into national security issues.

This is despite the fact that the first and perhaps the only official study of the forests and hills people of India by the independent Indian state in 1960s – the UN Dhebar Committee – had said that in pre-colonial times the forest and hills people in India were never isolated historically, civilisationally and culturally, and there was a free movement between them in the pre-colonial days. The committee, as mentioned earlier, had also relied on the common civilisational bonds between forest and plains and their peoples'. The committee had said that it was colonial rule that created reserved areas rules and brought about a physical isolation of the forest people. This became easier to accomplish with the colonists co-opting the people of the plains as their subordinates, and even as partners, in the administration of the state. The divide that is seen during the colonial period is a development divide caused by centuries of isolation between the two — the plainsmen and foresters.

WHAT THE INDIAN PLAINS PEOPLE REGARD AS SACRED, THE WESTERN ANTHROPOLOGISTS REGARD AS BACKWARD — THE GOAN AND SAHYADRI EXAMPLES

Here is a telling instance of contrast between the plainsmen of the West and the Indian plainsmen about how they see the forests and foresters

In the Portuguese rule of Goa, the colonial perspective that people living in the forests and hills were savage, uncivilised and backward, and this description was extended to hill and forest people of Sahyadri Range. The Portuguese regarded the people of the hills and forests in the Sahyadri Range as uncivilised and backward. But were they? The segregation as civilised and backward was on the basis of whether one was a Christian or Hindu. Ther former was considered as civilised and the latter was condemned as backward.

In his paper titled 'Rugged Hills', 'Dense Forests' and 'Backward People'. Imagining Landscapes in Nineteenth-Century Colonial Goa published in the International Journal for History Culture and Modernity, José Miguel Ferreira of the University of Lisbon, says that Goa's Portuguese rulers divided the Goans into two categories - the Old Conquests and the New Conquests. The first were converted to Christianity and the second were designated as Hindus. The Christian converts were recognised as civilised, but the Hindus were regarded as semi-savage and uncivilised.

Ferreira says "Well into the twentieth century both among the colonial administrators and the local elites, most authors were unanimous in describing the population of the New Conquests as backward, semi-savage and alienated from the values of modernity."

While in the Goan Christian establishment, some were willing to declare all Goans as belonging to the same race, Goan Catholics tended to emphasise the difference between the Old and New. They said the New Conquests were "semi savage people who lived in these rugged hills criss-crossed by deep gorges and ravines, shadowed by dense forests, and were physically morally superior to the Catholic elites of the Old Conquests".

Ferreira sums up how, even as late as 1961, this view prevailed in the abstract of his essay. He says: "The former Portuguese colony of Goa is best known nowadays as a tourist hotspot. To many, its iconic landscape is one of sandy beaches and whitewashed churches nestling among the paddy fields and coconut trees. But beyond this postcard image there is another lesser known landscape, epitomised by the rugged mountains and forests of the Sahyadri Range."

During the Portuguese colonial period, which lasted until 1961, this was the 'other landscape' of Goa, frequently portrayed as 'wild', 'backward' and inherently hostile to colonial rule.

The message is clear. If you convert you become civilised. If you don't you are savage and uncivilised.

What a contrast! The people of the plains, forests and the hills regard the Sahyadri hills and forests as sacred, while Western colonisers label it as backward and uncivilised. This brings out the paradigm difference between the two perspectives on not only forests and hills, but also about the people of forests and hills.

BHARATAVARSH CONCEPT: INTEGRATION OF ALL PEOPLE OF BHARAT – UNPARALLELED IN THE WORLD

The story of the millennial civilisational commonality of the foresters and plainsmen will be incomplete without the narrative of the millennial cultural and civilisational unity and integrity of Bharat. The history and geography as the world knows starting from the Greco-Roman times have been narration of wars, empires and conquests. All ancient history before the Greco-Romans are surmises based on archaeological excavations and epigraphy. The history of the even the Greco-Roman and later empires was not the history of a nation-state. It was a history of capturing territories and ruling over them and not of establishing a nation-state which meant an alignment between the people and the geography on which they lived with a commonalty. Henry Kissinger's treatise "Diplomacy" which traces the development of the idea of nation captures the absence of nation-states till the collapse of the Habsburg Empire. According to Eric Hobsbawm, the contemporary idea of a nation-state integrating geography with a people and a state, or a ruler, is a development of 18-19 century Europe. National Movements and Intermediary Structures in Europe (NISE) and the University of East London (UEL) conventionally say, "Nationalism is a doctrine invented in Europe at the beginning of the nineteenth century".

But the idea of a nation, or Rashtra, nation Rajya and Jana or subjects existed in Rig Vedic times, pointing to the existence of the idea of a nation-state. The Krishna Yajur Veda [in Bramhanam 1.8.3] says that the lives of the subjects must conform to the nation [Rashtra] and if a conflict arises between the interests of the nation and the interests of its subjects when the latter will have to yield to the former.

But, never before the 18th century has the concept of a nation and as a geographical entity been identified with a specific people, or a way of life, or with a ruler existed anywhere in the West. It is only so in Bharat. For millennia, India, that is Bharat, was known as Bharatvarsh. The term Bharat is as old as the Vedas. Iravatham Mahadevan even traces the idea of Bharat in the Indus Seals of 5000 years ago. The term Bharatvarsh as a nation of specific people living within geographical limits that match with the Bharat before the Islamic invasion occurs in Vishnu Purana, Vayu Purana, Linga Purana, Brahmanda Purana, Agni Purana, Skanda Purana and the Markandeya Purana. Two millennia before, the Puranas described the physical boundaries of Bharatvarsh, the way people lived, and their belief in Karma and rebirth with the goal of attaining Moksha.

The Vayu Purana, regarded as the oldest, and varyingly dated between 350 BCE and 203-300 CE, says "Bharatavarasha is bounded by the Himalayas to the north and by the ocean to the south. Bharatavarsha is divided into nine regions, or dvipas. These were Indradvipa, Kaserumana, Tamraparni, Gabhastimana, Navadvipa, Soumya, Gandharva and Varuna. This adds up to eight. The ninth region is an island that is surrounded by the ocean on all sides, [obviously Sri Lanka] it was not very easy to travel from one region of Bharatavarsha to another because transportation problems were enormous. The southern tip of Bharatavarsha is known as Kumarika (Cape Comorin or Kanyakumari). Beyond the boundaries of Bharatvarsha live the disbelievers, i.e., those who disbelieve in the Vedas. To the east live the Kiratas and to the west live the Yavanas. Bharatavarsha proper is populated by Brahmanas, Kshatriyas, Vaishyas and Shudras."

Bharatvarsha, according to the Puranas, is not just a geographic landscape in which specific people resided; it was also a nation-state with a condition. The Vayu Purana says, "He who conquers the whole of Bharatavarhsa is celebrated as a samrat.' That was why Asoka, who built an empire as vast as Bharatvarsha, including Sri Lanka, was called a Samrat. The cultural integration of Bharat and all of its residents, including the forest and hills people is as old as Bharatvarsha itself.

Yet even kings who ruled Bharat chose to go to the forest to meet their Vanaprastha responsibilities. The Vayu Purana also says, "This country is known as Bharatavarsa since the times King Dushyanta who handed over his kingdom to his son Bharata and went into the forests to practice ascetism.

This example reveals how even kings moved into the forests in search of their higher purpose in life, which again endorses the Indian fact that the forest is the place for higher knowledge and enlightenment. This again confirms that the Indian paradigm of forest-plains relation is totally opposite of the Western notion that the forest is backward and the foresters too are backward.

Against this background, is it not ridiculous to apply the Western move to divide and see the people of the forest and the plains people as two different peoples, i.e., the plainsmen as civilised and forest dwellers as backward.

INTERDISCIPLINARY & INTEGRATED APPROACH NEEDED

It is evident from testimonies from different disciplines– literary, epigraphic, historic, linguistic– and comparative civilisational and historic evidences explained above, that any study, or understanding of these relationships between the people of the plains and the people of the forests in India has to break the silos of individual discipline in which different testimonies is separately confined. Unless the silos are broken and an inter-silo, that is, an inter-disciplinary, study is undertaken an integral and comprehensive view will not emerge. To be comprehend the deeply underlying integration between the Indian plainsman and foresters, a multidisciplinary and interdisciplinary approach is a must. Otherwise getting fuller understanding of the forest and the hills people will be impossible. Unless the knowledge contained and confined in different silos and discipline are studied in an inter disciplinary way, looking at each silo of knowledge of the Indian civilisation in an isolated manner will be six blind people trying to comprehend an elephant, i.e., each one holding one relevant, but dismembered piece of evidence about the elephant, rather than comprehending it as a whole.

A geography with identified people, or even identifying itself as a nation-state for millennia encouraging migrations between the forests and the plains, where even Kings go to the forests in search of enlightenment and knowledge, cannot be seen as, or equated to the Americas, Europe, the Oceanias, or even Africa. Civilisational and historic integration between the forest and plains in India completely rules out the view that the forest people are or can be "other people". They are not and cannot be the other people in India.

One can understand what kind of bandwidth of diverse disciplines is needed to study and understand how different is the relation between forests and plains and between their respective peoples'.

CONCLUSION

In this background, it does not need a seer to say that there is a need for silo-free complete and comprehensive review and reversal of the current approach of the Indian establishment to study the relation between the foresters and plainsmen of India. For undertaking such a review, or considering the need for a reversal of thought and action, the establishment needs a complete psychological shift and makeover.

Here, I would like to recall an incident in the life of Maharishi Aurobindo, who went from Bengal to Pondicherry following the collapse of the revolutionary movement. After the revolutionary movement failed and till the mass political movement took off under Mahatma Gandhi, there was complete darkness in India. Many were looking towards Aurobindo, an intellectual giant, to show the way out of this darkness. But what did Aurobindo do? He was looking for inspiration from a mad-looking mystic Kullachami, on whom Subramania Bharati has written a number of poems. People were left surprised when the illiterate Kullachami revealed the path of enlightenment to Aurobindo by just pouring out tea from a cup onto the ground and showing the empty cup to Aurobindo. When Aurobindo's friends asked him what that message was, he said that Kullachami had asked him to empty his mind and begin thinking afresh.

That is how the exercise to review and reverse the Western anthropological approach to the forest and hill people of India should begin.

Bibliography

Abbi, B.L. and S. Saberwal, (1969). *'Urgent Research in Social Anthropology'.* Indian Institute of Advanced Study, Simla.

Aguilar, A. (1968). 'The Intellectuals and the Revolution', *Monthly Review.*

Aitchison, C.U. (1892). *'A Collection of Treaties, Engagements and Sanads: Relating to India and Neighbouring Countries',* Vol. I. Calcutta: Office of the Superintendent of Government Printing India.

Akhup, A. (2013). 'Revisiting tribal studies in India: an epistemological perspective', *Journal of Tribal Intellectual Collective of India,* vol. 1, pp. 1–14.

Ambedkar, B.R. (1948). *'Castes in India: Their Mechanism, Genesis and Development, paper presented at an anthropology seminar taught by Dr A.A. Goldenweizer at Columbia University, 1916, text first printed in: Indian Antiquary',* vol. XLI, May 1917, reprinted as Dr Babasaheb Ambedkar: Writings and Speeches, vol. I., Vasant Moon (ed.), Mumbai: Education Department, Government of Maharashtra, 1979.

Anil Kumar, K. (2006). 'Ethno-medicine, Indigenous Healers and Disease Healing Practices among the Kolam of Adilabad District of Andhra Pradesh', *Journal of Social Anthropology,* vol. 3, no. 1, pp. 75–88.

———, (2010). 'Dam and Displacement: A Review', *Journal of Humankind Indira Gandhi Rashtriya Manav Sangrahalaya, Bhopal,* vol. 4–6. pp. 101–135.

———, (2011). *Relevance of Local Environmental Knowledge in the Era Globalization,* New Delhi: Serial Publication.

———, (2012). 'Local Knowledge and Agricultural Sustainability: A Case Study of Pradhan Tribe in Adilabad District', *International Journal of Science and Research (IJSR),* vol. 1, no. 1, pp. 19–26.

Archana Prasad (2003). *Against Ecological Romanticism: Verrier Elwin and the Making of an Anti-Modern Tribal Identity,* New Delhi: Three Essays Collective. ISBN: 978-81-8878-903-0.

Atal, Y. (2013). 'A note on the concept of tribe', in *Tribes in India,* ed. V.K. Srivastava, Delhi: Serials Publications, pp. 36–48.

Aurora, G.S. (1972). *Tribe-Caste-Class Encounters.* Hyderabad: Administrative Staff College of India.

Bailey, F.G. (1960). *Tribe, Caste and Nation: A Study of Political Activity and Political Change in Highland Odisha.* Manchester: Manchester University Press.

———, (1961). 'Tribe' and 'Caste' in India. *Contributions to Indian Sociology.* Vol 5, P. 7–19.

Baker, D. (1991). 'State Polity, the Market Economy and Tribal Decline: The Central Provinces – 1861–1920', *Indian Economy and Social History Review,* vol. 28, no. 4, pp. 341–370.

Balakrishnan, V. (1980). Comment (pp. 4–5). In *Journal of the Indian Anthropological Society*, 15, 1–14 on the article by Basu, A. and Biswas, S. K. (1980). 'Is Indian Anthropology dead/dying?'

Balaram, A. (2021). 'Crafting New Narratives of Diasporic Resistance with Indo-Caribbean Women and Gender-Expansive People across Generations', *Societies*, vol. 2021, no. 11, p. 2.

Banarjee, M. (1989). 'An Historical outline of pre-British Chottanagpur, Ranchi Education Publications', quoted by Joseph Marianus Kujur and Sonajharia Minz, op. cit., 38.

Basu Mullick, S. (1992). 'The Concept of the Supreme Being in the Sarna System of Religion', in Cultural Chota Nagpur – Unity in Diversity, ed. S. Basu Mullick, New Delhi: Uppal Publishing House.

Basu, A. and S.K. Biswas, (1980). 'Is Indian Anthropology dead/dying?' *Journal of the Indian Anthropological Society*, vol. 15, pp. 1–14.

Bates, C. (1995). 'Race, caste and tribe in Central India: the early origins of Indian anthropometry', in *The Concept of Race in South Asia*, ed. P. Robb, Delhi: Oxford University Press, pp. 219–259.

Baviskar, A. (2023). 'Decolonising a Discipline in Distress: Anthropology's Pasts, Present and Futures in India', *American Ethnologists*, vol. 50, Issue 3, August, pp. 387–395.

Behera, M.C. (2000). *Tribal Religion Change and Continuity*, Commonwealth Publishers. University of Michigan.

Behera, M.C. (2010). 'Tribes in India: A Discourse of Temporal and Contextual Limitations', *The Eastern Anthropologist*, vol. 63, no. 2. April–June, pp. 184–187.

Behura, N.K. and N. Panigrahi, (2006). *Tribals and the Indian Constitution: Functioning of Fifth Schedule in the State of Odisha*, New Delhi: Rawat Publications.

Beteille, A. (1986). 'The Concept of Tribe with Special Reference to India', *European Journal Sociology*, vol. 27, pp. 297–318.

———, (1997). 'Newness in sociological enquiry'. *Sociological Bulletin*, 46(l): pp. 97–110.

———, (2004). *Society and Politics in India, Essays in a Comparative Perspective*, New Delhi: Oxford University Press.

Bhangya Bhukya. (2010). *Subjugated Nomads: The Lambadas under the Rule of the Nizam, Hyderabad*. New Delhi: Orient Black Swan.

Bhattacharya, R.K. and J. Sarkar, (2002). *Passage through Indian Civilization: N. K. Bose Thoughts and Work*, Kolkata: Anthropological Survey of India.

Bhukya, B. (2008). 'The Mapping of the Adivasi Social: Colonial Anthropology and Adivasis', *Economic and Political Weekly*, vol. 43, pp. 103–109.

———, (2017). *The Roots of the Periphery: A History of the Gonds of Deccan India*, New Delhi: Oxford University Press.

———, (2021). 'Featuring Adivasi/Indigenous Studies', *Economic and Political Weekly*, vol. 56, pp. 13–17.

Birinder, P.S. (2011). 'Defining the Tribe: Denotified Tribes of Punjab', *The Eastern Anthropologist*, vol. 63, No -3-4, July–December, pp. 418–419.

Biswaranjan, T. (2023). 'Decolonising Ethnography and Tribes in India: Toward an Alternative Methodology', *Frontiers Political Science*, vol. 5, pp. 1047276.

Biswas, S., R. Shaw, S. Bala and A. Mazumdar, (2017). 'Inventorization of Some Ayurvedic Plants and Their Ethnomedicinal Use in Kakrajhore Forest Area of West Bengal', *Journal of Ethnopharmacology*, vol. 197, pp. 231–241.

Bodhi, S.R. and B. Jojo, (2019). *The Problematics of Tribal Integration: Voices from India's Alternative Center*, Hyderabad: The Shared Mirror Publishing House.

Borofsky, R. (2004). *Conceptualizing Public Anthropology*, http://www.publicanthropology.org/Defining/definingpa.htm, accessed 24 December 2024.

Bose, N.K. (1961). *Cultural Anthropology*, Asia Publishing House, New Delhi.

———, (1941). 'The Hindu Method of Tribal Absorption', *Science and Culture*, vol. 7, pp. 188–194.

———, (1952). 'Current Research Projects in Indian Anthropology', *Man in India*, Vol 32(2) pp. 121–133.

———, (1967). 'The Hindu Method of tribal absorption' in *Culture and Society in India*, ed. N.K. Bose, Bombay: Asia Publishing House (1977 reprint).

———, (1967). *Peasant Life in India: A Study in Indian Unity and Diversity*, Delhi: Anthropological Survey of India (memoir no. 5).

———, (1971). 'Some Aspects of Indian Civilization', *Man in India*, vol. 51, no. 1, pp. 1–14.

———, (2006). 'Panchanan Mitra', *Current Science*, Vol 91(11) p. 1439.

Bose, P.K. (2007). 'The Anthropologists as 'Scientists' Nirmal Kumar Bose', in *Anthropology in the East*, eds. P. Oberoi, N. Sundari and S. Deshpande, New Delhi: Permanent Black.

Bosu Mullick, S. (1993). 'Jharkhand Movement: A Historical Analysis', In *Continuity and Change in Tribal Society*, ed. M. Miri, Shimla: Indian Institute of Advanced Study.

Buddhadeb, C. (1992). *Tribal Transformation in India: Ethno politics and Identity Crisis*, New Delhi: Inter-India Publications.

Bulke, C. (1950). *Ramkatha: Utpati aur Vikas*, Prayag: Hindi Parishad Prakashan.

Burling, R. (1963). *Rengsanggri: Family and Kinship in a Garo Village*, Philadelphia: University of Pennsylvania Press.

Burman Roy, B.K. (2000). Professor K.P. Chattopadhyaya: A Scientist with Social Concern', in *Life and Times of an Indian Anthro-pologist K.P. Chattopadhyaya: A Collection of Seminar Papers*, ed. G. Chattopadhyaya, Calcutta: The Asiatic Society, 2000, pp. 50–51.

Butler, C.J. (1875). Report of the Exploration Survey of the Naga Hills, Season 1874–75. Shillong: Assam Secretariat Press Eliot, J. (1794). Observations on the inhabitants of the Garrow Hills, made during a public deputation in the years 1788 and 1789. Asiatick Res. 3, 21–45.

Cécile, G.P. (2012). *Whose Centre? Title Gonasika—A Tribal Sacred Place and a Hindu Centre of Pilgrimage*. Voices from the Periphery.

Chakladar, H.C. (1972) Fifty years ago-the woes of a class of Bengal peasantry under European Indigo planters (First published in The Dawn and Dawn Society's Magazine, Calcutta July, 1905). Nil Durpan or The Indigo Planting Mirror, Edited with an Introduction by Sarkar Sen Gupta, 1972. Indian publications: Calcutta, pp. 187–205.

Chandra, P.K. (2022, December 8). 'Traditional Ecological Knowledge of Tribal Communities and Sustainability of Nature and Natural Resources in Pachmarhi Biosphere Reserve in India', *International Journal of Ecology*, vol. 2022, p. 13.

Chandran, M.D.S. and M. Gadgil, (1993). *Sacred Groves and Sacred Trees of Uttar Kannada (a pilot study)*. Report submitted to the Indira Gandhi National Centre for the Arts.

Channa, S.M. (2008). 'Concept of Mainstream', in Indian Tribes and the Mainstream, eds. S.K. Chaudhury and S.M. Patnaik, Jaipur: Rawat Publications.

Chaudhury, S.K. (2007). 'Civilisational Approach to the Study of Indian Society', *The Eastern Anthropologist*, vol. 60, pp. 501–508.

Chauhan, B.R. (1970). *Towns in the Tribal Setting*. Delhi: National Publishing House.

Chitrasen, P. (1997). 'Tribal and Non-Tribal Interaction in Odisha; A study of Samalei/ Samaleswari Devi in Sambalpur in Georg Pfeffer and Deepak Kumar Behera's Contemporary Society: Tribal Studies', *Development Issues Transition and Change*, vol. 2, New Delhi: Concept Publishing Company. Cohn, B. (1971). *India: The Social Anthropology of a Civilization*. Oxford University Press.

Chowdhury, M. and R. Mukherjee, (2012). Wild edible plants consumed by local communities of Maldah district of West Bengal, India. *Indian Journal of Science and Research*, vol. 3, no. 2, pp. 163–170.

Claerhout, S. (2014). 'Gandhi, Conversion and the Equality of Religions: More Experiments with Truth', *Numen* vol. 61, pp. 53–82.

Cohn, B. (1987a). *An Anthropologists among the Historian and other Essays*. New Delhi: Oxford University Press.

Cohn, B.S. (1987a). *An Anthropologists among the Historian and Other Essays*. New Delhi: Oxford University Press.

———, (1987b). 'Notes on the Study of Indian Society and Culture' in *An Anthropologists among the Historian and Other Essays*, ed. B.S. Cohn, New Delhi: Oxford University Press.

———, (1987b). 'Notes on the Study of Indian Society and Culture' in *An Anthropologists among the Historian and other Essays*, ed. B. S. Cohn, New Delhi: Oxford University Press.

Dalton, E.T. (1872). *Descriptive Ethnology of Bengal*, Calcutta: Office of the Superintendent of Government Printing.

Das, A.K. and M.K. Raha, (1967). *The Rabhas of West Bengal*, Calcutta: Government of West Bengal.

Das, B.M. (1967). 'Assamese Culture and the Hill People of north-eastern India', in *A Common Perspective for north-east India*, eds., R. Mitra and B. Das Gupta, Calcutta: Pannalal Das Gupta.

Das, N.K. (1988). 'Tribal Priesthood and Shamanism in Chattisgarh', *Journal of Indian Anthropological Society*, vol. 23, pp. 223–231.

Das, T.C. (1941). 'Cultural anthropology in the service of the individual and the nation', pp. 1-29. presidential Address delivered in the Section of Anthropology in the Twenty eighth Indian Science Congress: Benares.

Das, T.C. (1945). *The Purums: An Old Kuki Tribe of Manipur. Anthropological Paper No. 7*, Calcutta: University of Calcutta.

Dasgupta, P.K. (1961). 'A Note on Inter-ethnic Relationship and Certain Changes in the Life of the War Khasi of Shella', *Vanyajati*, vol. 9, no. 3. pp. 104–114.

Dasgupta, S. (2007). 'Recasting Oraons and the 'Tribe': Sarat Chandra Roy's Anthropology' in *Anthropology in the East*, eds. P. Oberoi, N. Sundar and S. Deshpande, New Delhi: Permanent Black, pp. 132–171.

Dattaniranjan, N. and A.S. Hallikeri, (2023). 'The Essence of the Tribal Knowledge System in the Indian Knowledge System, Shodh Drisht', *An International Peer Reviewed Refereed Research Journal*, vol. 14, no. 51. pp. 31–34.

Dave, P.C. (1960). *The Grasias*, Delhi: Bharatiya Adimjati Sevak Sangh.

Delphin, J.G., Jr. (1987, September 6–8). 'Philippines Ethnic Minorities: The Continuing Struggle for Survival and Self-Determination', In *Proceedings of the Conference on Forest Resources Crisis in the Third World*, Malysia: Sahabat Alam.

Dev, N. (1997). *From Tribe to Caste*, Shimla: Indian Institute of Advanced Study.

Devalle, S.B.C. (1992). *Discourses of Ethnicity: Culture and Protest in Jharkhand*, New Delhi and Newbury Park, CA: Sage.

Dorothy, L. and S. Reddy, (2010). 'Child Health Status in North Eastern States of India', *Indian Anthropologist*, vol. 40 (2) pp. 37–52.

Draft National Tribal Policy. (2006). *A Policy for the Scheduled Tribes of India*. Available at www.tribal.nic.in.

Dube, S.C. (1951). *The Kamar*, Lucknow: The Universal Publishers.

———, (1977). *Tribal Heritage of India, Vol 1: Ethnicity, Identity and Interaction*, New Delhi: Indian Institute of Advanced Study, Vikas Publication.

———, (1988). *Modernization and Development*, New Delhi: Sage Vistar.

Elwin, V. (1939). *The Baiga*, London: Wyman and Sons, Ltd.

———, (1942). *The Agaria*, London: Oxford University Press.

———, (1947). *The Muria and Their Ghotul*, London: Oxford University Press.

———, (1955). *The Religion of an Indian Tribe (Saoras)*, London: Oxford University Press.

———, (1960). *A Philosophy for NEFA*, Shillong: Government of Assam.

———, (1961). *When the World was Young*, New Delhi: National Book Trust.

———, (1964). *The Tribal World of Verrier Elwin: An Autobiography*, Bombay: Oxford University Press.

———, (1968). *The Nagas in the Nineteenth Century*, Bombay: Oxford University Press.

Elwin. (1943). *Muria Murder and Suicide*, London: Oxford University Press.

Epstein, S.T. (1967). 'Productive Efficiency and Customary System of Rewards in Rural South India', in *Themes in Economic Anthropology*, ed. R. Firth, London: Tavistock Publications.

Eschmann, A. (1986). 'Hinduization of Tribal Deities in Odisha: The Shakti Typology', In *The Cult: of Jagannath and Regional Tradition of Odisha*, eds., A. Eschmann, H. Kulke and G. Charan Tripathi, New Delhi: Manohar.

Eschmann, A., H. Kulke and G.C. Tripathy, (1978). *The Cult of Jagannatha and the Regional Tradition of Odisha*, New Delhi: Manohar.

Evans-Pritchard, E.E. (1955). *Theories of Primitive Religion*, London: Oxford University Press.

Fuches, S. (1960). *The Gend and Bhumia of Eastern Mandla*, Bombay: New Literature Publishing Company.

Fuller, C.J. (2017). 'Ethnographic Inquiry in Colonial India: Herbert Risley, William Crooke and the Study of Tribes and Castes', *Journal of the Royal Anthropological Institute*, vol. 23, no. 3, pp. 603–621.

Furer-Haimendorf, C.V. (1939). *The Naked Nagas*, London: Routledge and Kegan Paul.

———, (1943). *The Chenchus: Jungle Folk of the Deccan*, London: Macmillan.

———, (1945). *The Reddis of Bison Hills: A Study in Acculturation*, London: Macmillan.

———, (1948). *Raj Gonds of Adilabad: A Peasant Culture of Deccan*, London: MacMillan.

———, (1969). *The Konyak Nagas: An Indian Frontier Tribe*, New York: Holt, Reinhart and Winston.

———, (1977, October). 'The Changing Position of Tribal Populations in India', *Royal Anthropological Institute News*, no. 22.

———, (1982). *Tribes of India: The Struggle for Survival*, Univ. of California Press.

Gadgil, M. and M.D.S. Charan, (1992). 'Sacred Groves', In *Indigenous Vision: People of India-Attitudes to the Environment*, ed. G. Sen, New Delhi: Sage Publications.

Gadgil, M. and V.D. Vartak, (1976). 'Sacred Groves in Western Ghats in India', *Economic Botany*, vol. 30, pp. 152–1160.

Gayatri, B. (2013). 'Interrogating the Civilisational Approach of N.K. Bose', *The Eastern Anthropologist*, vol. 66, p. 1.

Ghosh, J. C. (1938). 'Hindu anthropology'. *Anthropological papers* (New Series),5: (27–33). Calcutta University Press: Calcutta.

Ghurye, G. S. (1963). *The Scheduled Tribes*, Bombay: Popular Prakashan.

———, (1959). *The Scheduled Tribes*, Bombay: Popular Prakashan.

———, (1963). *The Mahadev Kolis*, Bombay: Popular Prakashan.

Gopinath M.R. and K. Anil Kumar, P. Trinadha Rao and O. Springate-Baginski, (2010). *The Making of Andhra's Forest Underclass: An Historical Institutional Analysis of Forest Rights Deprivations, IPPG Discussion Papers Series 42*. Available at: www.ippg.org.uk. https://assets.publishing.service.gov.uk/media/57a08b29e5274a31e00009f2/dp42a.pdf, accessed on 22 February 2023.

———, *Obstructed Access to Forest Justice: An Institutional Analysis of the Implementation of Rights Reform in Andhra's Forested Landscapes, IPPG Discussion Papers Series 47*. Available at www.ippg.org.uk. https://assets.publishing.service.gov.uk/media/57a08b28ed915d622c000b41/dp47.pdf, accessed on 22 February 2023.

———, (2011, April 30). '*Issues Related to Implementation of the Forest Rights Act in Andhra Pradesh*', *Economic & Political Weekly*, vol. 46, no. 18.

Government of India. (1960–1961). *Report of the Scheduled Areas and Scheduled Tribes Commission*, U.N. Dhebar Commission Report, vol. I, New Delhi.

———, (1965). *Report of the advisory committee on the revision of the lists of Scheduled Castes and Scheduled Tribes (B.N. Lokur Committee)*, New Delhi: Department of Social Security.

Guha, A. (2025). 'Decolonisation Trends in Indian Anthropology', South Asian Anthropologist, 25 (1), pp. 87–90.

———, (2011). 'Tarak Chandra Das: A Marginalized Anthropologist', *Sociological Bulletin*, vol. 2011, pp. 245–265.

———, (2018a). 'Scrutinising the Hindu Method of Tribal Absorption', *Special article in Economic and Political Weekly*, vol. 53, no. 17, pp. 105–110.

———, (2018b, February 24). 'Nationalist Anthropology', *The Statesman*, p. 8.

———, (2019). 'Towards an Alternative Discourse: Colonial Legacy and Hindu Anthropology', *Frontier*, vol. 52, pp. 13–16.

———, (2023). *Nation-Building in Indian Anthropology: Beyond the Colonial Encounter*, London and New York: Routledge.

Guha, B.S. (1936). 'Dr Panchanan Mitra', *Current Science*, p. 98.

———, (1937). 'Progress of anthropology in India during the past twenty-five years'. pp. 300–335. Indian Science Congress Association: Calcutta.

———, (2021). 'Nation Building on the Margins: How the Anthropologists of India Contributed?' *Sociological Bulletin*, vol. 2021, pp. 59–75.

———, (2007). 'Between Anthropology and Literature: The Ethnographies of Verrier Elwin', in *Anthropology in the East*, eds., P. Oberoi, N. Sundar and S. Deshpande, New Delhi: Permanent Black.

Guha, R. and M. Gadgil, (1992). *This Fissured Land: An Ecological History of India*, Berkeley: University of California Press.

Gupta, P. (2021). *Role of Local Traditional Healers in Preservation of Traditional Knowledge and Biodiversity Conservation*, Spiritual Botany. https://www.spiritualbotany.com/emergingresearchers/role-of-local-traditional-healers-inpreservation-of-traditional-knowledge-and-biodiversityconservation/, accessed 1 November 2021.

Gurumurthy, S. (2023). *Need for an Indian Civilization Approach to Study India's Forest and Hill People*, 3, San Martin Marg, New Delhi: Vivekananda International Foundation.

Hardiman, David. (1987). *The Coming of the Devi: Adivasi Assertion in Western India*, New Delhi: Oxford University Press.

High Level Committee. (2014). *Report of the High-Level Committee on socio- economic, health and educational status of tribal communities of India*, Ministry of Tribal Affairs, Government of India.

Hivale, S. (1946). *The Pardhans of the Upper Narbada Valley*, Bombay: Oxford University Press (Published for Man in India).

Hockings, P. (1989). *Blue Mountains: The Ethnography and Biogeography of a South Indian Region*, Oxford: Oxford University Press.

Hoineilhing, S. (2017). *Deconstructing Colonial Ethnography: An Analysis of Missionary Writings on North East India*, New Delhi: Ruby Press.

Hunter, W.W. (1876). *A Statistical Account of Bengal: Chittagong Hill Tracts, Chittagong, Noakhali, Tipperah, Hill Tipperah VI*, London: Trubner and Co.

Inden, R. (1990). *Imagining India*, Oxford and Cambridge, MA: Basil Blackwell Ltd.

Jagannath, P. (1988). *Ethnic Minority in the Process of Development*, Rawat Publication.

Joshi, P.C. (1988). 'Traditional Medical System in Central Himalayas', *The Eastern Anthropologist*, vol. 41, no. 1, pp. 78–86.

———, (2023). *Indian Anthropology in the 21st Century Contemporary Concerns and Future directions, 12th Nirmal Kumar Bose Memorial Lecture*, New Delhi: IGNCA.

Kala, C.P. (2022). 'Traditional Ecological Knowledge of Tribal Communities and Sustainability of Nature and Natural Resources in Pachmarhi Biosphere Reserve in India', *Hindawi International Journal of Ecology*, vol. 2022, Article ID 5979024, p. 13.

Kalam, M.A. (1996). *Sacred Groves in Kodagu District of Karnataka (South India): A Socio-Historical Study*, Pondicherry: Institute Francais de Pondichery.

Kamei, R. (2021). *Uncivilizing the Mind: How Anthropology Shaped the Discourse on Tribes in India*, The Caravan. Available online at: https://caravanmagazine.in/books/Anthropologists-Tribes-India, accessed on 30 April 2022.

Kanato, C.G. (2021). *Critical Reflections on the Konyak Naga Ethnography*, The Oriental Anthropologist.

Karve, I. (1961). *Hindu Society: An Interpretation*, Poona: Deccan College.

———, (1969). *Yuganta: The End of an Epoch*, Poona: Deshmukh Prakashan.

Kaushal, M. (2021). 'Tribal Traditions of Ramkatha', in *Hinduism and Tribal Religions, Encyclopedia of Indian Religions*, eds., P. Jain et al., Springer Nature.

———, (2021). *Lakshman's Trial by Fire: Does the Gond Ramayani Invert the Ramayan?* https://indianculturalforum.in/2021/08/12/lakshmans-trial-by-fire does-the-gond-ramayani-invert-the-ramayan, accessed on 02 February 2024.

Kaushal, M., A. Bhalla and R. Pant, (2015). *Ramkatha in Narratives, Performance and Pictoral Traditions*, New Delhi: Publisher Indira Gandhi National Centre for the Arts and Aryan Book International.

Kosambi, D.D. (1956). *An Introduction to the Study of Indian History*, Rep. Ed., Bombay: Popular Prakashan.

———, (1975). *The Culture and Civilization of Ancient India in Historical Outline*, Delhi: Vikas Publishing House.

Kumar, S., J. Gupta, N. Kumar, K. Dikshit, N. Navani, P. Jain and M. Nagarajan, (2006, March). 'Genetic Variation and Relationships among Eight Indian Riverine Buffalo Breeds', *Molecular Ecology*, vol. 15, no. 3, pp. 593–600.

Kumari, B. and S. Hitesh, (2019). 'The Traditional Knowledge of Wild Edible Leaf used by Tribal People in Chhattisgarh', *International Journal of Plant and Environment*. Vol 5(4) pp. 1-6.

Lakiumong Yimchunger, T. (2006). 'Re-Perusal of the term 'Tribe' and its Redeemable Humanized potentiality. A liberative perspective', *Journal of Tribal Studies*, vol. X, no. 2. July–December, pp. 45–57.

Lewin, C.T.H. (1869). *The Hill Tracts of Chittagong and the Dwellers Therein: With Comparative Vocabularies of the Hill Dialects*, Calcutta: Bengal Printing Company, Limited.

Lewis, D. (1973). 'Anthropology and Colonialism', *Current Anthropology*, vol. 14, no. 5. pp. 581–602.

M'Cosh, J. (1837). *Topography of Assam*, Calcutta: G.H Huttmann, Bengal Military Orphan Press.

Mackenzie, A. (1884). *History of the Relations of the Government with the Hill Tribes of the north-east Frontier of Bengal*, Calcutta: Printed at the Home Department Press.

Madan, T.N. (1983). *Culture and Development*, Delhi: Oxford University Press.

Mahana, R. (2019). *Negotiating Marginality: Conflicts over Tribal Development in India*, New Delhi: Social Science Press and London: Routledge.

Majumdar, D.N. (1937). *A Tribe in Transition: A Study in Culture Pattern*, London: Longmans, Green and Co., Ltd.

———, (1937). *The Affairs of a Tribe: A Study in Tribal Dynamics*, Lucknow: Universal Publishers.

———, (1950). *The Affairs of a Tribe: A Study in Tribal Dynamics*, Lucknow: Universal Publishers.

———, (1967). 'Social Organisation of the Koch of Garo Hills', in *A Common Perspective for north-east India*, eds., R. Mitra and B. Das Gupta, Calcutta: Pannalal Das Gupta.

Majumder, P.P. (1980). Comment (pp. 9–10). In *Journal of the Indian Anthropological Society*, vol. 15, pp. 1–14. on the article by Basu, A. and Biswas, S.K. (1980). 'Is Indian Anthropology dead/dying?'

Malagi, S. and S. Malagi, (2022). 'Rights of Tribal Communities and Traditional Medical Practitioners of Vaids and Hakims on Traditional Knowledge: An Indian Context', *International Journal of Novel Research and Development*, vol. 7, no. 11. pp. 832–840.

Malhotra, K.C. (1990). 'Village Supply and Safety Forest in Mizoram: A Traditional Practice of Protecting Ecosystem', In *Abstracts of 5th International Congress of Ecology*, Yokohama, Japan, p. 439.

Mandelbaum, D.G. (1962). *Society in India (two volumes)*, Bombay Popular Prakashan.

Mann, R.S. (1993). *Culture and Integration of Indian Tribes*, New Delhi:MD Publications.

Mann, R.S. and K. Mann, (1989). *Tribal Cultures and Change*, New Delhi: Mittal Marques, B., Freeman, C. and Carter, L. (2021). 'Adapting Traditional Healing Values and Beliefs into Therapeutic Cultural Environments for Health and Wellbeing', *International Journal of Environmental Research and Public Health*, vol. 19, no. 1, p. 426.

Marriott, M. (1955). *Village India: Studies in the Little Community*, Chicago: The University of Chicago Press.

Max Weber. (1919). 'Wissenschaft als Beruf,' in Wolfgang J. Mommsen and Wolfgang Schluchter, eds., Max Weber-Gesamtausgabe, vol. I/17: Wissenschaft als Beruf 1917/1919 / Politik als Beruf 1919 (Tübingen, 1992).

Mehta, P.C. (1994). *Voluntary Organisations and Tribal Development*, Udaipur: Shiva Publishers Distributors.

Mishra, A. (2005). 'Insiders and Outsiders: Studying Tribal Kandha Villages', in *Behera's Contemporary Society: Tribal Studies, Identity, Intervention and Ideology in Tribal India and Beyond*, eds., G. Pfeffer and D. Kumar, vol. 7, New Delhi: Concept Publishing Company.

Misra, K.K. (2013). 'On 'Tribe' and 'Tribalism'', In *Tribes in India*, ed. V. K. Srivastava, Delhi: Serials Publications, pp. 3–18.

Misra, K.K. and K. Anil Kumar, (2004). 'Ethno-veterinary Practices among the Konda Reddi of East Godavari District in Andhra Pradesh', *Journal of Studies of Tribes and Tribals*, vol. 2, no. 1, pp. 37–44.

Misra, P.K. (2022). *De-Colonizing Toda Ethnography*, https://www.anthropologyindiaforum.org/post/de-colonizing-toda-ethnography

Mitra, P. (1933). Research leads in anthropology in India. Man in India, XIII (1): 1-16.

Mitra, S.C. (1911). 'A Plea for Nature Study in Indian Schools', *The Calcutta Review*, vol. 1911, pp. 48–64.

Morgan, L.H. (1877). *Ancient Society, United States.*

Mukherjee, B. and B.C. Roychoudhury and D. Ghosh, (1973). *The Chero of the Palamau*, Calcutta: Anthropological Survey of India.

Mukhopadhyay, K. (2002). 'A Brief History of Relationship Between the Jarawas and Others', In *Jarawa Contact, Ours with Them, Theirs with Us*, eds. K. Mukhopadhyay, R.K. Bhattacharya and B.N. Sarkar, Kolkata: Anthropological Survey of India, pp. 25–42.

Naga, R.C. and K. Anil Kumar, (2023). *Large Dams and Displacement Issues in India: Issues of Compensation, Rehabilitation and Resettlement*, New Delhi: Aayu Publications.

Naik, T.B. (1993). 'Rama-Katha among the Tribes of India' in *Rama-Katha in Tribal and Folk Traditions of India, Anthropological Survey of India*, eds. K.S. Singh & B. Datta, Calcutta: Seagull Books, pp. 31–48.

Nandini, S. (1997). *Subalterns and Sovereigns: An Anthropological History of Bastar, 1854–1996*, New Delhi: Oxford University Press, p. 296.

Nandini, S., D. Satish and U. Patricia, (2000, June 10–16). 'Indian Anthropology and Sociology: Towards a History', *Economic and Political Weekly*, vol. 35, no. 24, pp. 1998–2002.

Nandini, S.K. (2020). 'The Bhils in the Historic Setting of Western India', In *Tribal Studies in India Perspectives of History, Archaeology and Culture*, ed., M. C. Behera, Springer.

Nicholas, D.B. (2001). *Castes of Mind*, New Jersey: Princeton University Press.

Oommen, T.K. (1998) 'Society: Tradition and Autonomy', in *Independent India: The First Fifty Years*, ed. H. Karlekar, Delhi: Oxford University Press.

Ota, A.B. and S. Reddy, (eds.) (2023). *Indigenous Knowledge Systems and Practices among the Particularly Vulnerable Tribal Groups in India*. Bhubaneshwar: Mayur Publishers.

Pandey, H.N. (1962). 'Social Interaction in a Bastar Village', *Vanyajati*, vol. 10, no 1–2. pp. 17–23.

Pathy, J. (1982). *Agrarian Structure in Tribal Gujrat and its Implications for Tribal Policies (mimeo)*, New Delhi: Indian Council of Social Science Research.

Pathy, J., et al. (1976). 'Tribal Studies in India: An Appraisal', *Eastern Anthropologist*, vol. 29, no. 4, pp. 399–417.

Piplai, D. (1980). Comment (pp. 11–12). In *Journal of the Indian Anthropological Society*, vol. 15, pp. 1–14. on the article by Basu, A. and Biswas, S.K. (1980). 'Is Indian Anthropology dead/dying?'

Prabhakar, G. and S. Mishra, (2017). *The Gond Kingdom of Chanda*, Nisha Publications.

Prakash, C.M. (2006). *Development of Indian Tribes*, New Delhi: Discovery Publishing House, pp. 1–30.

Prasad Rao. (1971). 'Sahukar and Tribal Society', *Tribe*, vol. 8, nos. 3–4, Rastogi, P. N.

Prasad, S. (1974). *Where the Three Tribes Meet*, Allahabad: Indian International Publications. Radcliff-Brown, A. R.

Pratap Digal. (2016, December). 'De-Constructing the term "Tribe/Tribal" in India: A Post-Colonial Reading', *International Journal of Sociology and Social Anthropology (IJSSA)*, vol. 1, no. 1, pp. 45–57.

Publications.

Raghavaiah, V. (1979). 'Background of Tribal Struggles in India', In *Peasant Struggles in India*, ed., A. R. Desai, New Delhi: Oxford University Press.

Ramakrishnan, P.S. (1996). 'Conserving the Sacred: From Species to Landscapes', *Nature and Resources*, vol. 32, no. l, pp. 11–19.

Ramakrishnan, P.S. and R. Boojh, (1983). 'Sacred Groves and their role in environmental conservation', in *Strategies for Environmental Management*, Lucknow: Souvenir Vol. Dept. of Science and Environment of Uttar Pradesh, pp. 6–8.

Rawat, A.S. (1991). 'Indian Wild Life through the Ages', in *History of Forestry in India*, ed., AS Rawat, New Delhi: Indus Publishing Company.

Ray, N.R. (1972). 'Presidential Address', in *Tribal Situation in India*, ed. K. S. Singh, Simla: Indian Institute of Advanced Study, p. 8.

Raychaudhuri, T.C. (1958). 'Obituary of H.C. Chaklladar', *Man in India*, vol. 1958, pp. 138–139.

Reddy, N.S. (2007). 'The Anomaly of Slow Growth of Anthropology in South Indian Academia', *The Eastern Anthropologist*, vol. 60, nos. 3&4, pp. 327–338.

Reddy, S. (2008). 'Religion Beliefs and Practices among the Koyas in Andhra Pradesh, in *Ethnographic Discourse of the Other: Conceptual and Methodological Issues*, eds., P. Mohanty, R.C. Malik and E. Kasi, Cambridge Scholars Press.

Reddy, S. (2023). 'Revival of Local Health Traditions from Healers Perspectives: Urgency of Recognition and State Support'. In *Ethnomedicine and Tribal Healing Practices in India: Challenges and Possibilities of Recognition and Integration*, Singapore: Springer Nature Singapore, pp. 347–368.

Reddy, S., G. Nemthianngai and S. Bamdev, (eds.) (2022). *Ethno-medicine and Indigenous Healing Practices: Possibilities of Recognition and Integration*. Springers.

Redfield, R. (1953). *The Primitive World and Its Transformation*, Cornel University.

———, (1956). *The Little Community Peasant Society and Culture*, University of Chicago Press.

Redfield, R. and M. Singer, (1955). 'Foreword'. In *Village India: Studies in the Little Community.*

Richman, P. (ed.) (1992). *Many Ramayanas: the diversity of a narrative tradition in South Asia*, Delhi: Oxford University Press.

Risley, H. (1915). *The People of India*. [*Reprint 1969*], Delhi: Oriental Books Reprint.

———, (1892). *Tribes and Caste of Bengal*, Calcutta: Printed at the Bengal Secretariate Press.

Roy Burman, B.K. (1972a). 'Tribal Demography: A Preliminary Appraisal', in *Tribal Situation in India*, ed., K. Suresh Singh, Simla: Indian Institute of Advanced Study.

———, (1972b). 'Integrated Area Approach to the Problems of the Hill Tribes of Northeast India', in *Tribal Situation in India*, ed., K. Suresh Singh, Simla: Indian Institute of Advanced Study.

Roy Burman, B.K. and S.P. Thukral, (1970). *Demographic and Socio-economic Profiles of the Hill Areas of north-east India. Census of India 1961*, New Delhi: Office of the Registrar General, India.

Roy Burman, J.J. (1996). 'A Comparison of sacred groves among the Mahadeo Kolis and Kunbis of Maharastra', *Indian Anthropologist*, vol. 26, pp. 37–46.

Roy, S.C. (1912). *The Munda and Their Country*, Ranchi: City Bar Library.

———, (1915). *The Oraon of Chota Nagpur*, Ranchi: Bar Library.

———, (1925). *The Birhors: A Little-known Jungle Tribe of Chota Nagpur*, Ranchi: Man in India Office.

———, (1928). *Oraon Religion and Customs*, Delhi: Gyan Publishing House.

———, (1938). 'An Indian Outlook on Anthropology', *Man*, Vol 38, pp. 146–150.

Russell, R.V. and R.B. Hira Lal, (1916). *The Tribes and Caste of the Central Provinces of India*, London: Macmillan and Co., Limited.

Sachchidanand. (1964). *Culture Change in Tribal Bihar*, Calcutta: Bookland.

———, (1965). *Profiles of Tribal Cultures in Bihar*, Firma K.L. Mukhopadhyaya.

Sahay, B.N. (1962). *Pragmatism in Development*, New Delhi: Book Hive.

Sahay, K.N. (1962). 'Trends of Sanskritisation among the Oraon', *Bulletin of Bihar Tribal Institute*, vol. 4, no. 2.

Sahay, K.N. (1963). *The Impact of Christianity on the Oraons of Three Villages in Chotanagpur*, Ph.D. Thesis. Ranchi: Ranchi University.

———, (1975). *Hindu Shrines of Chotanagpur: Case Study of Tanginath*, Simla: Indian Institute of Advanced Study.

———, (1976). *Under the Shadow of the Cross: A Study of the Nature and Process of Christainization among Oraon of Central India*, Calcutta: Institute of Social Research and Applied Anthropology.

Said, E. (1978). *Orientalism*, New York: Routledge.

Salam, S. and N.S. Jamir, (2016, July). 'Common Spices Plant Used as Medicine by the Tangkhul Tribe of Ukhrul District, Manipur, India', *International Journal of Scientific and Research Publications*, vol. 6, no. 7.

Sandys, E.F. (2008). *History of Tripura. Agartala: Tripura State Tribal Research Institute and Museum*, Government of Tripura (First Print: 1915).

Sarana, G. and D.P. Sinha, (1976). 'Status of Social-Cultural Anthropology in India', *Annual Review of Anthropology*, vol. 5, pp. 209–225.

Saraswati, B. (1970). *Contributions to the Understanding of Indian Civilization*, Karnatak University.

———, (1978). *Pottery-making Cultures and Indian Civilization*, Abhinav Publications.

———, (1979). *Pottery-making Cultures and Indian Civilization*, New Delhi: Abhinav Publications.

———, (1997). 'Tribes as Caste in "From Tribe to Caste"', ed. D. Nathan, Shimla: Indian Institute of Advanced Study.

Sastry, V.N.V.K. and M. Sundara Rao, (2011). *Changing Patterns in Tribal Societies*, Ambala City: The Associated Publishers.

Sax, W.S. (2009). *God of Justice: Ritual Healing and Social Justice in the Central Himalayas*, New Delhi: Oxford University Press.

Shah, A. (2010). *In the Shadows of the State: Indigenous Politics, Environmentalism and Insurgency in Jharkhand, India*, Durham, NC: Duke University Press.

———, (2024). 'When Decolonisation is Hijacked', *American Anthropologist*, vol. 126, no. 4. pp. 553–566.

Sherring, M.A. (1872–1881), *Hindu Tribes and Castes* (Three Volumes), London: Thacker, Spink.

Shimray, R.A. and A. Lungleng, (2017, January–June). 'Ethnomedicinal Knowledge of Plants among the Tangkhul Nagas of Manipur', *Indian Journal of Research in Anthropology*, vol. 3, no. 1.

Singer, M. (1958). 'The Great Tradition in a Metropolitan Center: Madras', *The Journal of American Folklore*, pp. 347–388.

———, (1972). *When A great Tradition Modernizes*, Chicago: Chicago University Press.

Singh, K.R. and E.P. Orik Rallen, (2013, July). Elderly Adi Women of Arunachal Pradesh: "Living Encyclopedias" and Cultural Refugia in Biodiversity Conservation of the Eastern Himalaya, India, *Environmental Management*, vol. 52, no. 3, pp. 712–735.

Singh, K.S. (1989). *Jawaharlal Nehru, Tribes and Tribal Policy*, Calcutta: Anthropological Survey of India.

———, (1993). *Mahabharata in the tribal and Folk Traditions of India*, Rashtrapati Nivas, Shimla: Indian Institute of Advanced Study.

———, (1998). *People of India: India's Communities*, Anthropological Survey of India.

———, (2002). *Birsa Munda and His Movement (1872–1901). A Study of a Millenarian Movement in Chotanagpur*, Kolkata: Seagull Books.

———, (2003). *Hinduism and Tribal Religion in Culture, Religion and Philosophy: Critical Studies in Syncretism and Inter-Faith Harmony*, Jaipur: Rawat Publications.

Singh, K.S. and B. Datta, (1993). *Rama-Katha in Tribal and Folk Traditions of India: Proceedings of a Seminar, Anthropological Survey of India*, Calcutta: Seagull Books.

Sinha, R. (1962). *The Akas*. Shillong: Research Department, Advisers' Secretariat. Sinha, Surajit.

Sinha, S. (1957). 'Tribal Cultures of Peninsular India as a Dimension of Little tradition In the Study of Indian Civilization', *Man in India*, vol. 37, pp. 93–118.

———, (1959). 'Bhumij-Kshariya social movement in South Manbhum', *Bulletin of the Department of Anthropology, Government of India*.

———, (1965). 'Tribe-Caste and Tribe-Peasant Continnua in Central India', *Manin India*, vol. 42, no. 1, pp. 35–48.

———, (1978). *Foreword to Builders of Indian Anthropology 2*, Varanasi: N.K. Bose Memorial Foundation.

———, (1980). *India: A Western Apprentice. In Anthropology: Ancestors and Heirs. Edited by Stanley Diamond*. The Hague: Mouton Publishers.

———, (ed.) (1986). *Nirmal Kumar Bose: Scholar Wanderer*, New Delhi: National Book Trust.

Sinha, S.C. (1958). 'Tribal Culture of Peninsular India as a Dimension of Little Tradition in the Study of Indian Civilization – A Preliminary Statement', *Journal of American Folklore*, p. 71.

———, (1962). 'State Formation and Rajput Myth in Tribal Central India', *Man in India*, vol. 42, no. 1.

———, (1971). 'Is there an Indian tradition in social/cultural anthropology: Retrospect and prospect? Journal of the Indian Anthropological Society. 6: pp. 1–14.

———, (1987). *Tribal Politics and State System in Pre-Colonial Eastern and North Eastern India*, Calcutta: CSSS.

Sinha, S.P. (1871–1961). *Tribal Land Organisation in Chota Nagpur and its Development, Trends of Socio-economic Change in India*, Shimla: Indian Institute of Advance Study.

Sinha, V. (2005). 'Indigenizing' anthropology in India Problematic of negotiating an identity, in *Asian Anthropology*, eds., J. V. Bremen, E. Ben-Ari, S. F. Alatas, Routledge.

Skaria, A. (1999). *Hybrid Histories: Forests, Frontiers and Wilderness in Western India.* New Delhi: Oxford University Press, 1999, pp. 324.

Smith, L.T. (1999). *Decolonising Methodologies: Research and Indigenous Peoples*, London: Zed Books.

Srinivas, M.N. (1952). *Religion and Society among the Coorgs of South India*, Oxford: Clarendon Press.

Srinivas, M.N. (1976). *The Remembered Village*, Berkeley: University of California Press.

Srinivas, M.N. and M.N. Panini, (1973). 'The Development of Sociology and Social Anthropology in India', *Sociological Bulletin*, vol. 22, pp. 179–215.

Srivastava, S.K. (1958). *The Tharus: A Study in Culture Dynamics*, Agra University Press.

Srivastava, V.K. (2008). 'Concept of 'tribe' in the Draft National Tribal Policy", *Economic & Political Weekly*, vol. XLIII, no. 50, pp. 29–35.

———, (2010). 'Socio-economic Characteristics of Tribal Communities that Call Themselves Hindu', New Delhi: Indian Institute of Dalit Studies.

———, (2013). 'Introduction'. In *Tribes in India*, ed., V. K. Srivastava, Delhi: Serials Publications, pp. vii–xxxii.

———, (2013). *Tribes in India: Concepts, Institutions and Practices*, Serials Publication.

———, (2015). *Tribes in India: Symposium on People of India*, ed. P. C. Joshi, Department of Anthropology, University of Delhi.

———, (2016). 'Speaking of Caste: Merit of the Principle of Segmentation', *Sociological Bulletin*, vol. 65, no. 3, pp. 317–338.

———, (2018). 'The National Committee Report on Tribal People', *Social Change*, vol. 48, no. 1, pp. 120–130, Sage Publication.

———, (2018). 'The National Committee Report on Tribal People', *Social Change*, vol. 48, no. 1, pp. 120–130.

Subalternity and Empowerment in India, eds. M. Carrin and L. Guzy, Routledge India.

Subhadra, M.C. (2013). *The Inner and Outer Selves: Cosmology, Gender and Ecology at the Himalayan Borders*, New Delhi: Oxford University Press.

Suresh, M. (2019). *Tribal Revolts in 19th Century India*, Radha Publications.

Talal, A. (ed.) (1973). *Anthropology and the Colonial Encounter*, Ithaca Press.

Tamo, M. and M.C. Behera, (2007). *Tribal Studies – Emerging Frontiers of Knowledge*, New Delhi: Mittal Publications.

Tanuja, B. (2018, November). 'Ramkatha Tradition in North East India: An Unexplored Avenue', *OSR Journal of Humanities and Social Science (IOSR-JHSS)*, vol. 23, no. 11, Ver. 4, pp. 01–07.

Thangaraj Francis, X., K. Moorthy, L. Leyone, A. Anthonysamy, K.F.R. Antony and S.K. Subburaman, (2014, February 27). 'Ethnobotanical study of Kani tribes in Thoduhills of Kerala, South India', *Journal of Ethnopharmacology*, vol. 152, no. 1, pp. 78–90.

Thomas, M.M. and R.W. Taylor, (eds.) (1965). *Tribal Awakening*, Bangalore: Christian Institute for Study of Religion and Society.

Thurston, E. and K. Rangachari, (1909). *Castes and Tribes of Southern India*, Madras: Government Press.

Tiwari, B.K., S.K. Barik and R.S. Tripathi, (1996). *Sacred Groves of Megahalaya: Status and Strategies for their Conservation*, Shillong: north-eastern Hill University.

Toby E. Huff. (2011). Intellectual Curiosity and the Scientific Revolution: A Global Perspective, Cambridge, Cambridge University Press.

Trafzer, C.E., W. Sakiestewa Gilbert and A. Madrigal, (2008). "Integrating Native Science into a Tribal Environmental Protection Agency (EPA)", *American Behavioural Scientist*, vol. 51, no. 12, pp. 1844–1866.

Vashishtha, V.K. (1997). *Bhagat Movement: a study of cultural transformation of the Bhils of Southern Rajasthan*, Jaipur: Shruti Publications.

Venkata Rao, P.V. (2001). *Tribal Development: Policy and Practice*, New Delhi: Sarup & Sons.

Venkata Rao, P.V. (2019). 'Socio-cultural impact of non-tribal contact on tribes of Andhra Pradesh and Telangana, India', *Romanian Journal of Sociological Studies, Bucharest, New Series*, no. 2, pp. 139–151.

Venkata Rao, P.V. (2024). *13th Nirmal Kumar Bose Memorial Lecture on 'From Colonial to Post Colonial Anthropology in India: Reflections and Future Pathways'*, IGNCA Publications.

Venkatesan, S. (2002). *Savaging the Civilized: Verrier Elwin, His Tribals and India by Ramachandra Guha 23, Book Review*, Chicago: The Cambridge Journal of Anthropology.

———, (2012). 'The Social Life of a 'Free' Gift', *American Ethnologist*, vol. 38, no. 1, pp. 47–57.

Venkatesan, S., M. Ntarangwi, D. Mills, K. Gillespie, N. Dave and V. Backhaus, (2024). 'A Decolonial Anthropology: You Can Dismantle the Master's House with the Master's Tools', *Critique of Anthropology*, vol. 44, no. 2, pp. 99–140.

Verma, R.C. (1990). *Indian Tribes through the Ages*, Publications Division Ministry of Information & Broadcasting.

Vidal, D. (1997). *Violence and Truth: a Rajasthani Kingdom Confronts Colonial Authority*, Oxford: Oxford University Press.

Vidhyarthi, L.P. and B.K. Rai, (1976). *Religious life of the Tribals*, New Delhi: The Tribal Culture of India, Concept Publishing Company.

Vidyarthi L.P. (1963). *The Maler: A Case Study in Nature-Man-Spirit Complex of a Hill Tribe in Bihar*. Calcutta: Bookland.

Vidyarthi, L.P. (1978). *Rise of Anthropology in India: A Social Science Orientation*, Delhi: Concept Publishing Company, vol. 1, pp. 1–30.

Vidyarthi, L.P. and B.K. Rai, (1985). *The Tribal Culture of India*, New Delhi: Concept Publishing Company, pp. 1–10.

Vinita, D. and S. Dasgupta, (2022). 'Special Issue: Multiple Worlds of the Adivasi. An Introduction', *Modern Asian Studies*, vol. 56 no. 5. Cambridge University Press. https://www.cambridge.org/core/journals/modern-asian-studies/article/special-issue-multiple-worlds-of-the-adivasi-an-introduction/1F4F58D02E2C4FC8C6D5A94DAEB98B8D#fn23 22/02/24

Vyas, N.N. (1993). 'The Tribal View of the Ramayana; An Exercise in the Anthropology of Knowledge' in *Rama-Katha in Tribal and Folk Traditions of India, Anthropological Survey of India*, eds. K. S. Singh and B. Datta, Calcutta: Seagull Books, pp. 10–14.

Wade, J.P. (1800). *An Account of Assam*, Calcutta: The Kuntaline Press.

Walker, A. (1998). *Between Tradition and Modernity: A Study of Toda Adaptation*, New Delhi: Vikas Publishing House.

Wati Longchar, A. (2000). *An Emerging Asian Theology: Tribal Theology – Issue, Method and Perspective*, Jorhat, Assam: Tribal Study Centre, ETC.

———, (2001). *In Search of Identity and Tribal Theology*, Jorhat, Assam: Tribal Study Centre, ETC.

Watson, J.F. and J.W. Kaye, (1868–1875). *People of India: A Series of Photographic Illustrations of the Races and Tribes of Hindustan*, London: Indian Museum.

William H. McNeill. (1963) The Rise of the West: A History of the Human Community (Chicago, 1963) The University of Chicago Press.

Wouters, J.J.P. (2012). 'Reconfiguring colonial ethnography: the British gaze over India's north-east', in *north-east India: A Handbook of Anthropology*, ed. T. B. Subba. New Delhi: Orient Blackswan Private Limited, pp. 99–121.

Xaxa, V. (1999). 'Transformation of tribes in India', *Economic & Political Weekly*, vol. 34, no. 24, pp. 1519–1524.

———, (1999). 'Tribes as Indigenous People of India', Economic and Political Weekly, vol. 34, pp. 3589–3595.

———, (2001). 'Protective Discrimination: Why Scheduled Tribes Lag behind Scheduled Castes', *Economic and Political Weekly*, vol. XXXVI, no. 21. pp. 2765–72.

———, (2008). *State, Society and Tribes: Issues in Post-Colonial India*, New Delhi: Pearson Longman.

Yesodharan, K. and K.A. Sujana, (2007). 'Ethnomedicinal Knowledge among Malamalasar Tribe of Parambikulam Wildlife Sanctuary, Kerala', *Indian Journal of Traditional Knowledge*, vol. 6, pp. 481–485.

Ziipao, R.R. (2013). 'Tribes and tribal studies in North East: deconstructing the politics of colonial methodology', *Journal of Tribal Intellectual Collective India*, vol. 1, pp. 25–37.

https://amritmahotsav.nic.in/, accessed on 14 May 2024.

https://pib.gov.in/PressReleseDetailm.aspx?PRID=1977638, accessed on 15 May 2024.

https://pib.gov.in/FeaturesDeatils.aspx?NoteId=151692#:~:text=India%20will%20prosper%20when%20our,communities%20is%20our%20foremost%20priority.&text=Unity%20in%20diversity%20is%20one,tribal%20population%20in%20the%20world, accessed on 16 May 2024.

https://frontierweekly.com/articles/vol-52/52-13-16/52-13-16-Colonial%20Legacy%20and%20Hindu%20Anthropology.html, accessed on 16 May 2024.

https://rgu.ac.in/wp-content/uploads/2021/02/Download_637.pdf, accessed on 19 February 2024.

Index

Photographs

Photographs of brainstorming meetings and seminars held at various places in India

Plate 1: Brainstorming Meeting on 7th February 2023 at the Jharkhand Raksha Shakti University, Jharkhand

Plate 2: Brainstorming Meeting on 7 February 2023 at the Jharkhand Raksha Shakti University, Jharkhand

Plate 3: Brainstroming Meeting on 7 February 2023 at the Jharkhand Raksha Shakti University, Jharkhand

Plate 4: Brainstorming Meeting on 20th January 2023 at the Vivekananda International Foundation, New Delhi

Plate 5: Brainstorming Meeting on 20th January 2023 at the Vivekananda International Foundation, New Delhi

Plate 6: Brainstorming Meeting on 19th April 2023 at the Vivekananda International Foundation, New Delhi

Plate 7: Brainstorming Meeting on 19th April 2023 at the Vivekananda International Foundation, New Delhi

Plate 8: National Seminar: Inaugural Session organized at IGNCA during 21st–22nd November 2023

Plate 9: Keynote Address by S. Gurumurthy, Chairman, VIF, at the National Seminar, IGNCA

Plate 10: Address by Harsh Chauhan, former chairman, NCST, as the guest of honour

Plate 11: Address by Padma Bhushan Ram Bhadur Rai, President of IGNCA as the Chief Guest

Plate 12: Delegates at the National Seminar organized at IGNCA during 21–22 November 2023

Plate 13: National Seminar Valedictory Session on 22 November 2023: Chaired by Dr Sacchidanand Joshi; guests of honour—Prof. B.V. Sharma, Director, AnSi; Prof. Amitabh Pandey, Director, IGRMS; Prof. P.V. Rao, Former Dean, Hyderabad University

Plate 14: National Seminar—Valedictory session organized at IGNCA on 22 November 2023

Plate 15: Session at the National Seminar organized at IGNCA on 22 November 2023

Plate 16: Session at the National Seminar organized at IGNCA on 22 November 2023

Plate 17 : Panel Discussion on 'Decolonising Anthropology' at Indian Anthropology Congress (IAC)-2025 held at Kolkata, 22 February 2025

Plate 18: Prof. K. Anil Kumar speaking at a panel discussion at the Indian Anthropology Congress (IAC)-2025 held at Kolkata on 22 February 2025

Plate 19: Delegates attended the Indian Anthropology Congress (IAC)-2025 at Kolkata

Plate 20: Dr Sachchidanand Joshi, Member Secretary, IGNCA, delivering his address as the chief guest, on decolonising anthropology, during the valedictory session on 23 February 2025

Plate 21: Delegates attended Valedictory Session at IAC-2025 at Kolkata

About the Authors

DR. SACHCHIDANAND JOSHI serves as Member Secretary, Indira Gandhi National Centre for the Arts (IGNCA) New Delhi for the past decade. He is a distinguished academic and scholar in History and Mass Communication, as well as a writer, poet, and theatre artist. He was the founding Vice Chancellor of Kushabhau Thakre University of Journalism and Mass Communication in Raipur, where he served for ten years. Additionally, he was the founding Registrar of Makhanlal Chaturvedi National University of Journalism and Communication Bhopal and Dean of Academics at the same institution. Dr. Joshi has authored numerous works on Media, Communication, History, Culture, Education, and Policy. His significant contributions to culture and literature have earned him several national awards. He is a life member of INTACH and serves on multiple esteemed committees, including PMML.

RAGHVENDRA SINGH is a Senior Fellow at the Vivekananda International Foundation and is a former officer of the Indian Administrative Service. Over the course of his distinguished career he has held several prominent cultural and administrative positions, including Director General of the National Archives of India, Director of the Nehru Memorial Museum and Library, and Director General of the National Library of India. Additionally, he also served as Secretary in the Ministries of Culture and Textiles in the Government of India, making notable contributions to museology and cultural heritage management. Singh is the author of *India's Lost Frontiers: The Story of North-West Frontier Province of Pakistan* and is currently engaged in two major research projects titled *Gilgit* and *Syama Prasad Mukherjee.*

PROF. K. ANIL KUMAR currently serves as the Head of the Department of Janapada Sampada at the Indira Gandhi National Centre for the Arts (IGNCA) in New Delhi. From 2010 to 2022, he was Assistant Professor at IGNOU, New Delhi. His earlier experience includes serving at the Centre for Economic and Social Studies in Hyderabad from 2007 to 2010. Prof. Kumar has contributed significantly to academia, with numerous research papers and articles published in esteemed journals and edited volumes, and is the author of three books. He has actively participated in numerous national and international seminars, presenting his research findings, and undertaken several major and minor research projects and surveys in collaboration with organizations such as EPTRI, NIN, FHI, IPPG, UGC, DFID, and the Jamsetji Tata Trust.